DICKENS'S APPRENTICE YEARS
The Making of a Novelist

DICKENS'S APPRENTICE YEARS
YEARS
The Making of a Novelist

DUANE DeVRIES

The Harvester Press Limited

Barnes & Noble Books · New York

This edition first published in 1976 by
THE HARVESTER PRESS LTD
Publisher: John Spiers
2 Stanford Terrace, Hassocks, Sussex, England
and published in the USA 1976 by
HARPER & ROW PUBLISHERS, INC.
BARNES AND NOBLE IMPORT DIVISION
10 East 53rd Street, New York 10022

The Harvester Press Limited
ISBN 0 85527 179 5

Barnes and Noble
ISBN 0–06–491672–3

Filmset and Printed Offset Litho in Great Britain by
Cox & Wyman Ltd, London, Fakenham and Reading

Contents

To JoAnne

Preface

I HAVE always been fascinated by an author's development as a writer. In Dickens's career nowhere is such development more evident, I think, at least over a short period of time, than during the years 1833–36, when the young man was writing the sixty tales and essays all but one of which he collected in two series of *Sketches by Boz* in February and December 1836. And yet, surprisingly enough, nowhere in Dickens scholarship has a significant segment of the author's literary life been more neglected. This study of the making of the *Sketches* and of a young writer's development into a novelist will, I trust, help to remedy this oversight.

In analyzing Dickens's sketches and tales as apprentice exercises in the craft of fiction, I have limited myself largely to what I suppose is now something of an old-fashioned approach to the techniques of fiction: a study of plot, characterization, scene construction, setting, style, tone, and the interrelationship of all of these to provide form or structure for the works that are specifically tales. I have thus been more influenced by such now classic works as E. M. Forster's *Aspects of the Novel* and Percy Lubbock's *The Craft of Fiction* than by some of the more recent studies of the art of fiction or of Dickens's artistic accomplishments in the novels. I am not apologizing for my approach, however; I am convinced it is appropriate. It is just such basic matters as these that a novice writer must learn to master – first as techniques and then as techniques that work together to communicate and impress.

Moreover, it is always with the 21–24-year old writer, struggling to make his way out of the poverty into which his father had led the family, that I have attempted to remain and, where possible, identify. Although his first publications were, of course, important to him, Dickens could not have sensed their significance to his future or seen them clearly in the broader perspective of the writing of the time. He was simply struggling to write, as well as he could, pieces that were as good as those he saw performed on the stage or those he read in the magazines, newspapers, and popular books of his time and earlier. Accordingly, I have done little by way of comparing Dickens to his contemporaries and predecessors. In some instances, however (see Appendix D for a few examples), he must have suspected that certain of his sketches were superior to their models. But for the most part his concerns were practical, having to do with his immediate career, with the pleasing esteem of friends, and with his financial ability to maintain rooms of his own – and to support a wife and family in the near future.

In one respect, this study of Dickens's apprentice years is an examination of his yearly, and occasionally monthly, progress as a writer during a period when he was also involved with the perhaps more pressing concerns of a young man to achieve independence from his background and to establish a place of some sort for himself as an adult, preferably in a literary career. In regard to the writing itself, this is a study of a young author's somewhat un-directed groping toward a form, a style, a point of view, a *tone*, that was congenial to his image of himself or at least appropriate to the style of the publications in which his writings appeared. At the same time, he was learning with more conscious application to manipulate the techniques involved in creating life-like sets of characters, plots that made sense and had shape and direction, settings that contained and reinforced the action, a pleasing mixture of descriptive, narrative, and dramatized passages, some social criticism, some wit and humor, some melodrama, pathos, and anger. Since the movement of this apprenticeship to the novel is always toward *Pickwick Papers*, it has a happy, even sensational ending. But I am primarily interested in the process itself.

This volume is a considerable revision of my doctoral dissertation, and I am indebted to my Ph. D. committee for numerous suggestions (not all of which I have taken), and particularly to James D. Rust, whose kindness and encouragement were invaluable when the work was originally written. My reliance upon the volumes in the new Pilgrim Edition of Dickens's letters is, I trust, sufficiently indicated in the footnotes, but that upon the biographies by John Forster and Edgar Johnson is more pervasive than documentation can possibly suggest. I have been especially influenced by Butt and Tillotson's important study, *Dickens at Work*. Suggestions in the chapter on *Sketches by Boz*, largely the work of Professor Tillotson, I believe, had much to do with the direction that portions of this study have taken.

I must also express my gratitude for various kindnesses and services to the librarians of the New York Public Library and of the libraries of Michigan State University, Harvard University, Smith College, Ohio University, Ohio State University, the British Museum, the Victoria and Albert Museum, and particularly to Theodore Grieder, Curator of the Fales Collection of the New York University Library, and his competent staff. A portion of the expenses incurred in the course of revising this study for publication was provided by a grant from the Arts and Science Research Fund, New York University. The Southern Illinois University Press, holder of the copyright, has kindly granted permission to republish, in slightly revised form, my essay, 'Two Glimpses of Dickens' Early Develop-ment as a Writer of Fiction,' as part of Chapter II, below. It originally appeared in *Dickens Studies Annual*, Vol. I (1970), pp. 55–64.

I wish, finally, to thank Michael Slater, who introduced me to The Centenary Press, and my wife, whose assistance, patience, encouragement, and far too many personal sacrifices made this volume possible.
Polytechnic Institute of New York   Duane DeVries

CHAPTER ONE

1812–1833 : Beginnings and Preparations

E VER since July 1836, with the fourth installment of *Pickwick Papers*, scholars and critics have been expressing amazement at the apparently overnight metamorphosis of twenty-four-year old Charles Dickens into the polished, inventive, clever, professional author. Not all of the critics in 1836–37 cared for the work, it is true, but a good many were sufficiently impressed to predict a glorious future for the young author. Most were surprised that he should have staged such a grand entrance without adequate warning or fanfare. Even today scholars still seem baffled by the young man's sudden success. How was it possible for an obscure newspaper reporter to write such a brilliant, popular work as *Pickwick*? Where did he acquire what one reviewer rhapsodized about as 'the nicety of observation, the fineness of tact, the exquisite humour, the wit, heartiness, sympathy with all things good and beautiful in human nature, the perception of character, the pathos, and accuracy of description'?[1]

In *Dickens: From Pickwick to Dombey*, Steven Marcus explains the 'miracle' of *Pickwick* in terms of 'transcendence' – that is, Dickens somehow embodied in the novel 'a representation of life which fulfills that vision, which men have never yet relinquished, of the ideal possibilities of human relations in community, and which, in the fulfillment, extends our awareness of the limits of our humanity.'[2] Although the well-spring of artistic creativity

---

[1] *National Magazine and Monthly Critic*, December 1837. Reprinted in William Miller and E. H. Strange, *A Centenary Bibliography of the Pickwick Papers* (London: Argonaut Press, 1936), p. 169. For other reviews, see pp. 67–185, and also Walter Dexter and J. W. T. Ley, *The Origin of Pickwick: New Facts Now First Published in the Year of the Centenary* (London: Chapman and Hall, 1936), pp. 65–85. 'I well remember,' wrote Samuel Carter Hall in *Retrospect of a Long Life: From 1815 to 1883* (New York: D. Appleton and Company, 1883), 'my sensations of astonishment and interest when the first number of "Pickwick" was brought me, and I looked it over. Forster was with me at the time. How, on the introduction of Sam Weller [in No. 4 (July 1836)], the work took the town by storm, and its author, who, only a short time before, had been an unnoticed parliamentary reporter, reached at a bound the summit of success, and became *the* literary lion of the day, I need not here describe' (p. 394).

[2] Steven Marcus, *Dickens: From Pickwick to Dombey* (New York: Basic Books, 1965), p. 17.

remains as elusive as Ponce de Leon's fountain of youth, 'transcendence' need not serve as the sole explanation for the special virtues of this first novel. Sufficient evidence exists to offer at least a partial, more logical explanation for Dickens's rapid rise as an author. He had served a full apprenticeship in his writing of sixty tales, descriptive essays, and character studies for various magazines and newspapers between 1833 and 1836. These pieces, all but one of which were collected in two series in February and December 1836 as *Sketches by Boz*, have not merited the critical neglect they share with Dickens's other 'minor' writings.[3]

Whenever a scholar mentions the work at all, he generally points, as does Edgar Johnson in his biography of Dickens, to the young author's detailed, realistic, and frequently humorous observations of life as he knew it in the 1830's, to his sympathy with the oppressed poor and other victims of society, and to the early foreshadowing in style, characterization, and comic exuberance of the 'incredible fecundity that was to be.' Although Johnson concludes that *Sketches by Boz* has all the flaws of an apprentice work, he also recognizes it as an achievement that 'might well banish all surprise if its author, in his very next effort, leaped into the circle of the masters.'[4]

These are, inevitably, broad generalities. But the clue provided by Johnson will, I believe, lead to a productive investigation: these early writings were also exercises in the craft of fiction. An examination of them in approximately the order of their composition – an approach self-evident but new – should chronicle the early stages in Dickens's development as a writer of fiction, as he struggled with matters of craftsmanship and labored to write something of literary value. The investigation may well answer questions about how the young author, unpublished until December 1833, was able to leap into the 'circle of the masters' with *Pickwick Papers* less than three years later and to advance more rapidly than he might otherwise have as a novelist.

But the first chapter in the story of Dickens's development as a writer begins much farther back than 1833. His modest success with the early tales and essays would not have been possible if his early life, his growth and development as a human being, as a creative individual, had not had a special

---

[3] The First Series of *Sketches by Boz: Illustrative of Every-Day Life, and Every-Day People* was published in two volumes in London by John Macrone on 8 February 1836. Although it was not identified as the first series, I shall refer to it as such throughout. The Second Series, dated 1837, was published by Macrone in one volume on 17 December 1836. Fuller details of these and later editions, as well as the most up-to-date information about the earliest publication of the individual sketches, will be found in Appendix A, below. For a study of the publishing history of *Sketches by Boz*, with details about the revisions Dickens made in the various editions, see Ch. ii of John Butt and Kathleen Tillotson, *Dickens at Work* (London: Methuen, 1957), pp. 35–61. Hereafter cited as Butt and Tillotson. In the Preface, Professor Tillotson is identified as the main author of Ch. ii.

[4] Edgar Johnson, *Charles Dickens: His Tragedy and Triumph* (New York: Simon and Schuster, 1952), I, 110–14. Hereafter cited as Johnson. Wherever the reference is clear, page numbers will be given in the text. For a somewhat harsher, fuller, yet corroborating view, see Sylvère Monod, *Dickens the Novelist* (Norman: University of Oklahoma Press, 1968), pp. 50–62 – originally published in French as *Dickens romancier* (Paris: Hachette, 1953).

character. Only by familiarizing ourselves with the imaginative side of his childhood and youth can we appreciate the ease with which the young man did become a professional writer once he realized that for years he had been unconsciously preparing himself for such an occupation and moving in virtually inevitable stages toward it. The pattern of his development, emerging from the known biographical details and from his autobiographical essays, is consistent with modern theories of creativity.

To those in Chatham and London who knew Dickens as a child, the birth and development of the imagination at the heart of his literary achievements must have seemed significant only in retrospect. The boy himself must have felt simply that his reading, his visits to the theater, his day-dreaming, his pretending, his acting in plays, and his juvenile attempts at writing were more childhood prerogatives and efforts to bring amusement into an often lonely life than any preparation for a literary career. Nevertheless, the activities of these years, to 1827, when he completed what formal education he had managed to acquire, were an important part of just such preparation.

It is true that his father's financial troubles, which came to a head in 1824 but had been building for several years, deepened Charles's loneliness and frustrated his embryonic social pretensions and his more meritorious desire to acquire a decent education. In addition, having to work in a London shoe blacking factory while his father languished in debtors' prison and having to cope by himself at such an early age with the frightening, inhospitable city, may have produced in Dickens what Edmund Wilson termed 'a trauma from which he suffered all his life.'[5] Certainly the recurrent allusions in his writings to this side of his childhood and his bitter references to his father's mismanaged affairs attest at least to the lasting impression these experiences had upon his emotional life as child and adult. Very likely the desire, even the *need* to get ahead, to provide himself with a security that he had not felt as a growing boy, was a product of these difficult times. 'I know,' he wrote John Forster, his friend and first biographer, 'how all these things have worked together to make me what I am.'[6]

But a much more important influence on Dickens's future was one that modern biographers, even Johnson, greatly influenced by Wilson's long and persuasive study, do not sufficiently emphasize: the creative, imaginative side of the young boy's life. If Dickens himself claimed at times to be a lonely and a 'very small and not-over-particularly-taken-care-of boy,'[7]

---

[5] Edmund Wilson, 'Dickens: The Two Scrooges,' in his *The Wound and the Bow: Seven Studies in Literature* (Boston: Houghton Mifflin, 1941), p. 6. For the most recent criticism of Wilson's approach, see F. R. and Q. D. Leavis, *Dickens the Novelist* (London: Chatto & Windus, 1970), pp. xiii–xviii.

[6] John Forster, *The Life of Charles Dickens*, ed. J. W. T. Ley (London: Cecil Palmer, 1928), p. 35 – hereafter cited as Forster. Wherever the reference is clear, page numbers will be given in the text. Originally published in 3 vols. (London: Chapman and Hall, 1872–74).

[7] Madeline House and Graham Storey, eds. *The Letters of Charles Dickens*, The Pilgrim Edition, II (Oxford: Clarendon Press, 1969), 268, to Washington Irving, 21 April 1841. Hereafter cited as *Pilgrim Letters*. Also see Forster, pp. 3, 8–36.

he was also, as he describes David Copperfield (in several respects his fictional counterpart), 'a child of excellent abilities, and with strong powers of observation, quick, eager, delicate,' an 'innocent romantic boy, making his imaginative world out of . . . strange experiences and sordid things.'[8] And, contrary to Wilson's views and, earlier, Forster's, his father as much as his mother and other relatives and acquaintances permitted and frequently encouraged the life of fancy that the Dickens who wrote *Hard Times* would there advocate so strongly. His mother, he told Forster, awakened his 'first desire for knowledge' and his 'earliest passion for reading,' teaching him the rudiments of English and, a bit later, of Latin 'thoroughly well' (p. 3–4). Both she and Dickens's paternal grandmother introduced the boy to Little Red Riding-Hood, Jack the Giant-Killer, Robin Hood, Valentine and Orson, Bluebeard, The Yellow Dwarf, and 'all Mother Bunch's wonders,' as well as a multitude of sultans and Scheherazades, princes and princesses, dwarfs and fairies who filled, he later recalled, the pages of 'the most astonishing picture-books.' He remembered books about fortune-telling and dreams (*The Golden Dreamer* and the *Norwich Fortune Teller*), song books (the *Little Warblers* and *Fairburn's Comic Songsters*), and gaudily illustrated ballad sheets, all of which were 'infinite delights' to his younger self.[9]

He also listened avidly to other stories told by women in his life. His grandmother repeated narratives from the pages of history and reminisced about her past.[10] Mary Weller, the nurse of the Dickens children during the Chatham years (1817–22), related horrifying tales of murder and the supernatural, stories of Captain Murderer, a villain in the Bluebeard vein; of Chips, the shipwright who was fatally plagued by rats; of a ghastly child-craving Black Cat; of gigantic animals; and of ghostly apparitions.[11] His Aunt Fanny, who lived with the family in Chatham until her marriage, may also have participated in the story-telling. In 'The Holly-Tree,' an autobiographical piece, Dickens recalls sitting at the knee of a woman who not only told stories about a landlord who put his customers into pies and about a servant girl who married and then murdered an infamous housebreaker but also, more pointedly, about a brother-in-law who had all the virtues

---

[8] *The Personal History of David Copperfield* (London: Bradbury & Evans, 1850), pp. 111 and 122 (Ch. xi). Wherever reference to this novel is clear, chapter and page number will be given in the text. The first quotation is a slight variant of Dickens's description of himself as 'a child of singular abilities, quick, eager, delicate, and soon hurt, bodily or mentally' (Forster, p. 25) in the autobiographical fragment he wrote around 1846 (for date, see Johnson, I, iv [Notes], n. 63).

[9] See 'A Christmas Tree,' *Household Words*, 2 (21 December 1850), 289–92, and 'The Child's Story,' in *A Round of Stories by the Christmas Fire, Being the Extra Christmas Number of 'Household Words'* (Christmas 1852), p. 5 (both reprinted in editions of *Christmas Stories* and in *Reprinted Pieces*, The Nonesuch Dickens [Bloomsbury: Nonesuch Press, 1937–38]); and see 'Out of the Season,' *Household Words*, 13 (28 June 1856), 556 (reprinted in editions of *Reprinted Pieces*), and Harry Stone, 'Dark Corners of the Mind: Dickens' Childhood Reading,' *Horn Book Magazine*, 39 (1963), 313–15.

[10] Johnson, I, 8.

[11] 'The Uncommercial Traveller' ['Nurse's Stories'], *All the Year Round*, 3 (8 September 1860), 518–21. Reprinted as 'Nurse's Stories' in editions of *The Uncommercial Traveller*.

that Dickens's father did not (but whose escapades, he discovered later, were strongly reminiscent of incidents in *The Bleeding Nun, or Raymond and Agnes*, a popular romance of the time).[12] In another essay, he writes of ghost stories told around the Christmas tree, a scene that appears in more than one of his fictional works.[13] Such story-telling was apparently as much a part of the family life as were the father's financial troubles.

But John Dickens's contributions to his son's imaginative life were also considerable. In questioning Forster's harsh portrait of the father, J. W. T. Ley holds that Charles's walks with his father about the Chatham dockyard, their boating trips on the Medway, and their tramps along the Dover road helped to awaken the boy's imagination.[14] And what Edgar Johnson describes as John Dickens's love of 'the orotund gesture and the display of hospitality,' resulting in friends about 'the festal board – as he would have called it – a glowing hearth, songs and toasts' (I, 8), must have stimulated the boy's imagination even more. The father often called in his young son and daughter to recite the comic songs and stories he had taught them. If Charles did not acquire his father's weaknesses, he certainly was himself, in later life, the image of John Dickens in this more festive respect. According to Forster, Dickens felt that he must have been a 'horrible little nuisance' to the adults called on to admire such performances (p. 6), but some of these very adults recorded later – one trusts accurately – how enjoyable the recitations were.[15] 'He was proud of me, in his way,' Dickens himself recollected of his father, 'and had a great admiration of the comic singing.'[16]

Forster believed that the hardships of Dickens's childhood gave rise to the energy and determination to succeed that later helped to advance his career as a writer. But such energy would have been of little value without a highly developed fancy, what, for lack of a better word, may be called a 'producing' or 'creating' imagination; that is, one constantly manifesting itself in some form of overt, not necessarily logical or practical activity. Forster himself thought it a 'dangerous kind of wandering intelligence' (p. 7). But modern researchers into the origin and nature of 'creativity' generally seem to favor the 'highly creative' child over the 'highly intelligent' one. The latter is a 'converger'; that is, he tends to converge on right

---

[12] 'The Guest,' in *The Holly-Tree Inn, Being the Extra Christmas Number of 'Household Words'* (Christmas 1855), p. 4. Reprinted as 'The First Branch' of 'The Holly-Tree' in editions of *Christmas Stories*. According to Andrew Block, *The English Novel, 1740–1850*, new and rev. ed. (London: Dawson of Pall Mall, 1961), *The Bleeding Nun, or Raymond and Agnes* was published anonymously in 1820.

[13] 'A Christmas Tree,' pp. 293–95.

[14] Forster, p. 19, n. 10 (Ley). See also Philip Collins, 'Dickens on Chatham: An Uncollected Piece. With Introduction and Notes,' *Dickensian*, 59 (1963), 69–73.

[15] Robert Langton, *The Childhood and Youth of Charles Dickens: With Retrospective Notes, and Elucidations, from His Books and Letters*, rev. and enl. ed. (London: Hutchinson, 1891), p. 39 (hereafter cited as Langton); Forster, pp. 12 and 19, n. 14 (Ley); Johnson, I, 14–15. Mary Weller told Langton (p. 26) that a 'rather favourite piece for recitation by Charles at this time was "The Voice of the Sluggard" from Dr. Watts, and the little boy used to give it with great effect, and with *such* action and *such attitudes*.'

[16] Forster, p. 10. See also Stone, 'Dark Corners of the Mind,' pp. 306–10.

answers and does very well on standard intelligence tests. The former is a 'diverger,' with a tendency to 'think fluently and tangentially, without examining any one line of reasoning in detail,' and does well on 'open-ended' tests, requiring no correct answer.[17] Convergers, according to other studies, are fascinated with the known and the predetermined, the usual, the expected, and the certain. They exhibit intellectual acquisitiveness and conformity, among other qualities. Divergers, on the other hand, prefer to revise the known, explore the undetermined, and construct what might be. They prefer the novel and speculative and are further characterized by openness, risk-taking, intellectual inventiveness, and innovation.[18] A study of the details of his life quite clearly place the young Dickens in the camp of the 'diverger,' the highly creative child. The raw materials – the stimuli, the models – were there to begin with in the books, theaters (real and toy), and other entertainments of his youth. His books were basically those of David Copperfield: *Roderick Random, Humphry Clinker, Peregrine Pickle, Tom Jones, The Vicar of Wakefield, Don Quixote, Robinson Crusoe,* Lesage's *Gil Blas,* the *Arabian Nights, Tales of the Genii,* and several volumes of voyages and travels (Ch. iv, p. 41). Forster adds the *Tatler* and *Spectator* papers, Johnson's *Idler,* Goldsmith's *Citizen of the World,* Mrs. Inchbald's *Collection of Farces and Other Afterpieces* (7 vols., 1809), and a cheap series of novels then in the course of publication.[19] Still other works familiar to the boy were the essays of Benjamin Franklin (at least his paper on 'The Art of Procuring Pleasant Dreams'), a life of Lord Nelson, Sterne's *Sentimental Journey* and probably *Tristram Shandy,* the *Life* or *Memoirs* of Baron Trenck, *Philip Quarll, Gulliver's Travels,* many of Washington Irving's works, and others of which no record exists.[20]

Nor does much record remain of the books Dickens read in school, but

[17] Liam Hudson, *Contrary Imaginations: A Psychological Study of the Young Student* (New York: Schocken Books, 1966), pp. 36–37.

[18] Jacob W. Getzels and Philip W. Jackson, *Creativity and Intelligence: Explorations with Gifted Students* (London and New York: John Wiley & Sons, 1962), pp. 13–14, summarizing the conclusions of J. P. Guilford, C. R. Rogers, and A. H. Maslow.

[19] Forster, pp. 6 and 8. *Charles Dickens: An Exhibition to Commemorate the Centenary of His Death, June–September 1970* (London: Her Majesty's Stationery Office, 1970), the catalogue for the Victoria and Albert Museum's centenary exhibition, identifies the cheap series of novels as 'most probably' that published by John Cooke in 'Cooke's Pocket Library' (p. 3). The series included not only all of the novels listed above but, among some forty or more titles, such works as Walpole's *The Castle of Otranto,* Johnson's *Rasselas,* Voltaire's *Candide,* Fielding's *Jonathan Wild* and *Amelia,* Lesage's *The Devil on Two Sticks,* and Richardson's *Pamela.*

[20] See 'Lying Awake,' *Household Words,* 6 (30 October 1852), 145 (reprinted in editions of *Reprinted Pieces*); 'The Uncommercial Traveller' ['Nurse's Stories'], p. 517; 'Where We Stopped Growing,' *Household Words,* 6 (1 January 1853), 362–63 (reprinted in editions of *Miscellaneous Papers,* and in *Collected Papers,* The Nonesuch Dickens); 'A Christmas Tree,' p. 291; Forster, p. 464; and *Pilgrim Letters,* II, 267–68, to Washington Irving, 21 April 1841. In 'Where We Stopped Growing' (pp. 361–62), Dickens mentions many of the books also listed in Forster and in *David Copperfield.* According to Mary Weller, Dickens was 'a terrible boy to read, and his custom was to sit with his book in his left hand, holding his wrist with his right hand, and constantly moving it up and down, and at the same time sucking his tongue' (Langton, p. 25).

given the typical curriculum of the time, he encountered little in the way of English literature. Although once at William Giles's school he recited a piece about a Dr. Bolus from the *Humourist's Miscellany*, the selection could scarcely be called literary. However, when the Dickens family moved from Chatham, Giles presented his pupil with Goldsmith's *Bee*.[21] Dickens did have Latin instructors and presumably read the standard passages from Ovid, Virgil, Terence, Plautus, Cicero, and Horace. In general his school-days later evoked pleasant memories, although the picture he painted of Wellington House Academy had its more somber colors. He won prizes and 'great fame,' and was convinced of his cleverness.[22] But his education in literature advanced more rapidly out of school: Jane Porter's *Scottish Chiefs*, Holbein's *Dance of Death*, George Colman the Elder's *Broad Grins* and other works, again unrecorded, were loaned to him, Forster reports (p. 12), by the people who kept the bookshop under the Soho lodgings of his Uncle Thomas Barrow, whom the Dickens family frequently visited. Charles certainly knew such edifying volumes as Thomas Day's *Sandford and Merton* but also the more exciting *Portfolio of Entertaining and Instructive Varieties in History, Science, Literature, the Fine Arts, etc.*, a collection of parodies and miscellaneous literature, and *The Terrific Register; or, Record of Crimes, Judgments, Providences, and Calamities*, as well as a number of unnamed pamphlet romances.[23]

---

[21] Forster, pp. 7 and 9. For details about school curriculum, see Richard D. Altick, *The English Common Reader: A Social History of the Mass Reading Public 1800–1900* (Chicago: University of Chicago Press, 1957), pp. 141–87, and *passim*.

[22] *Pilgrim Letters*, I (Oxford: Clarendon Press, 1965), 424, to J. H. Kuenzel, [?July 1838]. This statement apparently refers to Dickens's days at Wellington House Academy, but, according to Langton (pp. 56–57), William Giles, Dickens's Chatham schoolmaster, also 'seems to have been much struck (could not fail to have been so) with the bright appearance and unusual intelligence of his little pupil, and, giving him every encouragement in his power, even to making a companion of him of an evening, he was soon rewarded by the marked improvement that followed. Charles made rapid progress, and there is no doubt whatever that his wonderful knowledge and felicitous use of the English language in after life was, in a great measure, due to the careful training of Mr. Giles, who was widely known as a cultivated reader and elocutionist.' Langton apparently received this information from Mrs. Godfrey, the eldest sister of Giles, whom he interviewed in connection with his study of Dickens's childhood and youth. See 'Our School,' *Household Words*, 4 (11 October 1851), 49–52 (reprinted in editions of *Reprinted Pieces*), for Dickens's description of student life at Wellington House Academy. For references to Dickens's Latin studies, see also 'A Christmas Tree,' p. 292; Forster, pp. 39–45 and 51, n. 55 (Ley); and Johnson, I, 47–51.

[23] 'New Uncommercial Samples: Mr. Barlow,' *All the Year Round*, N.S. 1 (16 January 1869), 156–59 (reprinted as 'Mr. Barlow' in editions of *The Uncommercial Traveller*); Forster, pp. 27, 36 (n. 37 – Ley), and 42–44 (note). Dickens must also have read pamphlet romances earlier than this. In the Preface to the Cheap Edition of *Pickwick Papers* (1847), he speaks of 'a dim recollection of certain interminable novels in [shilling numbers], which used, some five-and-twenty years ago, to be carried about the country by pedlars, and over some of which I remember to have shed innumerable tears, before I served my apprenticeship to Life.' Reprinted in *Posthumous Papers of the Pickwick Club*, ed. Robert L. Patten (Harmondsworth: Penguin Books, 1972), p. 44. For details about *The Portfolio*, see Gillian Thomas, 'Dickens and *The Portfolio*,' *Dickensian*, 68 (1972), 167–72; for more information about *The Terrific Register*, see R. D. McMaster, 'Dickens and the Horrific,' *Dalhousie Review*, 38 (1958), 18–28.

While books no doubt afforded young Dickens the greater amusement, the theater also enchanted him. As a child, he was frequently taken to performances at the Theatre Royal in Rochester by his father, by Mathew Lamert (soon to marry Charles's aunt), and a little later by James Lamert, Mathew's son by a former marriage.[24] Among the plays he saw there were Shakespeare's *Richard III* and *Macbeth*, William Barrymore's version of Pixérécourt's *Dog of Montargis*, Rowe's *Tragedy of Jane Shore*, and Lillo's *George Barnwell*.[25] He was also an awed spectator at pantomimes at the Rochester theater, as well as at those that 'came lumbering down in Richardson's waggons at fair-time to the dull little town in which we had the honour to be brought up,'[26] and, on at least one very special occasion, at the famous Christmas pantomimes in the great London theaters.[27] James Lamert occasionally got up private theatricals and, as Mary Weller told Robert Langton some sixty years later, the Dickens children and their friends sometimes 'would sing, recite, and perform parts of plays' at home.[28] No doubt Mrs. Inchbald's collection of farces came into heavy use on such occasions. Dickens also had a toy theater at Chatham, built for him by James Lamert, that kept him amused during the family's dark period in London prior to his father's imprisonment. For another such theater, built by the students at Wellington House Academy, he mounted productions of the *Dog of Montargis* (in which, he relates, a white mouse played the title role), the crusty *Miller and His Men* (Pocock), *Cherry and Fair Star*, and *Elizabeth, or the Exile of Siberia*, all standard items in the toy theater repertoire.[29]

Among the jumble in the playbox of the boy's imagination were toys that fascinated as well as frightened him – a roly-poly tumbler with horrible lobster eyes, and a jack-in-the-box 'in a black gown, with an obnoxious head of hair, and a red-cloth mouth, wide open,' who reappeared in his childhood nightmares. Drummer boys, toy soldiers, toy animals, miniature garden tools, doll houses, harlequin wands, and magic lanterns were also there.[30] In Chatham he became acquainted with an 'Orrery,' a portable model of the universe, with revolving planets and other

---

[24] Forster, pp. 7 and 19, n. 17 (Ley).

[25] 'The Uncommercial Traveller' ['Dullborough Town'], *All the Year Round*, 3 (30 June 1860), 276 (reprinted as 'Dullborough Town' in editions of *The Uncommercial Traveller*; 'A Christmas Tree,' p. 292.

[26] Introductory Chapter to *Memoirs of Joseph Grimaldi*, edited by 'Boz' (London: Richard Bentley, 1838), I, xii (reprinted in *Collected Papers*, The Nonesuch Dickens). Also see the description in 'Greenwich Fair,' *Evening Chronicle*, 16 April 1834 (reprinted in *Sketches by Boz*, First Series, I, 322–26).

[27] Forster, p. 104.

[28] Langton, p. 25.

[29] Forster, pp. 10, 40, and 44; Johnson, I, 49. For fuller descriptions, see 'Our School,' pp. 50–51, and 'A Christmas Tree,' p. 292.

[30] 'A Christmas Tree,' pp. 289–90; 'New Year's Day,' *Household Words*, 19 (1 January 1859), 97 (reprinted in editions of *Miscellaneous Papers*, and in *Collected Papers*, The Nonesuch Dickens); 'The Uncommercial Traveller' ['Birthday Celebrations'], *All the Year Round*, 9 (6 June 1853), 350 (reprinted as 'Birthday Celebrations' in editions of *The Uncommercial Traveller*); Langton, p. 25.

such astronomical features; stared open-mouthed at Indian sword swallow-ers, and was regaled at fairs and circuses.[31] Later he also remembered his mother telling stories from the Bible, his nurse singing the 'Evening Hymn,' and Christmas carollers passing from door to door.[32] In London he viewed Punch and Judy shows; conjurors and strong men; show vans with fat pigs, wild Indians, and lady midgets; and a street band that came around the neighborhood on Monday mornings playing such tunes as 'Begone Dull Care!' and 'I'd Rather Have a Guinea than a One-Pound Note.'[33] Although there were unhappy months in Dickens's young life, the glamour, excitement, and adventure implicit in the physical world in which he moved impressed itself emphatically upon his imagination. From Chatham he later remembered longing examinations of colorful displays in booksellers' windows, and an environment of 'barracks and soldiers, and ships and sailors' and of 'all sorts of parties, junketings, and birthday cele-brations, and . . . Fifth of November festivities round the bonfire.' London provided an atmosphere of prisons, pawnshops, dark and twisted alleys, Covent Garden market, inns and taverns, mad women in black or white flitting through the streets.[34]

Obviously the books, plays, childhood amusements, and the very world in which Dickens grew up influenced the subject matter of his novels, and in the case of the books and plays something of the manner, style, and form as well. But a listing of the activities available to the boy affords but a start-ing point for a discussion of his creative life. Of far greater importance is what his mind made of these raw materials. Later he described himself as 'a very odd little child with the first faint shadows of all my books in my head – I suppose.'[35] The first stage in the creative process from the initial experience to the creative act of writing fiction he described in *David Copperfield*. There the older David, narrating his own story, states that his childhood reading was his only and his constant comfort. 'When I think of it,' he writes, 'the picture always rises in my mind, of a summer evening, the boys at play in the churchyard, and I sitting on my bed, reading as if for life. Every barn in the neighbourhood, every stone in the church, and every foot of the churchyard, had some association of its own, in my mind, connected with these books, and stood for some locality made famous in them.' The books kept alive his fancy, and his 'hope of something beyond that place and

---

[31] 'The Uncommercial Traveller' ['Birthday Celebrations'], p. 349; 'The Uncommercial Traveller' ['Dullborough Town'], p. 276; Introductory Chapter to *Memoirs of Joseph Grimaldi*, I, xii–xv.
[32] 'A Christmas Tree,' p. 292; Forster, p. 2 (note); Langton, p. 29.
[33] 'An Unsettled Neighbourhood,' *Household Words*, 10 (11 November 1854), 289–90 (reprinted in editions of *Miscellaneous Papers*, and in *Collected Papers*, The Nonesuch Dickens); Forster, p. 31.
[34] 'The Uncommercial Traveller' ['Dullborough Town'], p. 277; 'Where We Stopped Growing,' pp. 362–63; Langton, p. 58.
[35] Walter Dexter, ed., *The Letters of Charles Dickens*, 3 vols., The Nonesuch Dickens (Bloomsbury: Nonesuch Press, 1938), II, 743, to Miss Coutts, 9 February 1856. Hereafter cited as *Nonesuch Letters*.

time' (Ch. iv, pp. 41–42). Dickens himself told Forster that his comparable set of books had given his ailing little life in Chatham 'its picturesqueness and sunshine' (p. 8). Indeed, the world in which the boy lived is, in important respects, much more adequately pictured through his fanciful impressions of the realities around him than through the realities themselves. If Dickens's own, later, account is to be believed, the imaginative process began very early. In 'New Year's Day,' he describes one of his earliest memories, 'the sensation of being carried down-stairs in a woman's arms, and holding tight to her, in the terror of seeing the steep perspective below.' The group of family and friends seated in a row along the wall in the room downstairs were, as he recalled, 'very like my first idea of the good people in Heaven, as I derived it from a wretched picture in a Prayer-book.'[36] Such associations are as characteristic of the adult author as of the infant. Their intensity and frequency in childhood were no doubt responsible for the remarkable imagination evident on every page of the adult's novels. Certainly the ability 'to play spontaneously with ideas, colors, shapes, relationships – to juggle elements into impossible juxtapositions, to shape wild hypotheses, to make the given problematic, to express the ridiculous, to translate from one form to another, to transform into improbable equivalents'[37] are characteristics of the highly creative child – and of the novelist.

Young Dickens created a large portion of his child's world from his favorite books. Sometimes the real world transformed itself into one in which Little Red Riding-Hood was his first love and the only villains were 'the real original roaring giants.'[38] Or he imbued his life with Eastern magic from the pages of the *Arabian Nights* and *Tales of the Genii*. 'Oh, now all common things become uncommon and enchanted to me!' he writes in 'A Christmas Tree' of his childhood experiences. 'All lamps are wonderful; all rings are talismans. Common flower-pots are full of treasure, with a little earth scattered on the top; trees are for Ali Baba to hide in. ... My very rocking-horse, – there he is, with his nostrils turned completely inside-out, indicative of Blood! – should have a peg in his neck, by virtue thereof to fly away with me, as the wooden horse did with the Prince of Persia, in the sight of all his father's Court.'[39] At other times, as he grew in years, Dickens conceived of the world in terms of the picaresque novel, recalling in later years a child with his head full of Partridge, Strap, Tom Pipes, and Sancho

---

[36] 'New Year's Day,' p. 98. As Forster points out (pp. 1–2), Dickens always claimed to have a remarkable faculty for remembering childhood experiences in great detail, another characteristic that he gave to Copperfield (see Ch. ii, p. 10).

[37] Carl R. Rogers, 'Toward a Theory of Creativity,' in *Creativity and Its Cultivation: Addresses Presented at the Interdisciplinary Symposia on Creativity, Michigan State University, East Lansing, Michigan,* ed. Harold H. Anderson (New York: Harper and Brothers, 1959), p. 76. Quoted in Getzels and Jackson, p. 53. The other two qualities that Rogers finds to be characteristic of a creative person are an openness to experience and an internal locus of evaluation.

[38] 'A Christmas Tree,' p. 290, and 'Where We Stopped Growing,' p. 362.

[39] 'A Christmas Tree,' p. 291.

Panza.[40] Then, again, in London, intoxicated with reading 'The Elder Brother,' a poem in Colman's *Broad Grins*, he hurried to Covent Garden market to compare it with the poem's description of it. 'He remembered,' Forster states, 'as he said in telling me this, snuffing up the flavour of the faded cabbage-leaves as if it were the very breath of comic fiction.'[41] The theatrical influence was also strong, particularly that of the pantomime. He wanted to live forever 'in the bright atmosphere' of the pantomime, and found the return to the 'dull, settled world' most difficult.[42] He would return from such a performance full of questions about the clowns, harlequins, pantaloons, and Columbines he had been dazzled by, all of whom, he informed readers in his introduction to *The Memoirs of Joseph Grimaldi* (pp. xi–xii), he believed to be real personages.

A much fuller description of the child's mind responding to external stimuli is found in Dickens's imaginative reconstruction of his mental condition on the occasion of being lost in London. Since no other record exists to verify even that the incident itself took place, one cannot, of course, assume that the essay necessarily treats of an actual experience. But there is, surely, validity in the *nature* of the response, and possibly in many of the details; 'Gone Astray,' the essay in which the experience is described, is clearly autobiographical, and Dickens does insist that this was 'literally and exactly how I went astray.'[43]

As he describes the incident, he was taken as a child of eight or nine, 'but newly come . . . out of the hop-grounds of Kent,' to see the outside of St. Giles's Church. But becoming separated from his guide, he unexpectedly found himself 'gone astray.' After overcoming his initial fright (an 'unreasoning terror' that 'comes as freshly on me now as it did then,' Dickens writes), he sat down on a step 'to consider how to get through life,' the idea of asking his way home never occurring to him. 'I had no eyes for the nearest and most obvious course,' he points out. For some time he moved in a world that he formed from the Dick Whittington legends. He made his way from the Strand toward Guildhall in the City, by way of Temple Bar, St. Dunstan's, a toyshop, and St. Paul's, the object of his interest at Guildhall being the Giants, the grotesque statues known as Gog and Magog. 'While I knew them to be images made of something that was not flesh and blood,' he tells us, 'I still invested them with attributes of life – with consciousness of my being there, for example, and the power of keeping a sly

---

[40] Preface to the Cheap Edition of *Nicholas Nickleby* (1848). Reprinted in *Nicholas Nickleby*, The Nonesuch Dickens, p. xvi.

[41] Forster, p. 12. The description of Covent Garden market in Colman's poem occupies four lines. To anyone familiar with the piece, Dickens must have been more interested initially in searching out the disreputable comic characters whom Colman described than in 'snuffing up' the market odors.

[42] 'A Christmas Tree,' p. 292.

[43] 'Gone Astray,' *Household Words*, 7 (13 August 1853), 557; see pp. 553–57 for the entire essay. Reprinted in editions of *Miscellaneous Papers*, and in *Collected Papers*, The Nonesuch Dickens.

eye upon me.' Wandering about later, he saw the City in terms of an imaginative response associated with his early reading. It was to him 'a vast emporium of precious stones and metals, casks and bales, honour and generosity, foreign fruits and spices.' He even imagined (though here one suspects the adult of self-indulgence) Rothschild sitting in the bazaar at Bagdad with rich stuffs for sale. He wandered about for a good part of the day, 'in and out of yards and little squares – peeping into counting-house passages and running away.' He peered into the kitchen window at Mansion House until one of the cooks chased him away; he was pursued by a group of boys. These are details close to the realities of a lost child's aimless movements. Here, too, he responded imaginatively, even wishfully: 'In such stories as I made,' Dickens relates, 'to account for the different places, I believed as devoutly as in the City itself. I particularly remember that when I found myself on 'Change, and saw the shabby people sitting under the placards about ships, I settled that they were Misers, who had embarked all their wealth to go and buy gold-dust or something of that sort, and were waiting for their respective captains to come and tell them that they were ready to set sail. I observed that they all munched dry biscuits, and I thought it was to keep off sea-sickness.'

The boy strayed into a theater, where he became completely caught up in the performance, only half-recognizing the nature of theatrical machinery, duplication of acting roles, and other such realities of theatrical life. At the same time he envisioned an elaborate future in which he, winning a donkey supposedly being raffled off, had to cope with such problems as how to get the animal home, where to keep him, what to feed him. It was only on leaving the theater later in the evening that he fully allowed reality to intrude, when he sought out the watch and was eventually reunited with his family. 'They used to say I was an odd child,' he concludes, 'and I suppose I was. I am an odd man perhaps.'

The 'odd' child is obviously a highly imaginative one, still confusing fiction and reality, though not always unconsciously so, one suspects – treating each new experience in life in the light of the vicarious 'experience' derived from books and plays. The persistence of this process is surely one of the prerequisites of creativity. The child who can see such wonders in commonplaces will later, as an adult, have little difficulty in creating not only such comparable beings as Oliver Twist, David Copperfield, and Pip, but also Mr. Pickwick, who is endowed with much of the same wonder. The exciting mixture of imagination and reality will also produce hundreds of other memorable characters living in worlds modified by their imaginations and will create such settings as *Pickwick's* Fleet Prison, *Barnaby Rudge's* London, *Martin Chuzzlewit's* America, the Chancery Court and environs of *Bleak House*, and the Circumlocution Office of *Little Dorrit*, to mention only a few. Such characters, such scenes are, as Edgar Johnson observes, all 'realities in which the commonplace, the comic, the pathetic, and the grotesque are inseparably blended' (I, 22).

But it is a long way from the 'odd' child to the writer of fiction. The next, and still very preliminary stage, that of a more overt merging of reality and the imaginative life, is seen largely in the boy's making up of games usually related to his reading, retelling tales he has heard or read, and creating his own stories about real people and places. Like David Copperfield he no doubt pretended to be Roderick Random or Tom Jones '(a child's Tom Jones, a harmless creature) for a week together.' Or, 'armed with the centre-piece out of an old set of boot-trees,' he stalked the region of his parents' house for days, 'the perfect realisation of Captain Somebody, of the Royal British Navy, in danger of being beset by savages, and resolved to sell his life at a great price' (Ch. iv, p. 41). Duelling grounds, the dungeons of Seringapatam (a haystack), the Spanish Main, fields tainted by the blood of murderers' victims – all were topographical details of the landscape in which young Dickens, the duellist (defending the honor of the 'youngest Miss Clickett but one'), the prisoner, the pirate, the adventurer, created and acted out his childhood dramas.[44]

These were Chatham activities. In London, under far less congenial circumstances, the lonely, neglected child was even more stimulated to exercise his imagination in disguising the frightening realities of his family's misfortunes. To entertain both himself and his fellow workers at Warren's Blacking, he retold the stories he had earlier read, stories, he claimed, which were 'fast perishing' out of his mind.[45] While waiting in the early morning outside the Marshalsea prison for the gates to open, Dickens also told the orphanage servant whom the family still maintained what he later described as some 'quite astonishing fictions about the wharves and the tower.' In describing the 'fictions' to Forster, Dickens added, 'I hope I believed them myself.'[46]

Similar manifestations of creativity continued during his years at Wellington House Academy. Owen P. Thomas, one of Dickens's schoolmates, wrote Forster that Dickens 'invented what we termed a "lingo," produced by the addition of a few letters of the same sound to every word; and it was our ambition, walking and talking thus along the street, to be considered foreigners.' Henry Danson, another classmate, remembers Dickens leading him and other boys in pretending to be poor and impudently begging charity of old ladies. They hoped to produce indignant reactions, and when they were successful, 'Dickens would explode with laughter,' Danson relates, 'and take to his heels.'[47] The idea for this prank came to

---

[44] 'New Year's Day,' p. 99; 'The Uncommercial Traveller' ['Dullborough Town'], p. 275; K. J. Fielding, ed., *The Speeches of Charles Dickens* (Oxford: Clarendon Press, 1960), pp. 326–27.

[45] Forster, p. 29.

[46] Forster, p. 30. Dickens uses virtually the same words in *David Copperfield* (Ch. xi, p. 120).

[47] Forster, pp. 42, 44. Yet another schoolfellow denied that Dickens invented the 'lingo' described above, claiming it was already in use when Dickens entered the school. See Forster, p. 51, n. 52 (Ley). Whatever the case, the use to which Dickens put the 'lingo' is significant.

Dickens, one suspects, from the *Life and Adventures of Bampfylde Moore Carew*, so-called 'King of the Beggars,' a work with which he was well-acquainted in one edition or another.[48] Owen Thomas also remembered himself 'extemporising tales of some sort, and reciting them offhand,' with Dickens and Danson or Tobin (another classmate) walking on either side of him (Forster, p. 42). Surely Dickens had his turn at such tale-spinning, too.

An incident from the days of John Dickens's imprisonment for debt gives, I believe, the clearest picture of this important stage between the manifestation of a free-flowing imagination and the actual disciplining of it in the form of creative writing. Release from prison being imminent, John Dickens drew up a petition for a bounty to be paid the prisoners to drink the king's health on the monarch's forthcoming birthday. Young Charles was present on the occasion of the signing of the document. From his post in a corner, he observed each prisoner file in to sign his name while a Captain Porter read the petition to the assemblage in his most sonorous tones. In the autobiographical fragment from which Forster quotes, Dickens states:

> Whatever was comical in this scene, and whatever was pathetic, I sincerely believe I perceived in my corner, whether I demonstrated or not, quite as well as I should perceive it now. I made out my own little character and story for every man who put his name to the sheet of paper. I might be able to do that now, more truly: not more earnestly, or with a closer interest. Their different peculiarities of dress, of face, of gait, of manner, were written indelibly upon my memory. I would rather have seen it than the best play ever played; and I thought about it afterwards, over the pots of paste-blacking, often and often. When I looked, with my mind's eye, into the Fleet-prison during Mr. Pickwick's incarceration, I wonder whether half-a-dozen men were wanting from the Marshalsea crowd that came filing in again, to the sound of Captain Porter's voice! (p. 33).

Describing essentially the same scene in *David Copperfield*, where Mr. Micawber draws up a far more significant social document calling for the abolishment of imprisonment for debt, Dickens has David state: 'I set down this remembrance here, because it is an instance to myself of the manner in which I fitted my old books to my altered life, and made stories for myself, out of the streets, and out of men and women; and how some main points in the character I shall unconsciously develope, I suppose, in writing my life, were gradually forming all this while' (Ch. xi, p. 121). Here, certainly, is the adult Dickens's own acute interpretation of the sources of his genius as a writer. Though his development into a literary artist of the first rank was obviously a complex process, his molding of reality to suit himself, particularly in terms of his literary interests, was an important part of the procedure.

The final stage in Dickens's youthful creative development, when he

---

[48] See 'New Year's Day,' p. 99, and 'Gone Astray,' p. 553.

actually transcribed some of his imaginative flights, came quite early. Although copies are not extant, his first attempts at authorship were 'certain tragedies achieved at the mature age of eight or ten' in which he got other children to act and which, he tells us, were 'represented with great applause to overflowing nurseries.'[49] In these productions he had obviously been influenced by his reading, by the performances he had witnessed at the Theatre Royal in Rochester, perhaps indirectly by compositions he may have been assigned at school, but most immediately, one suspects, by the theatrical ventures of James Lamert. Only the name of one of these plays has been preserved: 'Misnar, the Sultan of India,' founded on one of the narratives in *Tales of the Genii*.[50] Around 1822 or 1823 the young boy wrote at least two sketches. The first, Forster tells us, depicted a very old barber who shaved Thomas Barrow, the boy's uncle, and who 'was never tired of reviewing the events of the last war, and especially of detecting Napoleon's mistakes, and re-arranging his whole life for him on a plan of his own.' The second, modeled on a description of the canon's house-keeper in *Gil Blas* (see Bk. II, Ch. i), portrayed a 'deaf old woman who wait-ed on them in Bayham-street, and who made delicate hashes with walnut-ketchup.' Dickens never had the courage to show either of these sketches to anyone, Forster relates, though he was apparently very proud of them.[51]

Dickens's amateur writing career expanded during his years at Welling-ton House Academy. The influence of the cheap penny and Saturday magazines, the pamphlet romances, the toy theater performances, his earlier reading and theater-going, and no doubt the admiration of the other boys stimulated his creativity. 'I think at that time Dickens took to writing small tales,' Henry Danson wrote to Forster, 'and we had a sort of club for lend-ing and circulating them' (p. 44). This was substantiated by yet another classmate, John Bowden: 'He and I, in conjunction with one or two others, used to write short tales on scraps of paper, pin them together so as to form books with a few leaves, and lend them to the other boys to read for the small charge of a piece of slate-pencil, etc.' They also occasionally issued what Bowden referred to as a 'small morning newspaper containing comic advertisements and scraps of news.'[52] Langton, who corresponded with him, printed two of the advertisements that Bowden could recollect:

---

[49] Preface to the Cheap Edition of *Sketches by Boz: Illustrative of Every-Day Life and Every-Day People* (London: Chapman and Hall, 1850), p. [vii]; also see *Pilgrim Letters*, I, 424, to J. H. Kuenzel, [?July 1838].

[50] Forster, p. 6. For a description of Rev. James Ridley's *The Tales of the Genii; or, The Delightful Lessons of Horam, the Son of Asmar*, see Jane W. Stedman, 'Good Spirits: Dickens's Childhood Reading,' *Dickensian*, 61 (1965), 150–54.

[51] Forster, pp. 12–13. Forster does not reveal his source for this information. Although his descriptions show that he had some idea of their contents, it seems unlikely that he had actually read the sketches. Probably this information came from Dickens's autobiographical fragment.

[52] Frederic G. Kitton, *Charles Dickens by Pen and Pencil, Including Anecdotes and Reminis-cences Collected from His Friends and Contemporaries* (London: Frank T. Sabin, 1890), p. 128. This information originally appeared in the London *Daily News*, 21 December 1871.

Lost. Out of a gentleman's waistcoat pocket, an acre of land; the finder shall be rewarded on restoring the same.

Lost. By a boy with a long red nose, and grey eyes, a very bad temper. Whoever has found the same may keep it, as the owner is better without it.[53]

Dickens's father, who had learned shorthand, was a Parliamentary reporter at this time for a newspaper called the *British Press*. Charles occasionally contributed to the paper brief 'penny-a-line' notices of accidents, fires, and the like that the regular reporters had no time to cover.[54]

Another ex-schoolmate, C. F. Walsh, remembered Dickens's fondness for theatricals. 'I have some recollection of his getting up a play at Dan Tobin's house, in the back kitchen – but not a written play,' he stated. 'We made a plot, and each had his part; but the speeches every one was to make for himself. When we had finished, we were quite sure that if there had only been an audience they would all have cried, so deep we made the tragedy.'[55] In 'Our School,' Dickens himself describes another play that he wrote based partly on his reading and partly on his imaginative impression of yet another schoolfellow, whom he characterizes as a rich but rather idiotic boy. Like Steerforth in *David Copperfield*, 'Dumbledon' had extra privileges as a parlor-boarder:

[T]here was a belief among us that . . . he was too wealthy to be 'taken down.' His special treatment, and our vague association of him with the sea, and with storms, and sharks, and Coral Reefs, occasioned the wildest legends to be circulated as his history. A tragedy in blank verse was written on the subject – if our memory does not deceive us, by the hand that now chronicles these recollections – in which his father figured as a Pirate, and was shot for a voluminous catalogue of atrocities: first imparting to his wife the secret of the cave in which his wealth was stored, and from which his only son's half crowns now issued. Dumbledon (the boy's name) was represented as 'yet unborn' when his brave father met his fate; and the despair and grief of Mrs. Dumbledon at that calamity was movingly shadowed forth as having weakened the parlor-boarder's mind. This production was received with great favor, and was twice performed with closed doors in the dining-room. But, it got wind, and was seized as libellous, and brought the unlucky poet into severe affliction. (p. 50)

Commenting in 1851 on his great interest in acting, Dickens wrote to Bulwer-Lytton: 'Assumption has charms for me – I hardly know for how many wild reasons – so delightful, that I feel a loss of, oh! I can't say what exquisite foolery, when I lose a chance of being someone in voice, etc. not at

---

[53] Langton, p. 89. Bowden also reports here that the work he and Dickens called *Our Newspaper* was 'written on scraps of copy-book paper.'

[54] Hall, *Retrospect of a Long Life*, p. 64. See also William J. Carlton, 'John Dickens, Journalist,' *Dickensian*, 53 (1957), 5–11.

[55] Forster, p. 835 (note). Also see William J. Carlton, 'Postscripts to Forster,' *Dickensian*, 58 (1962), 87–88.

all like myself.'[56] The roots of such a response lie, obviously, in Dickens's childhood. Not only did such 'assumption' make reading, play-going, and the like most attractive to the young child and fill many of his days with great happiness and pleasure, it gave him at least vicarious experience far beyond the range of many children of his time and place. It also enabled him to escape momentarily from the terrifying realities of the dark days in London. Most important, by a complex process (simplified, obviously, in this chapter) it led to actual creative writing of stories, sketches, and plays, much more tangible evidence of the course his life might take, the right opportunities opening for him at the right time. The investigations of modern researchers into the origin, nature, and nourishing of creativity reveal at every point, at every turn, that Dickens's childhood provided full opportunity for creativity to flourish in the boy. He must be considered a model of the truly 'divergent,' the 'highly creative' child.

The reading and theater-going were the raw materials, the sources of stimulation for the imagination. As such, they largely determined the form and content of his imaginative dreaming, his creative play, his earliest writing and, because of their enormous formative influence, his later writing as well. But if these sources were important, even more so was the lively imagination itself that used them to create a world in which an often lonely boy could live happily and securely, engaging in the make-believe that was equally an activity of his happier days and that was to be a lifelong habit, delight, and necessity. Observed from the vantage-point of the future, the creative activities of his childhood clearly moved Dickens slowly but with some appearance, at least, of inevitability toward the occupation in whose service he would enchant successive generations of readers.

★

Although Dickens's creativity flourished in a variety of activities after he left Wellington House Academy as well as before, the period of his life between 1827 and 1833 is particularly characterized by an intensive search for a vocation conducive to his need for a full life of the imagination. In the course of his search, he not only continued to prepare himself unconsciously for a future as a writer but conscientiously procured a more thorough education for himself, particularly in literature. Most important of all, he continued to write.

The beginning of his working life was by no means promising. Shortly after leaving Wellington House Academy in 1827, he became a minor clerk, or office boy, with Charles Molloy and with Ellis and Blackmore, all solicitors. However, soon discovering that he was not temperamentally suited to office work, he began casting about for a more felicitous, remunerative, and challenging vocation, a task that was to occupy him for the next six years or so.

---

[56] *Nonesuch Letters*, II, 262, to Sir Edward Bulwer Lytton, 5 January 1851. A variant of this quotation is in Forster, p. 839, but without proper attribution.

Since his father was a Parliamentary reporter (by 1828 he had moved from the *British Press* to the *Morning Herald*) and an uncle a reporter for the *Times*, Dickens's first tentative movements were toward a similar career. He had heard apparently, as later did David Copperfield (Ch. xxxvi, p. 372), that many wealthy and influential men had begun as members of the Parliamentary press corps. Accordingly, as David was also to do, he labored over Gurney's *Brachygraphy* until he had mastered that popular system of shorthand. But he found no employment as a Parliamentary reporter; he was, after all, but a novice and just turned sixteen. Instead, abandoning his clerkship, he set himself up as a freelance shorthand writer for the proctors in the Consistory Court of Doctors' Commons.[57] He soon tired of this, too. 'It wasn't,' he told Forster much later, 'a very good living (though not a *very* bad one), and was wearily uncertain' (p. 380). He had fallen in love with Maria Beadnell, the daughter of a banker, and so was even more acutely conscious of his social position than before. Of his efforts to make himself at least financially respectable, he wrote, 'I went at it with a determination to overcome all the difficulties, which fairly lifted me up into that newspaper life, and floated me away over a hundred men's heads. . . .'[58] But already in late 1832 Maria was in Paris, where her parents obviously hoped she would forget her young lover. Shortly after her return, she rewarded their hopes.[59]

In the meantime, Dickens had been attracted to acting as a possible profession. His earlier interest in the theater had been reactivated when he became a clerk with regular pay. This taste for theatricals, Edward Blackmore recalled later for Forster (p. 46), was much encouraged by a fellow clerk named Potter – a name given, interestingly enough, to one of the comic young clerks on the town in the sketch entitled 'Making a Night of It' (*Bell's Life in London*, 18 October 1835), although, it is true, the other clerk is named Smithers, not Dickens. 'They took every opportunity, then unknown to me,' stated Blackmore, 'of going together to a minor theatre, where (I afterwards heard) they not unfrequently engaged in parts.' George Lear, another clerk with Ellis and Blackmore, claimed that Potter, not Dickens, was the stage-struck young man. Potter acted at the Minor Theatre but, according to Lear, had no talent whatsoever. While Lear admits that he and Dickens went to see Potter perform two or three times, he adds, 'I do not for a moment think that Dickens ever acted at this theatre, and I know that his opinion agreed with mine, that the sooner Potter quitted the boards of "The Minor," the better.'[60] Certainly the early sketch entitled

---

[57] Among the archives of St. Bartholomew's is a transcript of two cases of 1830 in Dickens's handwriting. These are the originals on which the law suit in 'Doctors' Commons,' one of the pieces in *Sketches by Boz*, is based. For an account of these documents, see William J. Carlton, *Charles Dickens, Shorthand Writer: The 'Prentice Days of a Master Craftsman* (London: Cecil Palmer, 1926), pp. 57–71.

[58] Forster, p. 49.

[59] Johnson, I, 72. For the course of the affair between Dickens and Maria Beadnell, see I, 67–83, and *Pilgrim Letters*, I, 2–30.

[60] Kitton, *Charles Dickens by Pen and Pencil*, p. 132.

'Private Theatres' (*Evening Chronicle*, 11 August 1835) reveals extensive knowledge of the kind of place where neophyte actors paid for roles. Dickens may not have engaged in such activity, but it is true that between 1828 and 1832, while he labored by day in Doctors' Commons, his play-going continued unabated and with increased purpose at night: he was indeed seriously considering acting as a career. 'I went to some theatre every night, with a very few exceptions,' he later told Forster, 'for at least three years; really studying the bills first, and going to where there was the best acting: and always to see [Charles] Mathews whenever he played. I practised immensely (even such things as walking in and out, and sitting down in a chair); often four, five, six hours a day: shut up in my own room, or walking about in the fields. I prescribed to myself, too, a sort of Hamiltonian system for learning parts; and learnt a great number.'[61]

Dickens's acting ability, particularly in comic imitation, is verified by some of the people who knew him then. George Lear recalled that Dickens's imitations of the speech, ways, and manners of the charwoman at Ellis and Blackmore's were 'to the very life.' But more than this, Dickens 'could imitate, in a manner that I have never heard equalled, the low population of the streets of London in all their varieties, whether mere loafers or sellers of fruit, vegetables, or anything else.' He could do old clerks who presided over the public offices, mimic the popular singers, declaim Shakespeare 'by the ten minutes,' and imitate all the leading actors. Dickens told Lear that he had often taken part in amateur theatricals and that his father knew many of the well-known actors, among whom Lear particularly recollected Young Macready (later to become one of Dickens's closest friends) and John Pritt Harley.[62]

Dickens also became more closely associated with the world of actors and singers through his sister Fanny. By 1827, following four years of study at the Royal Academy of Music, Fanny had begun to move on the fringes of the theatrical crowd; for example, in 1827 and 1828 she sang at benefits for Harley, for whom Dickens wrote *The Strange Gentleman* and *Is She His Wife?* a few years later. She also introduced her brother to John Hullah, with whom he collaborated in 1835–36 on *The Village Coquettes*, a reasonably successful comic operetta. She and Hullah both studied singing under the same teacher at the Royal Academy and sang more than one concert together. Often she and her brother gathered around the piano with friends for an evening of songs and fun.[63] Charles must frequently have been the bright light of the evening. Henry Burnett, whom Fanny also met at the Royal Academy and whom she married in 1837, reported that on such

---

[61] Forster, p. 380. For descriptions of Mathews's 'At Homes,' see *The Memoirs of Charles Mathews, Comedian*, ed. Mrs. Charles Mathews (London: R. Bentley, 1838–39, II–IV, *passim*, and Earle Davis, *The Flint and The Flame: The Artistry of Charles Dickens* (Columbia: University of Missouri Press, 1963), pp. 37–53.

[62] Kitton, *Charles Dickens by Pen and Pencil*, pp. 131–32.

[63] See William J. Carlton, 'Fanny Dickens: Pianist and Vocalist,' *Dickensian*, 53 (1957), 133–39, and Johnson, I, 54–55.

evenings Dickens occasionally sang 'serio-comic' songs that were 'highly successful, and gave great pleasure even to the most sedate among his friends, for it was his habit to give very amusing, droll, and clever sketches of character between the verses, comic and quaint, but never vulgar.'[64] Some of these sketches must have been based on material from the 'At Home' performances of Charles Mathews.

Early in 1832, believing himself ready for a career in the theater, Dickens applied to George Bartley, the stage manager at Covent Garden, for an audition. '[I] told him,' Dickens recalled for Forster, 'how young I was, and exactly what I thought I could do; and that I believed I had a strong perception of character and oddity, and a natural power of reproducing in my own person what I observed in others.' Bartley was interested and eventually arranged an audition, the young aspirant to do something by Mathews. But on the scheduled day, Dickens was incapacitated with a dreadful cold and an inflammation of the face. He wrote Bartley to say that he would renew his application the following season. He never did so; by then his career had taken a new direction. 'I never told you this, did I?' he wrote Forster. 'See how near I may have been to another sort of life' (pp. 59–60). He insisted that he never thought of the stage but as a means of getting money. Knowing of his intense interest in the theater from an early age, one can scarcely credit such an explanation.

Although he abandoned his projected career as an actor and comic singer, Dickens did not abandon his interest in the theater. A year later, in 1833, he was the moving spirit behind two evenings of amateur theatricals with his family and a few friends. The first, which took place on 27 April, consisted of performances of John Howard Payne's opera, *Clari, the Maid of Milan*, P. P. O'Callaghan's *The Married Bachelor*, and R. Brinsley Peake's *Amateurs and Actors*. From the printed playbill and letters written at the time of rehearsals, we learn that Dickens not only wrote a prologue (later destroyed) for the evening but, as stage manager, was responsible for directing the plays, getting the actors to rehearsals, pleading with them to finish the pieces of scenery they had agreed to construct, renting costumes, and other such matters. He also acted in all three plays. A letter to Henry Kolle, lamenting his not having come to a rehearsal, gives a few details: 'Thursday is a Rehearsal of Clari with the Band & Friday week a dress Rehearsal. You shall have your Bills [that is, playbills] when I see you – an immense audience are invited, including many Judges. . . . The family are busy, the *Corps dramatique* are all anxiety, the scenery is all completing rapidly, the machinery is finished, the Curtain hemmed, the Orchestra complete – and the manager *grimy*.'[65] Sometime later in the year Dickens repeated the process

---

[64] Kitton, *Charles Dickens by Pen and Pencil*, p. 137.

[65] *Pilgrim Letters*, I, 19. On the playbill, headed 'Private Theatricals,' Dickens is listed as stage manager. He, his father, an uncle, two brothers, and two sisters, as well as a number of acquaintances – the Urquharts, the Austins, Miss Oppenheim, and Messrs. Bramwell, Mitton, Kolle, and Boston – are listed as the actors. According to the playbill, 'The Band which

for another evening of theatrical entertainment, of whose feature attraction, a burlesque extravaganza entitled *The O'Thello*, he was the proud author. No information about the degree of success of either production has come down to us, but Dickens's portrait in 'Mrs. Joseph Porter, "Over the Way,"' a tale published in January 1834, of a catastrophic amateur production of Shakespeare's *Othello* may contain glimpses of reality. Since Fanny Dickens, already a professional musician, sang the title role in *Clari*, the evening must have had its finer moments, however. Charles himself would also have handled his roles professionally. So far as it is possible to determine, the other actors and singers were strictly amateurs.

But even before 1832 Dickens was turning to other interests. He had already joined *The Mirror of Parliament*, a serious rival to *Hansard* in recording Parliamentary debate. John Barrow, an uncle, had founded the publication in 1828 and apparently took his nephew on, perhaps first in some minor capacity and then, when he had acquired sufficient experience in the Gallery, as a regular shorthand reporter. By 1832 he was well set in this career. He worked for the *True Sun* in a similar position for a few months in 1832 but continued with his uncle's paper until 1834.[66] He spent a good portion of his time in the cramped quarters reserved for reporters in the two Houses, his pad balanced on his knee as he strained to hear the orators below.[67] As his biographers indicate, these years provided him with a liberal education. 'Even a casual glance at Hansard for those years, or a brief examination of one of those ponderous three-volumed Victorian biographies, say the biography of Henry Brougham, would reveal a galaxy of powerful personalities and a solid amount of epoch-making legislation,' concludes John Manning. 'Where is the college graduate who would not envy such an opportunity?'[68]

---

will be numerous and complete' was under the direction of his uncle Edward Barrow. The playbill has been reproduced frequently, most recently in Lola L. Szladits, ed., *Charles Dickens, 1812–1870: An Anthology* (New York: New York Public Library, 1970), p. 8. For other letters referring to the production, see *Pilgrim Letters*, I, 18–21 – and I, 31, for a reference to the theatricals later in the year.

[66] The dates of Dickens's service on these papers are still somewhat speculative. See Gerald G. Grubb, 'Dickens's First Experience as a Parliamentary Reporter,' *Dickensian*, 36 (1939/40), 211–18, and *Pilgrim Letters*, I, 2, n. 3.

[67] Fielding, ed., *The Speeches of Charles Dickens*, p. 347. 'In the old House of Commons,' states Samuel Carter Hall, in *Retrospect of a Long Life* (p. 65), 'the conditions of parliamentary reporting were as follows: The reporter pushed his way with the crowd to the Strangers' Gallery. The seat provided for him and the other representatives of the Press was the back seat of that gallery, into which he had to squeeze himself through a doorway about two feet wide. Seated there, he took his notes. There were, perhaps, a hundred seats under him, benches filled by "strangers," and in this back bench it was very difficult to hear. When he sought egress he had a hard fight with intervening legs and arms to reach his own door; often jaded, heated, and laden with anxiety, he had absolutely to push his way in or out – struggling to make room for his successor who was pushing his way in. Having had his "hour," and been relieved, he made his way as fast as he could to the office to write out his notes for the printer.'

[68] John Manning, *Dickens on Education* (Toronto: University of Toronto Press, 1959), pp. 40–41. Also see Forster, pp. 61–63 and 66, n. 72 (Ley), and Johnson, I, 63–66, 87–89.

In August 1834, having risen to the top of his profession for accuracy and rapidity in transcribing debate (the considered opinion of one of his colleagues in the Gallery),[69] Dickens was finally asked to join the staff of the *Morning Chronicle* through the good offices of Thomas Beard, a close friend who had himself been recently hired. The *Chronicle* was a Liberal paper with which Dickens had unsuccessfully sought employment a year earlier on the recommendation of John Payne Collier.[70] Although he worked on the paper until November 1836, this reward for his industriousness and persistence really came too late. Sometime in the spring or early summer of 1833 he had written a short work of fiction, a rather crudely conceived tale about a London bachelor imposed upon by boorish suburban cousins. Its publication in the December 1833 issue of the *Monthly Magazine* must have forced him to re-examine his goals and turned him, as a result, more sharply toward the writing career that was to make him famous.

Over the course of the next year or so, as Dickens continued to write stories for the *Monthly Magazine* and, beginning in September 1834, descriptive essays for the *Morning Chronicle*, he may have felt that these early pieces were only 'side issues' of his journalistic career, as F. J. H. Darton maintains.[71] Certainly, the five essays he wrote for the *Morning Chronicle* were considered part of his expected weekly output as a full-time reporter. Nor did he receive payment from the *Monthly Magazine*. But given the methodical way in which he had practiced acting techniques and studied shorthand, signs of similar preparation for a career as a writer are evident in the quantity and variety of his early writings. It may be that his position on the *Chronicle* simply provided him with the minimal financial security that a budding literary artist needs while serving his apprenticeship to the craft. Even Darton concedes that there is 'an odd mixture of sanguine confidence and caution' in certain letters that Dickens wrote to Henry Kolle at this

---

[69] See James Grant, *The Newspaper Press: Its Origin – Progress – and Present Position* (London: Tinsley Brothers, 1871), I, 295–96 and 301. Dickens 'occupied the very highest rank among the eighty or ninety reporters for the press then in Parliament,' Grant states (I, 296). In the 1830's Grant was a reporter for the *Morning Advertiser* and the *Morning Chronicle*.

[70] John Payne Collier, *An Old Man's Diary, Forty Years Ago* [in four parts] (London: Printed by Thomas Richards for 'strictly private circulation,' 1871–72). According to the entry for 24 July 1833 (IV, 12–14), Dickens's uncle John Barrow asked Collier to recommend his nephew, pointing out that 'he was extremely clever' and 'wished of all things to become one of the parliamentary reporters of the *Morning Chronicle*.' Barrow also said that Dickens had written advertising verses for Warren's Blacking and, when inviting Collier to dinner to meet Dickens, that his nephew 'was cheerful company and a good singer of a comic song.' Collier was sufficiently impressed by the young man to recommend him for the desired position, but nothing came of it at the time. Also see the entry for 27 July 1833, containing a description of the merry dinner at which Dickens sang two songs, one, about 'Sweet Betsy Ogle,' apparently of his own composition (IV, 14–15).

[71] F. J. Harvey Darton, 'Dickens the Beginner: 1833–1836,' *Quarterly Review*, 262 (1934), 61.

time about his future literary plans.[72] When George Hogarth asked him to write a sketch for the *Evening Chronicle*, a new thrice-weekly paper, similar to those he was writing for the morning paper, his answer indicated that he was already separating his reportorial and his literary careers in his own mind. He spoke of commencing 'a series of articles under some attractive title' for remuneration beyond his salary from the parent paper. 'I merely wish to put it to the Proprietors,' he deferentially wrote Hogarth, ' – first whether a continuation of light papers in the style of my 'street sketches' would be considered of use to the new paper; and secondly, if so, whether they do not think it fair and reasonable, that – taking my share of the ordinary reporting business of The Chronicle besides – I should receive something for the papers beyond my ordinary Salary as a Reporter.'[73]

Of course, one can only speculate about what ambitions, what dreams for financial security and literary prestige were running through Dickens's mind in 1834–35. His future must have held out a variety of pleasant possibilities to him. His career as a reporter was skyrocketing, his literary pieces were being published regularly, and he had met and successfully courted Hogarth's daughter Catherine (to whom he became engaged in May 1835). What might he not accomplish? He certainly knew by 1835 – and probably by the end of 1833 – that he had the capacity for good hard work, the potential and initiative to advance in any of several fields, and the imaginative resources and the basic technical knowledge necessary to flourish in the kind of creative endeavor that had always attracted him, perhaps to write works of fiction, even three-decker novels. That he accepted the challenge, met it, and triumphed is, of course, a matter of record.

But Dickens's occupations between 1827 and 1833 did more than move him slowly toward a career as a novelist. Not only had the persistence of his search for an amenable outlet for his creative imagination been rewarded, in the process he had actually been unconsciously preparing for the new career. All occupations obviously furnished additional subject matter for his writings, but this was really a minor acquisition. His work as a shorthand reporter in Doctors' Commons and Parliament must have contributed greatly to the improvement and variety of his writing style. In going through the process of recording in shorthand and then recopying in long-hand whatever was said, Dickens constantly reproduced, in Doctors' Commons, the speech patterns of people of various classes and, in Parliament, the rhetorical patterns of sometimes educated, often officious, and frequently pompous men, surely an invaluable preparatory exercise for fictional dialogue and characterization. Moreover, the portraits he drew of a number of these figures and of various functionaries associated with the Houses of Parliament, in 'The House' and 'Bellamy's,' two

---

[72] Darton, p. 62. See letters to Kolle, *Pilgrim Letters*, I, 33–34, 38, and 39. For the earliest, the editors suggest a date of 10 December 1833, and of April and Spring of 1834 for the other two.
[73] *Pilgrim Letters*, I, 55, to George Hogarth, 20 January [1835].

sketches of 1835, were apparently close enough to reality to require him to tone down several of the portraits when he combined the two as 'A Parliamentary Sketch' for the Second Series of *Sketches by Boz*.[74] In addition, the tales and sketches contain a number of parodies of the florid language of public speakers. He may also have implemented an early fluency with English while recording Parliamentary debate, for he was responsible for making sense out of incompletely heard and inaccurately constructed sentences. A Parliamentary reporter had to make 'at least tolerable English for even the worst speaker,' a colleague wrote; 'otherwise the inaccuracies and slovenliness of the style would be ascribed to the reporter, not to the speaker.' He was also expected to correct any errors the speaker made in dates, names, and other such information.[75]

His preparation for an acting career also aided Dickens considerably as a writer. His wide reading of plays with an eye to acting in them greatly increased the models at his disposal when he did begin to write for publication. While such an influence was not always in the best interests of the young writer, his early and thorough familiarity with the ingredients and forms of tragedy, comedy, and particularly farce and melodrama gave him a certain facility from the start: he knew what effects the various forms were capable of producing and, no doubt from memorizing parts if from nothing else, had some idea of how to achieve such effects. As an actor, he had surely become adept at projecting himself, with accuracy and exaggeration, into the characters of imaginary as well as real people, and had mastered certain theatrical types, especially the vast catalogue of Charles Mathews characters. And again, through memorizing and speaking the lines of numerous characters, he had valuable practice in a variety of conventional and unusual speech patterns. It was not a terribly long step to what the literary artist needed – the ability to create original characters who, while maintaining a resemblance to real people, still manage to have lives of their own within the stories for which they have been conceived. At least it was not a long step for an imaginative young man. In addition, his leadership in the amateur theatricals in 1833 gave him some experience in the manipulation of all the facets of a creative performance, an ability he would find useful when he sat down to write a fictional piece.

Even more important preparation for a writing career, though still largely unconscious preparation, I think, lay in the plays, essays, and novels that Dickens read between 1827 and 1833 and in his more conscious desire to acquire a general education for himself beyond that which his limited

---

[74] 'The House' was published in the *Evening Chronicle*, 7 March 1835; 'Bellamy's' appeared there on 11 April. For details of the alterations made in the combined version, see William J. Carlton, 'Portraits in "A Parliamentary Sketch,"' *Dickensian*, 50 (1953/54), 100–109.

[75] Grant, *The Newspaper Press*, II, 203; also see 201–204. In *Retrospect of a Long Life*, S. C. Hall states: 'It is needless to say that the printed speeches were frequently far better than the speeches spoken' (p. 65).

schooling had provided. The plays he saw, read, and acted in must have represented a fairly thorough survey of eighteenth- and nineteenth-century drama. He continued to reread the books familiar to him from childhood, a pleasure that he never outgrew. And he devoured the contents of numerous magazines and newspapers now that he no longer had to go without dinner to purchase them, as had been necessary earlier – the *True Sun*, the *Mirror of Parliament*, the *Morning Chronicle*, the *Evening Chronicle*, and the *Times* undoubtedly; the *British Press* and the *Morning Herald*, for which his father had worked; and also, from the nature of his early allusions to them, at least the *New Monthly Magazine*, the *Thief*, the *Metropolitan Magazine*, the *Athenaeum*, the *Literary Gazette*, the *Court Journal*, the *Morning Post*, *Blackwood's*, *Frasers*, and the *Examiner*.[76] There were no doubt others, among them (some then, some a bit later), the magazines in which his tales and essays were first published: the *Monthly Magazine*, *Bell's Weekly Magazine*, *Bell's Life in London, and Sporting Chronicle*, the *Carlton Chronicle*, and the *Library of Fiction*.

On his eighteenth birthday Dickens became eligible for a reader's ticket at the British Museum. Here, old request slips show, he at least glanced at such works as Goldsmith's *History of England* (with continuation), Addison's *Miscellaneous Works*, two collections of Shakespeare's plays (one with notes, the other with a life by Symmons), Holbein's *Dance of Death*, Burgess' *A Short Account of the Roman Senate*, *Lights and Shadows of Scottish Life* (an anonymous work), and *Volunteers: A Letter to Wm. Wyndham on the Subject of Exercising Volunteers on the Sabbath Day*.[77] These records are obviously not complete. '[I] devoted myself for some time to the acquirement of such general literature as I could pick up in the Library of the British Museum,' Dickens himself testified.[78]

A list of other works that Dickens read at about this time would very likely comprise a catalogue of mainly early nineteenth-century authors, major and minor, with the exception of Jane Austen. Besides reading numerous sensational novels, Dickens read the works of Scott, Bulwer-Lytton, Mrs. Radcliffe and other Gothic novelists, and James Fenimore Cooper. He also read Ainsworth's *Rookwood*, Richardson's *Sir Charles*

---

[76] For listings of the plays Dickens knew, see J. B. Van Amerongen, *The Actor in Dickens: A Study of the Histrionic and Dramatic Elements in the Novelist's Life and Works* (London: Cecil Palmer, 1926), *passim*, and Earle R. Davis, 'Literary Influences upon the Early Art of Charles Dickens,' Diss. Princeton, 1935, pp. 114–16 and *passim*. Davis includes the list of plays from his dissertation (but excluding farces, melodramas, and operas) in his *The Flint and the Flame: The Artistry of Charles Dickens*, pp. 315–16; see also pp. 54–74. For the allusions to the magazines and newspapers, see *Pilgrim Letters*, I, 32 [*New Monthly Magazine*], 33–34 [*Thief* and *Metropolitan*], 54 [*Athenaeum* and *Literary Gazette*], 129 [*Court Journal*], 140 [*Morning Post*], 161 [*Fraser's*]. The allusion to the *Examiner*, canceled in *Sketches by Boz*, First Series, is in 'The Boarding House – No. II,' *Monthly Magazine*, N. S. 18 (August 1834), 181.
[77] William Miller, 'Dickens Reads at the British Museum,' *Dickensian*, 43 (1946/47), 83–84, and *Pilgrim Letters*, I, 9–10, n. 4.
[78] *Pilgrim Letters*, I, 423, to J. H. Kuenzel, [?July 1838].

Grandison, Godwin's *Caleb Williams*, probably Miss Mitford's *Our Village*, Pierce Egan's *Life in London*, Robert Surtees's *Jorrocks' Jaunts and Jollities* (as it was serialized in the *New Sporting Magazine*, 1831–34; the first edition was not published until 1838), some of the writings of Theodore Hook, More's *Utopia*, Bunyan's *Pilgrim's Progress*, and Pepys's *Diary*. He also knew particularly well the comic poems of Thomas Hood and the works of Byron, Thomas Moore, and George Colman the Elder. Long attracted to the essayists, Dickens read at this time, if not earlier, writings of Leigh Hunt, William Hazlitt, Charles Lamb, Walter Savage Landor, Thomas DeQuincey, and others,[79] including John Poole and John Wight, two now virtually forgotten authors who greatly influenced his early writing. Poole's *Sketches and Recollections* (1835) had been irregularly serialized between 1825 and 1834 in the *New Monthly Magazine*, where Dickens apparently read the pieces. Wight's popular police reports for the *Morning Herald* were collected as *Mornings at Bow Street* (1824) and *More Mornings at Bow Street* (1827).[80] Now, or possibly earlier, Dickens read Boswell's *Life of Johnson* and also Johnson's own works, at least the *Life of Savage*.[81] Finally, he read or at least glanced at such diverse publications at Belzoni's *Observations and Discoveries, within Pyramids, Tombs, etc. in Egypt and Nubia* (1820), *The Newgate Calendar*, and Scott's *Letters on Demonology and Witchcraft* (1830).[82]

Dickens's career as a shorthand reporter, his great interest in the theater, and his considerably expanded literary education were certainly important during this period to his preparation as a writer. But most significant, once again, was the writing he continued to do. Interestingly enough, with the variety of literary models at his disposal, he turned first to poetry. The extant pieces – 'The Devil's Walk,' 'The Churchyard,' 'Acrostic,' and 'Lodgings to Let,' from Maria Beadnell's album; 'A Fable (Not a Gay One),' from Ellen Beard's album; 'The Bill of Fare,' a 358-line imitation of Goldsmith's 'Retaliation,' concerned with the Beadnells and their friends; and 'The Ivy Green,' included in *Pickwick Papers* (Ch. vi) – were written during this period, some as early as 1831. *The O'Thello*, Dickens's 'travestie' on Shakespeare's play, was also in verse, as extant fragments

---

[79] See Philip Collins, 'Dickens's Reading,' *Dickensian*, 60 (1964), 136–51; Earle R. Davis, 'Literary Influences upon the Early Art of Charles Dickens,' and *The Flint and the Flame: The Artistry of Charles Dickens*, *passim*; Harry Stone, 'Dickens's Reading,' Diss. University of California, at Los Angeles, 1955, *passim*; and T. W. Hill, 'Books that Dickens Read,' *Dickensian*, 45 (1948/49), 81–90, 201–207.

[80] Butt and Tillotson, p. 37, n. 5, and p. 40, n. 6; *Nonesuch Letters*, I, 702, to Miss Coutts, 17 September 1845; Wilhelm Dibelius, *Charles Dickens*, 2nd ed. (Leipzig and Berlin: B. G. Teubner, 1926), p. 80.

[81] *Pilgrim Letters*, I, 85, to Catherine Hogarth, [?29 October 1835].

[82] See allusions in 'Seven Dials,' *Bell's Life in London*, 27 September 1835, and 'Some Account of an Omnibus Cad,' *ibid.*, 1 November 1835 (both reprinted in *Sketches by Boz*, Second Series, pp. 147 and 306, the latter as the second half of 'The Last Cab Driver and the First Omnibus Cad'), and Shabby-Genteel People,' *Morning Chronicle*, 5 November 1834 (reprinted in *Sketches by Boz*, First Series, II, 103).

indicate. Inevitably, these early compositions are marred by trite and often borrowed poetic ideas, awkward syntax, and crude rhythm, as these melancholic lines from 'The Churchyard' illustrate:

> How many tales these Tombstones tell
> Of life's e'er changing scene,
> Of bygone days spent ill or well
> By those who gay have been;
> Who have been happy, rich, and vain,
> Who now are dead, and cold,
> Who've gone alike to dust again,
> The rich, poor, young, and old.[83]

Surely Thomas Gray, whose name should be added to the list of poets with whose works Dickens was familiar, turned over in his grave at the time.

While the poetry is atrocious, the prose that Dickens wrote between 1827 and 1833 is somewhat more promising, and certainly more significant for the future of the novelist. He apparently wrote a 'monopolylogue' in imitation of similar one-man, quick-change playlets that were a speciality of Charles Mathews and also scribbled certain rough sketches of people and things in a notebook,[84] but these writings have not come down to us. However, some of the letters that Dickens wrote before 1834 have survived. They illustrate that even this early in his writing career he had surprising control over the English language and a promising ability to express himself formally, colloquially, seriously, humorously. For example, the following angry lines are from the letter that ended his relationship with Maria Beadnell:

Our meetings of late have been little more than so many displays of heartless indifference on the one hand while on the other they have never failed to prove a fertile source of wretchedness and misery and seeing as I cannot fail to do that I have engaged in a pursuit which has long since been worse than hopeless and a further perseverance in which can only expose me to deserved ridicule I have made up my mind to return the little present I received from you sometime since (which I have always prized as I still do far beyond anything I ever possessed) and the other enclosed mementos of our past correspondence which I am sure it must be gratifying to you to receive as after our recent situations they are certainly better adapted for your custody than mine. Need I say that I have not the most remote idea of hurting your feelings by the few lines which I think it necessary to write with the accompanying little parcel? I must be the last person in the world who could entertain such an intention but I feel that this is neither a matter nor a time for

---

[83] *Collected Papers*, The Nonesuch Dickens, II, 281. For the fragment from *The O'Thello* and the other poems, see II, 61–63, 279–98. Also see Alain de Suzannet, 'Maria Beadnell's Album,' *Dickensian*, 31 (1934/35), 161–68.
[84] See Frederic G. Kitton, *The Minor Writings of Charles Dickens: A Bibliography and Sketch* (London: Elliot Stock, 1900), pp. 221–22, and Ralph Straus, *Charles Dickens: A Biography from New Sources* (New York: Cosmopolitan Book Corporation, 1928), p. 68.

cold deliberate calculating trifling. *My* feelings upon any subject more especially upon this must be to you a matter of very little moment still I *have* feelings in common with other people – perhaps as far as they relate to you they have been as strong and as good as ever warmed the human heart, – and I do feel that it is mean and contemptible of me to keep by me one gift of yours or to preserve one single line or word of remembrance or affection from you. I therefore return them and I can only wish that I could as easily forget that I ever received them.[85]

The language is obviously stilted and the sentence structure unnecessarily complex, surely in part a heritage from the language of Parliament and the law courts, a language that Dickens had been transcribing and correcting for several years. But one also perceives a conscious stylist at work: the cold cruelty of the tone of voice is obviously intentional, however much disclaimed by the hurt lover who declares he has 'not the most remote idea' of hurting Miss Beadnell's feelings by the 'few lines' he thinks it necessary to include with the letters and mementos he is returning to her. The wonder is that she did not angrily destroy this amazing composition.

Passages from other letters are more light-hearted in tone, more colloquial in style, and more humorous in intent. Surely here the young man's extensive reading in the comic literature of his time as well as of the past shows its early influence. A child does not learn to write in school or a young man in a law office or court with the verve of the following:

> In reply to your enquiry respecting a sizeable poney, I have also great satisfaction in being enabled to say that I can procure you a 'oss' which I have had once or twice since I have been here. I am a poor judge of distance but I should certainly say that your legs would be off the ground when you are on his back. To look at the animal in question you would think (with the exception of Dog's Meat) there was no earthly purpose to which he could be applied but *when* you try him joking apart I will pledge my veracity he will beat any horse hired or private that you would see in a Morning's ride. I am his especial patron but on this occasion I will procure something smaller for myself.[86]
>
> . . . – By the bye if I had many friends in the habit of marrying which said friends had brothers who possessed an extensive assortment of choice hock I should be dead in no time. Yesterday I felt like a Maniac – to day my interior resembles a Lime Basket.[87]

The humor here is obvious, relying on some exaggeration and highly pictorial images, but it is not exorbitant and, most likely because of its spontaneity, is superior to much of the humor Dickens attempted in his earliest published tales. Here, I believe, in the letters the promising future is first clearly indicated.

★

---

[85] *Pilgrim Letters*, I, 16–17, to Maria Beadnell, 18 March [1833].
[86] *Pilgrim Letters*, I, 5, to H. W. Kolle, [?April–May 1832].
[87] That is, a basket of quick-lime. *Pilgrim Letters*, I, 30, to H. W. Kolle, [19 May 1833].

By 1833, then, Charles Dickens was ready to launch his literary career. He had much to learn about basic techniques of fiction-writing, obviously, and, for that matter, may have just become conscious of budding professional ambitions in the authorial line. But, all things considered, his preparation as a writer was surprisingly extensive, if largely unplanned. His reading, theater-going, acting, and other youthful activities, particularly his daydreaming and imaginative games, contributed greatly to the development of his creative imagination. And so, in their way, did his many days of loneliness and depression. A few years later the assiduity with which Dickens acquired an education for himself in the British Museum reading room and conscientiously prepared himself as a legal and Parliamentary reporter and as an actor suggests the care he would now shortly take to ready himself as a writer of fiction. More significantly, these activities themselves were important influences on his writing. He was intimately familiar with two Londons – the dark, frightening city of his youth and the fascinating playground of his young manhood, a London of theaters and inns, Parliament, Doctors' Commons, criminal courts, Seven Dials and Monmouth Street, Vauxhall Gardens and Astley's Circus. 'Having been in London two years,' wrote George Lear, 'I thought I knew something of town, but after a little talk with Dickens I found that I knew nothing. He knew it all from Bow to Brentford.'[88] Dickens also read armloads of novels, plays, poems, and essays. Thus, by the time he stealthily dropped his first manuscript of a story 'with fear and trembling, into a dark letter-box, in a dark office, up a dark court in Fleet Street,' one evening in 1833,[89] he not only had a head full of possible subjects for future papers, he had numerous literary models available to aid him in giving form to his experiences and observations. Moreover, he had been acting and writing for years. 'Do you care to know,' he wrote to a friend in 1859, 'that I was a great writer at 8 years old or so – was an actor and a speaker from a baby – and worked many childish experiences and many young struggles, into Copperfield?'[90] Crude though his early poems are, and his lost plays and sketches must have been, though the letters show promise, the act of imitative creation was surely an important first step in his formal training as a writer. Supplemented by a determination not to emulate John Dickens and a strong desire to gain eminence and financial success in some field, Dickens's extensive, though mainly unconscious preparation for a writing career made his resolution to become an author more easily attainable than otherwise and his advancement in this new profession more rapid – and, for us, more understandable.

---

[88] Kitton, *Charles Dickens by Pen and Pencil*, p. 131.
[89] See quotation from the Preface to the Cheap Edition of *Pickwick Papers* (1847) at the beginning of Chapter II of this study, below.
[90] *Nonesuch Letters*, III, 122, to Mrs. Howitt, 7 September 1859.

CHAPTER TWO

The *Monthly Magazine* Tales

I was a young man of three-and-twenty, when the present publishers [Chapman and Hall], attracted by some pieces I was at that time writing in the Morning Chronicle newspaper (of which one series had lately been collected and published in two volumes, illustrated by my esteemed friend Mr. George Cruikshank), waited upon me to propose a something that should be published in shilling numbers – then only known to me, or I believe, to anybody else, by a dim recollection of certain interminable novels in that form, which used, some five-and-twenty years ago, to be carried about the country by pedlars, and over some of which I remember to have shed innumerable tears, before I served my apprenticeship to Life.

When I opened my door in Furnival's Inn to the managing partner who represented the firm, I recognized in him the person from whose hands I had bought, two or three years previously, and whom I had never seen before or since, my first copy of the Magazine in which my first effusion – dropped stealthily one evening at twilight, with fear and trembling, into a dark letter-box, in a dark office, up a dark court in Fleet Street – appeared in all the glory of print; on which occasion, by-the-bye – how well I recollect it! – I walked down to Westminster Hall, and turned into it for half-an-hour, because my eyes were so dimmed with joy and pride, that they could not bear the street, and were not fit to be seen there. I told my visitor of the coincidence, which we both hailed as a good omen; and so fell to business.[1]

Even as Charles Dickens was negotiating in February 1836 with the publishing firm of Chapman and Hall about his writing *Pickwick Papers*, the figure of William Hall reminded him of that moment in December 1833, described above, when he saw his first story, 'A Dinner at Poplar Walk,' in print. *Pickwick Papers* was to be gloriously successful, signaling the beginning of the author's long career as novelist. But its success would not have been possible without the essential – and productive – period of apprenticeship between 1833 and 1836 in which Dickens wrote 'A Dinner

---

[1] Preface to the Cheap Edition of *Pickwick Papers* (1847), p. viii, reprinted in the Penguin Edition, ed. Patten, pp. 43–44. For 'one evening at twilight,' Dickens had originally written 'one summer's night.' See facsimile of corrected proof of p. viii of the Preface in ' "In All the Glory of Print," ' *Dickensian*, 30 (1933/34), 2.

at Poplar Walk' and fifty-nine other tales and essays. Collected in two series of *Sketches by Boz*, these early pieces were important and necessary exercises in the craft of fiction.[2]

Dickens began his professional apprenticeship with eight (as ten) farcical tales. All but one of these appeared in the *Monthly Magazine*, a publication of small circulation and declining reputation.[3] As might be expected from the writer's inexperience, the tales are for the most part crudely conceived and executed. Yet in certain respects the later ones show significant improvement over the earlier, and individual tales have occasional merit. We know from his reading, play-going, and youthful writing that Dickens was not completely unprepared for the career that he embarked upon in 1833; he had simply had little practice in the writing of fiction itself. We can be certain that he did not write *in vacuo* but at every turn joyously inundated himself in the flood of theatrical, popular, and journalistic literature produced for the early nineteenth-century reading audience.[4] Although the influence of the eighteenth- and early nineteenth-century novel was not much evident until Dickens began to write longer fiction himself, the one-act farces then extremely popular as afterpieces were an important influence, as were the short comic tales with which the magazines were filled and the comic verse narratives of Hood, Combe, and George

---

[2] Most of the tales and sketches had originally appeared in the *Monthly Magazine, Bell's Weekly Magazine, the Morning Chronicle, the Evening Chronicle, Bell's Life in London, and Sporting Chronicle, the Library of Fiction,* and the *Carlton Chronicle.* For a list of the first publication of the pieces in *Sketches by Boz,* see Appendix A. An earlier detailed listing is in Thomas Hatton and Arthur H. Cleaver, *A Bibliography of the Periodical Works of Charles Dickens: Bibliographical, Analytical, and Statistical* (London: Chapman and Hall, 1933), pp. 91–103; but see the three additions to this list in William J. Carlton, '"The Story without a Beginning": An Unrecorded Contribution by Boz to the *Morning Chronicle,*' *Dickensian,* 47 (1950/51), 67; in Hilmer Nielsen, 'Some Observations on *Sketches by Boz,*' *Dickensian,* 34 (1937/38), 243; and in Appendix B, below. Fifty-nine of the sketches and tales were published as fifty-five in the two series of *Sketches by Boz* – the two parts of 'The Boarding House' and of 'Passage in the Life of Mr. Watkins Tottle,' both *Monthly Magazine* tales, being published as stories of two chapters each; 'The House' and 'Bellamy's,' two of the *Evening Chronicle* sketches, being combined as 'A Parliamentary Sketch'; and 'Hackney Cabs, and Their Drivers,' from the *Carlton Chronicle* (see Appendix B, below), and 'Some Account of an Omnibus Cad,' from *Bell's Life in London,* being combined as 'The Last Cab Driver, and the First Omnibus Cad.' 'The Tuggs's at Ramsgate,' originally published in the *Library of Fiction,* was first included in *Sketches by Boz* in the 1837–39 issue in parts.

[3] See F. J. Harvey Darton, *Dickens, Positively the First Appearance: A Centenary Review* (London: Argonaut Press, 1933), p. 10, for a fuller description of the *Monthly Magazine.* The tales that appeared in it were 'A Dinner at Poplar Walk' (retitled 'Mr. Minns and His Cousin' in the Second Series of *Sketches by Boz*), December 1833; 'Mrs. Joseph Porter, "Over the Way"' (retitled 'Mrs. Joseph Porter' in the First Series), January 1834; 'Horatio Sparkins,' February 1834; 'The Bloomsbury Christening,' April 1834; 'The Boarding House,' May 1834; 'The Boarding House – No. II,' August 1834; 'The Steam Excursion,' October 1834; and 'Passage in the Life of Mr. Watkins Tottle,' January (Chapter the First) and February (Chapter the Second) 1835. In addition, 'Sentiment!' appeared in *Bell's Weekly Magazine,* 7 June 1834, under the title of 'Original Papers.'

[4] See Altick, *The English Common Reader,* and Walter Graham, *English Literary Periodicals* (New York: Thomas Nelson & Sons, 1930), *passim.* Both works have an extensive bibliography.

Colman. From these sources Dickens acquired the farcical situations, the lower- and middle-class characters, and the punning, obtrusively clever style of writing that all too frequently define his early tales.[5] Thus, when he sat down to write his first story, apparently in the spring or summer of 1833, he must have been reasonably conscious of what he was about to attempt. The finished work was not below the quality of many of the stories published at about that time in the *Monthly Magazine*, and superior to some I have read.

While Dickens himself was naturally elated and even tearful when he saw his first story in 'all the glory of print,' he had recovered sufficiently by mid-1836 to make numerous revisions in the tale before allowing it in the Second Series of *Sketches by Boz*.[6] But he seems to have responded objectively even earlier; his fourth story, 'The Bloomsbury Christening,' was enough like his first and yet a decided enough improvement upon it to suggest not only that he had already discovered deficiencies in his earlier piece but that the later tale was essentially a completely redesigned version of his first. A study of the revisions that he made in 'A Dinner at Poplar Walk' and an examination of the improvements evident in 'The Bloomsbury Christening' should provide us with our first important glimpses of Dickens's early development as a writer of fiction. And these will also introduce the fuller study, in the second half of this chapter, of the flaws and merits of the other early tales.

The revisions that Dickens made in 'A Dinner at Poplar Walk' in 1836 are largely attempts to achieve fluency and clarity of style, to create a fuller, more chronologically consistent scene, and to give the whole story greater form. The revisions in style dispense first of all with a number of literary

---

[5] Perhaps the closest influences were the 'At Homes' of Charles Mathews and the essays of John Poole that appeared in the *New Monthly Magazine* between 1825 and 1834, collected as *Sketches and Recollections*, 2 vols. (London: Henry Colburn [for Richard Bentley], 1835). Although only pirated versions of Mathews's performances have been published, descriptions of his various one-man shows can be found in *The Memoirs of Charles Mathews, Comedian*, by his wife, who discounts the accuracy of the pirated editions. These descriptions, mainly in Vol. 4, suggest that Dickens, a devout admirer of Mathews, may very likely have consciously imitated in his early writings some of the characters and situations created by the famous comedian, as he had earlier in the amateur entertainments for his friends. Dibelius, in *Charles Dickens*, pp. 68ff., discusses the influence of the theater, and particularly of Mathews, on Dickens's early writing, as does Earle Davis, in *The Flint and the Flame: The Artistry of Charles Dickens*, pp. 37–53. For a more general, more philosophically oriented discussion of the theatrical influence, see Ch. iii ('*Sketches by Boz* and the *Theatrum Mundi*') in William F. Axton, *Circle of Fire: Dickens' Vision & Style & the Popular Victorian Theater* (Lexington: University of Kentucky Press, 1966), pp. 37–59. For some evidence of Poole's influence, see Appendix D.

[6] The original version is reprinted in '"In All the Glory of Print,"' pp. 3–10, and in Darton's *Dickens, Positively the First Appearance*, pp. 53–68. Darton deals briefly with the revisions that Dickens made in 'A Dinner at Poplar Walk,' as do Butt and Tillotson in Ch. ii of *Dickens at Work* and Siegfried Benignus in his early and largely neglected *Studien über die Anfänge von Dickens*, Diss., University of Strasbourg, 1895 (Esslingen: Langguth, 1895). 'A Dinner at Poplar Walk' is, as Butt and Tillotson indicate (p. 43), 'the most thoroughly revised of all the tales.' Its title in manuscript was 'A Sunday Out of Town' (see *Pilgrim Letters*, I, 32).

affectations (but by no means all of them), such as the frequent use of italics and quotation marks to indicate the author's cleverness ('Mr. Minns ... was always exceedingly clean, precise, and *tidy*, perhaps somewhat priggish, and the most "retiring man in the world"' – *Monthly Magazine*, N.S. 16, 617). Dickens also deleted a number of extravagant, even grotesque figures of speech (for example, Minns 'looked as merry as a farthing rush-light in a fog,' his boots 'were like pump-suckers,' had he 'been stung by an electric eel, he could not have made a more hysteric spring through the door-way'). But he left several others (Minns 'leaped from his seat as though he had received the discharge from a galvanic battery,' he was 'looking forward to his visit of the following Sunday with the feelings of a pennyless poet to the weekly visit of his Scotch landlady,' he was as happy as 'a tom-tit upon bird-lime') and added yet another ('the first gleam of pleasure he had experienced that morning, shone like a meteor through his wretchedness'). He made numerous other stylistic revisions to clarify meaning, eliminate wordiness, and, in a few instances, sharpen the humor, as in the description of a poodle who, 'with his hind legs on the floor, and his fore paws resting on the table, was dragging a bit of bread and butter out of a plate, preparatory to devouring it, with the buttered side next the carpet' (*Sketches by Boz*, Second Series, pp. 262–63). In the original version, the dog 'was dragging a bit of bread-and-butter out of a plate, which, in the ordinary course of things, it was natural to suppose he would eat with the buttered side next the carpet' (*Monthly Magazine*, N.S. 16, 618).

F. J. H. Darton associates such changes, even what he characterizes as 'a more self-conscious, dramatised system of stops' (p. 76), with an undesirable shift in the narrative tone of voice. They show Dickens, he claims, 'now, ever so slightly, looking at the effect of his words, instead of writing fluently,' trying, 'not too successfully, to feign an artlessness which was merely natural a little earlier in his career' (p. 75). I think Darton is mistaken. As I believe the examples above and the longer one below illustrate, the stylistic revisions help to produce a tone of voice that is, instead, often more mannered than that of the original, but perhaps therefore more appropriate to the artificiality of farcical characterization and plot. If the story suffers even in revision – and it does not compare favorably with the much less fully revised versions of Dickens's other early tales – it is not because the style is ostentatiously artless or too artfully mannered but because it is neither with any great consistency. Although Dickens was enough of a craftsman by 1836 to recognize some of the stylistic weaknesses in the original version, he was still not sufficiently experienced as an artist to recognize or know how to make all the changes requisite to creating a consistent, appropriate, and artistically satisfying tone of voice.

In addition to stylistic changes, Dickens made two other important alterations in 1836 that illustrate his development as a craftsman. The first of these is a thorough revision of a scene in a coach. Having waited an excessively long time for the coach to Poplar Walk to get underway (the coachman is attempting to find additional passengers), Minns, the tale's protagonist, voices his irritation. The two versions proceed as follows:

Original

'Going this minute, Sir,' was the reply; – and, accordingly, the coach trundled on for a couple of hundred yards, and then stopped again. Minns doubled himself up into a corner of the coach, and abandoned himself to fate.

'Tell your missis to make haste, my dear – 'cause here's a gentleman inside vich is in a desperate hurry.' In about five minutes more missis appeared, with a child and two band-boxes, and then they set off.

'Be quiet, love!' said the mother – who saw the agony of Minns, as the child rubbed its shoes on his new drab trowsers – 'be quiet, dear! Here, play with this parasol – don't kick the gentleman.'

The interesting infant, however, with its agreeable plaything, contrived to tax Mr. Minns's ingenuity, in the 'art of self-defence,' during the ride; and amidst these infantile assaults, and the mother's apologies, the distracted gentleman arrived at the Swan, when, on referring to his watch, to his great dismay he discovered that it was a quarter past five.

(*Monthly Magazine*, N.S. 16, 620)

Revision

'Going this minute, Sir,' was the reply; – and, accordingly the machine trundled on for a couple of hundred yards, and then stopped again. Minns doubled himself up into a corner of the coach, and abandoned himself to fate – as a child, a mother, a bandbox, and a parasol became his fellow passengers.

The child was an affectionate and an amiable infant; the little dear mistook Minns for its other parent, and screamed to embrace him.

'Be quiet, dear,' said the Mamma, restraining the impetuosity of the darling, whose little fat legs were kicking, and stamping, and twining themselves into the most complicated forms, in an ecstasy of impatience. 'Be quiet dear, that's not your Papa.'

'Thank heaven I am not' – thought Minns, as the first gleam of pleasure he had experienced that morning, shone like a meteor through his wretchedness.

Playfulness was agreeably mingled with affection in the disposition of the boy. When satisfied that Mr. Minns was not his parent, he endeavoured to attract his notice by scraping his drab trousers with his dirty shoes, poking his chest with his Mamma's parasol, and other nameless endearments, peculiar to infancy, with which he beguiled the tediousness of the ride, apparently very much to his own satisfaction.

When the unfortunate gentleman arrived at the Swan, he found to his great dismay, that it was a quarter past five.

(*Sketches by Boz*, Second Series, pp. 269–71)

In the revision Dickens not only creates a more artfully mannered narrative voice but also fills in the confusing gaps in the continuity of the narrative and produces humor that is less strained, more the natural if slightly exaggerated outgrowth of reality. He reports the child's behavior more directly and in greater descriptive detail and allows his narrator to indulge in humorous irony, hyperbole, and litotes – and even a touch of anthropomorphism as the bandbox and parasol, along with mother and child, become Minns's fellow passengers. Finally, he gives the scene more of a reason for its existence: it effectively dramatizes an earlier description of Minns's character and becomes less a transitional scene and more noticeably one in a series of frustrating encounters for Minns.

The other important change that Dickens made in 1836 – a thorough revision of the conclusion – gives the story the focus that the original version lacks. The conflict in the tale, as we know from a brief scene between the Bagshaws, Minns's cousin and his wife, revolves around their plan to persuade Minns to make their young Alick the heir to his modest fortune. In the original version, Dickens soon loses sight of this plot line while trying to derive as much humor as possible from Minns's harassment by Bagshaw and his undisciplined poodle, by the cabman and the child in the coach, and by the adults and young Bagshaw at the dinner party. This series of humiliations for Minns provides a secondary structure for the story along a line tangential, though not contradictory, to what seems to be the announced direction of plot movement. Toward the conclusion of the story, Dickens makes a crude attempt to regain his initial emphasis by having the Bagshaw child, in the confusion resulting from Minns's attempt to make a hasty departure from the party, cry out, 'Do stop, godpa' – I like you – Ma' says I am to coax you to leave me all your money!' (*Monthly Magazine*, N.S. 16, 624). But he fails to maintain the focus at the very end:

> Never from that day could Mr. Minns endure the name of Bagshaw or Poplar Walk. It was to him as the writing on the wall was to Belshazzar. Mr. Minns has removed from Tavistock Street. His residence is at present a secret, as he is determined not to risk another assault from his cousin and his pink-eyed poodle.
>
> (*Monthly Magazine*, N.S. 16, 624)

The revision, while still structuring the major portion of the story as before, brings the focus back at the end to the main conflict. Minns makes a definite decision about his will, and the reader, if not the Bagshaws (Dickens changed their name to Budden in 1836), is aware that the scheme of Minns's cousins has failed:

> He made his will next morning, and his professional man informs us, in that strict confidence in which we inform the public, that neither the name of Mr. Octavius Budden, nor of Mrs. Amelia Budden, nor of Master Alexander Augustus Budden, appears therein.
>
> (*Sketches by Boz*, Second Series, p. 282)

It seems likely that Dickens made these specific changes in the tale's resolution because he realized that in its main outline the original version was essentially formless. It did not take much to give form to the story, for the secondary structure held most of it together, but once again the alterations show Dickens learning to write better fiction.

Despite the young author's obviously greater awareness of his craft, and a developing ability in using the techniques of it, the revised version of 'A Dinner at Poplar Walk' is not a completely effective story. Its style lacks polish and much of the writing is uninspired. Though somewhat more fully developed in one scene and better structured overall, it is, like the original version, little more than a farcical and rather sterile *jeu d'esprit*. However, in revising the tale in 1836, Dickens must have found himself considerably hampered not only by time – he was, after all, writing *Pickwick Papers* in monthly parts, holding down a full-time position as a reporter for the *Morning Chronicle*, and doing other writing besides – but also by his original conception of the work. To have made anything more of the story would have involved a thorough redesigning and a complete rewriting of it.

*

In several important respects, 'The Bloomsbury Christening' can be considered as the very redesigned and rewritten tale that perhaps the young author should have made of 'A Dinner at Poplar Walk' in 1836. The stories themselves are very much alike. Each has as its central character a grumpy, ill-natured, fastidious bachelor-misanthropist (Minns, Dumps). He is visited by a relative (Bagshaw, Kitterbell) who invites the man to his home for a special occasion from which the host hopes to benefit tangibly. The bachelor accepts with reluctance. Following a disagreeable ride in a public conveyance, he arrives at the home, where he spends several boring hours replete with arid conversation and long-winded dinner speeches in the company of people who only exacerbate his misanthropic inclinations. In the end he manages to escape, vowing to have nothing more to do with his relatives. Dickens was at least reusing a standard plot structure of the sort encountered in the theatrical farces and the comic magazine tales with which he was all too familiar. But he made important changes and refinements in writing 'The Bloomsbury Christening' that seem to point to a dissatisfaction with 'A Dinner at Poplar Walk' and to a new insight into the potentialities of the basic story. While little improvement in the more technical aspects of style is to be noted or expected, the very *telling* of 'The Bloomsbury Christening' is a bit smoother, more continuous, perhaps because of the greater length of the tale (twelve pages as opposed to seven). But whether the cause or the effect of the additional pages, the interlinks between scenes and between actions and speeches within scenes are better developed, the main characters are presented in fuller detail and the minor characters somewhat more colorfully, the conflict is more evident throughout, and characterization, plot, and tone of voice work together to produce a much more structurally unified story.

A scene in an omnibus provides examples of some of these improvements.

36

It is three times as long as the parallel coach scene in the original version of 'A Dinner at Poplar Walk,' and more effective. The narrative transitions within it are smoother and the progression of events more naturally sequential and a bit more dramatic. Beginning with a long description of a rainy, miserable London day, the narrator then introduces us to Mr. Dumps, who, pausing at the corner in search of transportation to his nephew's, is immediately stolen by an aggressive omnibus 'cad,' or conductor, from beneath the noses of two others, and unceremoniously thrust into the middle of an already crowded vehicle. The discomfort of the wet passengers, newly augmented by the addition of Dumps, quite naturally becomes the subject of conversation and leads to the bachelor's argument with the cad. As a result the young man deliberately allows the omnibus to dash past Dumps's stop. Losing a second altercation, with cad and driver, over the fare, Dumps departs for the Kitterbells' in a vile mood. It is true that narrative progression in the 1836 version of the coach scene in 'A Dinner at Poplar Walk' is handled at least as well, perhaps even better. But, of course, when Dickens completely revised this scene then, he was able to utilize everything that he had learned about writing fiction between 1834 and 1836.

What is particularly important about the scene in 'The Bloomsbury Christening' is that Dickens is working in it with a larger number of characters – the scene is conceived on a slightly grander scale than is that of 'A Dinner at Poplar Walk' and requires that the author exercise greater control over his materials. The result is not perfect, but it is a notable accomplishment for a young writer's fourth story and a striking improvement over the scene in the original version of his first tale. Several of the characters in the Bloomsbury-bound omnibus momentarily spark into life, and the occupants of the vehicle, operating as a group in one of life's numerous petty conflicts, produce a scene whose humor, arising largely out of consistency of character, is at least suggestive of what the more experienced author would produce a few years later.

The techniques of characterization are necessarily simple – a descriptive touch, a suggestion of dialect, a mannerism, a gesture, an action briefly sketched – but the result is surprisingly good. A lawyer's clerk, who may be a satirical self-portrait of the author, is concisely depicted as a damp, constantly smirking young man in a red-and-white-striped shirt. His part in the conversation consists largely of puns. For example, when one of the passengers requests that Dumps sit anywhere but on his chest, the clerk replies, 'Perhaps the *box* would suit the gentleman better.'[7] The description is sketchy, the characterization flat, but when combined with the comic tone of voice in which the clerk delivers and reacts to his own witticisms

---

[7] *Monthly Magazine*, N.S. 17, 379. Describing a conversation with Dickens (*ca.* 1833–34), J. P. Collier relates, 'He informed me, as we walked through it, that he knew *Hungerford* Market well, laying unusual stress on the two first syllables' (Collier, *An Old Man's Diary*, IV, 15), a pun not unworthy of the lawyer's clerk.

(he chuckles audibly at his second effort, blithely oblivious of the discomfort of Dumps that occasioned it), the result is a young man bursting with self-satisfaction and *joie de vivre*. The omnibus driver appears in one brief paragraph, but his speech, apparently an accurate reproduction, and the brief description of his nonchalant stance on the box that belies at the same time that it reinforces the determination of his remarks reveal more than one might expect about the confidence of the man. The Cockney omnibus cad, who is the major antagonist in the scene, is a notorious trouble-maker, as is revealed by the false solicitousness of his tone of voice and by actions clearly expressive of his independence: slamming the door once he knows it bothers Dumps, deliberately allowing the omnibus to go far past Dumps's corner, and joining with the driver in demanding full fare nevertheless. After each incident he appears all innocence – and all arrogance.

Like its counterpart in 'A Dinner at Poplar Walk,' this scene in the omnibus provides a transition between the two main episodes in the story and is an important structural element if the story is viewed largely as a character sketch. Here again 'The Bloomsbury Christening' is an improvement upon the original version of the first tale. Dickens, flexing his new authorial muscles, builds onto his earlier characterization of Minns by making Dumps a more colorful, more fully conceived, more humorously depicted, more complex character than Minns. A cross, cadaverous, odd, ill-natured, tall, fifty-year-old bachelor, Dumps is initially described as delighting in being miserable and in making others miserable, too. He takes, we are told by the narrator, a perverse pleasure in cemeteries, funeral services, fretful and impatient whist players, and King Herod's massacre of the innocents – and hates children, cabs, old women, doors that will not shut, musical amateurs, harmless amusements, people who find comfort in religion, and omnibus cads. The scene in the omnibus helps to dramatize this description by showing Dumps confronting unsuccessfully (thus, of course, contributing to his love of misery) two of the antipathies listed, as well as rain, wet umbrellas and people, a crowded omnibus, a window that will not shut, annoying passengers, and an unsympathetic coachman.

But let us go beyond an examination of the scene in the omnibus for its own sake to a more general consideration of the importance of Dickens's characterization of Dumps to the structure and purpose of the entire story. Unlike Minns, Dumps is aggressive; thus the rudeness with which he is treated during his ride in the omnibus, and his failure to reciprocate fully, reinforce his misanthropy and, what is more important, further motivate him to unleash the full force of his frustration on the Kitterbells, who he believes beguiled him in some way into serving as their infant's godfather. In 'A Dinner at Poplar Walk,' Minns's mild triumph over the Bagshaws is an unexpected windfall, for he is predominantly a victim, a passive receptor of the incivilities of others. Even in deciding finally to have nothing more to do with his relatives – and in the revised version to leave the Bagshaw boy out of his will – he is not acting in a way contrary to how he might have behaved under less harassing circumstances. As a result, even the 1836 version of the story contains very little dramatic tension. Mr. Dumps, on the other hand, does not have such an easy time of it. There is no immediate question of whether or not the godson is to be Dumps's heir. So far as tangible benefits are concerned, Kitterbell desires only the traditional silver christening cup, and he is understandably upset when it is discovered that a thief has deftly removed it from his uncle's coat pocket.

But this is a minor disappointment; the story does not end here. Dumps must himself take steps to upset the family and guests at the christening party, to make them at least as miserable as he feels they have made him. He conscientiously sets about this through his understanding of the psychology of newly-made parents, dwelling at great length in his toast at supper upon such sensitive matters as infant mortality, wasting childhood diseases, and filial ingratitude. Mrs. Kitterbell goes into hysterics, her husband is almost as greatly upset, and the christening party ends in shambles. Thus Dumps is a far more effective protagonist than Minns, and the plot of the story, held together by the reader's desire to see whether or not Dumps will behave in a way consistent with his early established character and whether or not he will manage to revenge himself upon the Kitterbells, has a greater suspense, force, and vitality to it. Again, Dickens elaborates upon the basic plot line used in his first tale, makes slight changes, shifts emphases, develops a closer relationship between character and structure, and comes up with a noticeably improved and redesigned version in 'The Bloomsbury Christening.'

In connection with the improvements already described, Dickens makes a basic change in the narrative tone of voice that produces a consistent satiric effect in 'The Bloomsbury Christening.' The change is achieved through a shift in the attitude of the narrator toward the characters in his tale. In 'A Dinner at Poplar Walk,' the Bagshaws are crude, boorish, unattractive fortune-hunters, but Minns, their victim, is entitled to some sympathy. Even though the reader is not attracted by the man's irritability and fastidiousness, he is inclined to enjoy the bachelor's triumph at the end because of the indignities to which the Bagshaws have subjected Minns. The narrator himself seems to be a young man who thinks he is terribly clever, and more often is not, but whose sympathy for Minns's desire to be left alone and whose even more intense dislike of the Bagshaws' greed and provinciality guide the reader's responses to the characters and to the final working out of the story.[8] While the narrator of 'The Bloomsbury

---

[8] In 'Comic Viewpoints in *Sketches by Boz*,' *English: The Magazine of the English Association*, 12 (1958/59), C. B. Cox states that the important theme of the tale is implicit in the contrast that Dickens draws between the coldness and drabness of Minns's 'ordered existence' and the 'exuberant joy in life' of Bagshaw (pp. 133–34). In addition to the evidence that I have already given in the text, one need only contrast the relationship between Scrooge and his nephew in *A Christmas Carol* (which does, it seems to me, illustrate the contrast of which Cox speaks) with that between Minns and his cousin to realize that Dickens does *not* favor the Bagshaws to Minns.

Christening' shares an often tasteless cleverness with Minns's narrator, he is a more objective observer of human behavior; as a result, the reader is not allowed to extend his sympathy, at least not for long, to any character in the tale. If at one moment he feels that Dumps has been unduly insulted, a page later he encounters Dumps inflicting similar insults on others. If he begins to sympathize with the Kitterbells (it is their child's christening day, after all, and Dumps's vindictiveness seems a bit of an overcompensation), he must remind himself of their greed, smug middle-classness, unattractive physiognomies, unpleasant mannerisms, silliness, and general dullness.

What Dickens much more successfully and perhaps more intentionally produces in 'The Bloomsbury Christening' than in 'A Dinner at Poplar Walk' is a satire on human relationships. The aloof, unsympathetic narrator forces the reader to see that both men are foolish, foible-ridden, and at times disgusting human beings, that in the end neither man triumphs, that no good, no human understanding, results from their interaction. This conscious satiric intent is most evident in the ironic juxtaposition of the reactions of the men to each other at the end, Dumps gloating in mad triumph, Kitterbell happy to be rid of 'the most miserable man in the world.' Certainly the final effect comes closer than that of 'A Dinner at Poplar Walk' to what its youthful author considered an accurate picture of life, for in the Preface to the First Series of *Sketches by Boz*, he proudly characterized the collection as 'little pictures of life and manners as they really are.' The 'little pictures' are surprisingly dark, as dark in some respects as the view of life in the novels of Dickens's maturity, and darker than that in his early novels. Mr. Pickwick, Mrs. Nickleby, and Mr. Micawber, for example, are products of a far more sympathetic understanding of man's frailties than are Dumps, the Bagshaws, the Kitterbells, and even Minns. Compared with the satirical effectiveness of the short pieces that Dickens wrote in the next two years and certainly of *Pickwick Papers* itself, the satire in 'The Bloomsbury Christening' is coarse-grained. Nevertheless, the emphasis that it gives to Dickens's early impression of reality defines, it seems to me, another important if still primary stage in the young man's progress as a writer.

Thus, in the slightly greater vitality and import of its subject (a christening as opposed to a Sunday dinner), in its more fully and more colorfully realized characters, in its greater dramatic tension, and in the satirical suggestiveness produced by improvements in structure and tone of voice, 'The Bloomsbury Christening' stands as a significant early work in Dickens's career.

As his work on 'A Dinner at Poplar Walk' and 'The Bloomsbury Christening' illustrates, Dickens's early development was largely associated with a search for effective style and form. We get intimations (particularly, of course, in the 1836 version of his first tale) of the style that, from *Pickwick Papers* on, would be recognized as 'Dickensian.' We see Dickens working conscientiously with various stylistic elements to improve the quality of humor, to redeem characters from utter flatness, to create fuller and more colorfully detailed scenes, and to maintain a more consistently satiric tone of voice. At times his attempts are reasonably successful. But Dickens was, I think, always less troubled by style than by form. As his novels became increasingly complex, they reflected his developing artistic facility and maturity as well as a more serious assumption of the responsibilities of social critic, moral philosopher, and artist. Inevitably, the structural problems demanding solution merely increased in number and difficulty. In these early tales, his problems with form are of a lower order but certainly as troublesome for the young writer to resolve satisfactorily. In 'The Bloomsbury Christening' and the 1836 version of his first tale, he managed to correct some of the flaws in structure that marred 'A Dinner at Poplar Walk,' both in regard to the development of individual scenes and, especially in 'The Bloomsbury Christening,' to the artistic unity of the entire tale.

But we should also realize that the improvements in his fourth tale came earlier and more easily than might otherwise have been the case because it was conceived and worked out from the beginning essentially as a redesigned version of his first story. While we cannot discount the favorable effect that such a reworking must have had upon Dickens, the other tales he wrote in late 1833 and in 1834 were new, not redesigned, and, in each instance, presented most of the same old problems of inspiration, construction, and development that confronted the twenty-one year old author when he first sat down to write 'A Dinner at Poplar Walk.'

Dickens may even have been hampered in his development by the generally favorable reception of his early work. A week after its appearance in the *Monthly Magazine*, his first tale was pirated, as he proudly informed his friend, Henry Kolle, for publication in the *London Weekly Magazine* (still known to Dickens by its former title, *The Thief*). He had also received 'a polite and flattering communication from the Monthly people requesting more papers,' and he was in the midst of planning or writing two short tales, a series of papers to be called 'The Parish,' and a 'proposed Novel,' which he was considering cutting up into magazine sketches, 'as publishing is hazardous.'[9] A few months later, the *Weekly Dispatch* listed 'The Bloomsbury Christening' as among 'the amusing papers' in the April issue of the *Monthly Magazine* and the following month indicated that the first part of 'The Boarding House' was 'excellent in [its] way.'[10] Dickens may not have seen these pleasant notices, but surely he

---

[9] *Pilgrim Letters*, I, 33, to H. W. Kolle, [?10 December 1833]. For a note on the *London Weekly Magazine*, see Walter Dexter, 'When Found: The Pirates,' *Dickensian*, 30 (1933/34), 239.

[10] Quoted in Walter Dexter, 'Contemporary Opinion of Dickens's Earliest Work,' *Dickensian*, 31 (1934/35), 106.

heard no unfavorable comments from relatives, friends, and editorial acquaintances.

Even so, when we read the tales in the order of their publication (presumably also the order of their composition), we notice active efforts to improve, to experiment, to learn the craft of writing. We see the budding writer attempting, not always successfully, to come to grips with the complex process of interweaving the strands of plot, scene development, characterization, and tone into a coherent, vibrant, and meaningful fictional pattern.

Although Dickens grouped these early pieces under the heading of 'tales' in the first combined edition of the two series of *Sketches by Boz*,[11] most are fictional 'sketches,' 'episodes,' or 'scenes' – and not very good ones at that. The structural flaws of 'A Dinner at Poplar Walk' haunt these pieces, too. Most lack convincing focus. At the beginning of 'Horatio Sparkins,' Dickens's third tale, the Maldertons are concerned about the social status of Sparkins, their daughter's suitor. But in the middle section, this concern is completely ignored (by Dickens as well as the Maldertons) in favor of a lengthy satire of snobbery and, on the part of the grocer uncle, reverse snobbery. As a matter of fact, the Maldertons now stand in awe of Sparkins's affected social graces. At the end, when mother and daughter discover that the elegant young man is really Mr. Samuel Smith, the lowly clerk and junior partner in a 'cheap' store, which they happen to be patronizing, the reader is not horrified, delighted, or amused but simply annoyed by the unfocused satire.

Dickens also fails to develop scenes essential to the plot and to the total comic or satiric effect. At the denouement in 'Horatio Sparkins,' the Malderton women no sooner recognize Sparkins than the narrator intrudes with '"We will draw a veil," as novel writers say, over the scene that ensued.' This should, surely, be the climactic moment; it should tie together whatever loose plot ends are about and give final unifying focus to the author's views on human nature. There should, perhaps, be painful explanations, indignant remonstrances, or even laughter. After all, what a series of blows to affectation, snobbery, and hypocrisy! And 'drawing a veil' is not, in this instance, comic in itself. In the first part of 'The Boarding House,' such a device works fairly successfully, but this story has other flaws. In 'Mrs. Joseph Porter, "Over the Way,"' Dickens prepares the reader for a comic *tour de force*, an amateur performance of *Othello* to be accompanied *sotto voce* by devastatingly clever critical commentary. But he passes over the scene with 'It would be useless and tiresome to quote the number of instances in which Uncle Tom, now completely in his element, and instigated by the mischievous Mrs. Porter, corrected the mistakes of

---

[11] This was the edition issued by Chapman and Hall in monthly parts, November 1837–June 1839, and in one volume, May 1839. For details, see Butt and Tillotson, pp. 56–57, and Appendix A, below.

the performers. . . .' Only a year or two later Dickens would have developed this scene fully, but in 1833–34 he seems to have thought the idea comic enough in itself.

Much of the blame for such plot inadequacies lies, I suspect, in Dickens's attraction to the popular farces of the late eighteenth- and early nineteenth-century, an influence noticed and praised, unfortunately, by a number of the reviewers of *Sketches by Boz* in 1836.[12] Dickens himself contemplated a 'dramatic destination' for 'The Bloomsbury Christening,' as he pointed out in a letter printed in the *Monthly Magazine* complaining of an unauthorized dramatization of his story by John Buckstone, a popular actor and play-wright.[13]

'The Christening,' Buckstone's version of the tale, is typical of the farcical afterpieces performed at that time and resembles Dickens's tale only in a few speeches, two or three characters, and the fact that it has some-thing to do with a baby's christening. Major modifications produced new characters and altered relationships between others. Assigned, by a curious coincidence, to review Buckstone's one-act farce for the *Morning Chronicle*, Dickens wrote in part:

> A new trifle, in one act, by Mr. Buckstone, was produced here last night [13 October 1834], and met with complete success. It would be hardly fair to detail the plot of an amusing interlude, which is principally made up of unlooked-for situations, and humorous *equivoques*. We will, therefore, only say that the principal features of the peace [*sic*] are the distresses of *Grum* (Mr. Wilkinson), a surly misanthrope, who is entrapped into becoming sponsor for the first child of *Mr. Hopkins Twiddie* (Mr. Buckstone), and the confusion arising from certain mistakes occasioned by a changing of children, and con-

---

[12] Among them was George Hogarth, soon to become Dickens's father-in-law, who wrote in the obviously partisan *Morning Chronicle* (5 February 1836) as follows: 'These tales are in general very interesting and entertaining; and several of them are so ingenious in their plot, so full of *ris comica*, and told in so dramatic a manner, that they want little more than a division into scenes to become excellent theatrical pieces. To one of them, "The Bloomsbury Christening," Mr. Buckstone is indebted for his very popular piece of "The Christening," and the admirable tales, "The Great Winglebury Duel" [first published in the First Series], "The Boarding House," "Horatio Sparkins," and the "Passage in the Life of Mr. Watkins Tottle," are equally rich in dramatic materials.' This and other reviews are quoted in W[alter] D[exter], 'The Reception of Dickens's First Book,' *Dickensian*, 32 (1935/36), 44, 45–50.

[13] Quoted in W[alter] D[exter], 'A New Contribution to "The Monthly Magazine" and an Early Dramatic Criticism in "The Morning Chronicle,"' *Dickensian*, 30 (1933/34), 224. In a note appended to the letter, the editor corroborated Dickens's statement: 'We know that he [Boz] has already prepared a farce on the subject, which Mr. Buckstone has so unceremoniously appropriated; and ... we think such literary larceny most unwarrantable.' J. B. Buckstone's 'The Christening' was published in 1834 and in '*John Jones*,' and '*The Christening*,' Dicks' Standard Plays, No. 816 (London: John Dicks, n.d.). If such a script actually existed – and it may not have – it is no longer extant. In all editions of *Sketches by Boz*, through the Cheap Edition (1850), Dickens placed the following note at the beginning of his tale: 'The Author may be permitted to observe that this sketch was published some time before the Farce entitled "The Christening" was first represented.'

founding of people, which frequently take place on the stage, and never occur elsewhere.[14]

Dickens obviously recognized the unrealistic, ephemeral nature of a farce in calling Buckstone's effort a 'trifle' and an 'interlude' and in stating that the plot contrivances of 'The Christening' could happen only on the stage. While these remarks might be applied equally well to 'The Bloomsbury Christening,' the concluding statement suggests that Dickens thought his tale came closer than Buckstone's dramatic version to reality. It does avoid some of the worst excesses of the Buckstone script. Dickens also realized that a farce's vitality depends not only upon the manipulation of the basic plot to produce typical farcical situations but also upon exaggerated characters, clever stage business, and witty dialogue not urgently related to the plot. One can see Buckstone, always the actor, working just such business into his script. In the delight of the moment, the audience scarcely notices whether or not the plot is weak. Yet in a printed tale, capable of being studied at leisure, plot deficiencies that mar the movement of the story soon catch the eye of the critical reader. Only vivid characterization or a dazzling style could possibly put the critic in a forgiving mood. While such brilliancy flashes out from time to time in these early tales, it is scarcely often enough to compensate for flawed plot construction.

In placing emphasis on the comic scene rather than on plot motivation, Dickens followed in the tradition of the stage farce. But he had to write a number of tales before he at all mastered even the techniques of scene development. Unexplainably abrupt jumps in time, omission of necessary details, crudity of humor, and inadequately developed characterizations are some of the flaws already indicated in reference to 'A Dinner at Poplar Walk.' These and others are too often typical of the remaining tales as well. Characters carry on conversations (thereby creating scenes) merely because

---

[14] D[exter], 'A New Contribution to "The Monthly Magazine" and an Early Dramatic Criticism in "The Morning Chronicle,"' pp. 223–24. Grum was Dickens's Dumps and Mr. Hopkins Twiddy (the correct spelling) his Kitterbell. Dickens pointedly remarked in his review: 'We hailed one or two of the characters with great satisfaction – they are old and very particular friends of ours. We met with them, and several of the jokes we heard last night, at a certain "Bloomsbury Christening" described in "The Monthly Magazine" some little time since' (p. 224). When the play was revived for the 1835 season, the *Morning Chronicle* review of 29 September stated: 'The excellent burletta of *The Christening* followed. It was admirably acted, particularly by Buckstone, Mrs. Keeley, and Wilkinson, and, from beginning to end, kept the house in a roar. Who is the author of this piece? We read a tale in the *Monthly Magazine*, a couple of years ago, we believe [actually April 1834], of which *The Christening*, as represented, seems to be little more than a transcript, with a change in the names of the characters.' Quoted in William J. Carlton, 'Charles Dickens, Dramatic Critic,' *Dickensian*, 56 (1960), 14. The play was withdrawn a week later, Carlton states (p. 14). The review was probably not by Dickens, but he or his friends were obviously protecting his interests.

Dickens knows he must not merely *tell* a story[15] but, as of necessity did his dramatic models, *show* his characters in action by creating a series of scenes in roughly chronological order, occupying a certain amount of space and time, and unfolding largely through dialogue – even though there might be no obvious structural necessity for some of the scenes. Compare the stilted, extraneous dialogue of a dinner scene in 'The Boarding House' (May 1834) with the forceful exuberance of a passage from *Pickwick Papers* (No. IX, December 1836) in which Sam Weller discovers details of Mrs. Bardell's plan to prosecute Pickwick for breach of promise. Not only will the comparison pinpoint Dickens's limitations as a writer in 1834 but also reveal something of his development as a craftsman in the next two years:

From 'The Boarding House'

'Soup for Mrs. Maplesone, my dear,' said the bustling Mrs. Tibbs. She always called her husband 'my dear' before company. Tibbs, who had been eating his bread, and calculating how long it would be before he should get any fish, helped the soup in a hurry, made a small island on the tablecloth, and put his glass upon it, to hide it from his wife.

'Miss Julia, shall I assist you to some fish?'

'If you please – very little – oh, plenty, thank you;' (a bit about the size of a walnut put upon the plate.)

'Julia is a *very* little eater,' said Mrs. Maplesone to Mr. Calton.

.   .   .

'Ah,' said Mr. Calton, filling his glass, 'Tom Moore is my poet.'

'And mine,' said Mrs. Maplesone.

'And mine,' said Miss Julia.

'And mine,' added Mr. Simpson.

'Look at his compositions,' resumed [Mr. Calton].

'To be sure,' said Simpson, with confidence.

(*Monthly Magazine*, N.S. 17, 485–87)

From *Pickwick Papers*

'Ven is it expected to come on?' inquired Sam.

'Either in February or March,' replied Mrs. Bardell.

---

[15] The best example of Dickens's early ability with narrative description occurs at the end of the first chapter of 'Passage in the Life of Mr. Watkins Tottle' (*Monthly Magazine*, N.S. 19, 21–24) in Gabriel Parsons's account of the complications arising on his wedding night from his and his bride's desire to keep their marriage secret. Beginning with 'I spent my wedding-night in a back-kitchen chimney,' Parsons's narrative succeeds largely through its felicitous phrasing, the tension and humor of the sentence structure and diction, the avoidance of puns and extravagant word-play, and primarily the wild absurdity of the action itself. Yet even this passage lacks the brilliancy of Tony Weller's almost incidental description of his encounter with 'the shepherd' who is the bane of his life in Ch. xxii of *The Posthumous Papers of the Pickwick Club* (London: Chapman and Hall, 1837), pp. 224–25 (identical to the publication in monthly parts, April 1836–May 1837, July–November 1837). Unless otherwise specified, references to *Pickwick Papers* are to this edition.

'What a number of witnesses there'll be, won't there?' said Mrs. Cluppins.

'And won't Mr. Dodson and Fogg be wild if the plaintiff shouldn't get it?' added Mrs. Cluppins, 'when they do it all on speculation!'

'Ah! won't they!' said Mrs. Sanders.

'But the plaintiff must get it,' resumed Mrs. Cluppins.

'I hope so,' said Mrs. Bardell.

'Oh, there can't be any doubt about it,' rejoined Mrs. Sanders.

'Vell,' said Sam, rising and setting down his glass. 'All I can say is, that I vish you *may* get it.'

'Thanke'e, Mr. Weller,' said Mrs. Bardell, fervently.

'And of them Dodson and Fogg, as does these sort o' things on spec,' continued Mr. Weller, 'as vell as for the other kind and gen'rous people o' the same purfession, as sets people by the ears free gratis for nothin', and sets their clerks to work to find out little disputes among their neighbours and acquaintance as vants settlin' by means o' law-suits – all I can say o' them is, that I vish they had the revard I'd give 'em.'

'Ah, I wish they had the reward that every kind and generous heart would be inclined to bestow upon them,' said the gratified Mrs. Bardell.

'Amen to that,' replied Sam, 'and a fat and happy livin' they'd get out of it. Vish you good night, ladies.'

(Ch. xxvi, pp. 273–74)

In the scene from *Pickwick* Dickens relies upon his reader's knowledge of Sam's character to effect the delightfully cutting irony of the situation, and through dialogue and only the briefest touch of description allows the naïveté, vindictiveness, and self-righteous indignation of the women to show through. He does not stop to explain what is happening, as he does in the passage from 'The Boarding House'; the conversation is meaningful in its own right, moving the story forward the desired amount. But unlike the dialogue in 'The Boarding House,' this is also colorful and rich enough in itself (in its specific details and character-revealing words, phrasing, and mannerisms) to merit its existence for aesthetic reasons alone.

One would expect *Pickwick Papers* to show considerable improvement in technique. But a few scenes in the early tales show some improvement also, if not as much as does the larger work. Two or three such scenes are to be found in 'The Steam Excursion' (October 1834), one of the better *Monthly Magazine* tales. While it, too, has a weak, unfocused plot, it re-deems itself by being a charming, frequently humorous sketch of an outing on the Thames that ends disastrously in rough water – and seasickness. One of the scenes (others will be described later) was created primarily to get Percy Noakes, the planner of the outing, from shore to the excursion boat. The dialogue here is relatively effective in bringing this about and also is sufficiently well-handled to make the scene entertaining in itself:

'Boat, Sir!' cried one of the three watermen who were mopping out their boats, and all whistling different tunes. 'Boat, Sir!'

THE *MONTHLY MAGAZINE* TALES

'No,' replied Mr. Percy Noakes rather sharply, for the inquiry was not made in a manner at all suitable to his dignity.

'Would you prefer a wessel, Sir?' inquired another, to the infinite delight of the 'Jack-in-the-water.'

Mr. Percy Noakes replied with a look of the most supreme contempt.

'Did you want to be put on board a steamer, Sir?' inquired an old fireman-waterman very confidentially. He was dressed in a faded red suit, just the colour of the cover of a very old Court-guide.

'Yes, make haste – the Endeavour; off the Custom-house.'

'Endeavour!' cried the man who had convulsed the 'Jack' before. 'Vy, I see the Endeavour go up half an hour ago.'

'So did I,' said another; 'and I should think she'd gone down by this time, for she's a precious sight too full of ladies and gen'lmen.'

Mr. Percy Noakes affected to disregard these representations, and stepped into the boat, which the old man, by dint of scrambling, and shoving, and grating, had brought up to the causeway. – 'Shove her off,' cried Mr. Percy Noakes, and away the boat glided down the river, Mr. Percy Noakes seated on the recently mopped seat, and the watermen at the stairs offering to bet him any reasonable sum that he'd never reach the 'Custum-us.'

(*Monthly Magazine*, N.S. 18, 366)[16]

More successful, however, and more reminiscent of the later Dickens is the well-conceived scene in the 'social room' of the sponging house from 'Passage in the Life of Mr. Watkins Tottle' (Chapter the Second). Having been informed of Tottle's arrest for debt, Gabriel Parsons, his fair-weather friend, has reluctantly come with the money for his release; their greater purpose, entrapping the comfortably wealthy Miss Lillerton, remains to be accomplished. Admittedly the scene, viewed largely through Parsons's eyes, does not really forward the story, and even detracts from it – that is, we are aware of Tottle's financial straits from the preceding scenes, and the characters created for the sponging house scene do not reappear later in the story. But it may have some value as a background against which we are to understand the pathetic figure Tottle will cut later in the story. Because the conversation and action occur between minor characters, Dickens was forced to make quick and clear distinctions between characters. Although he selected stereotyped characters – Ikey, one of the assistants of the establishment; a destitute young married couple abandoned by their parents; a horse-dealer from Islington; a cheerful, healthy-looking couple in their forties; Willis, a 'young fellow of vulgar manners,' smoking a cigar and frequently imbibing from a pint pot; and Walker, something of a realist – they come to life for a moment through a fully dramatized scene, of which the following exchange between Willis and Walker is but a brief excerpt:

---

[16] Interesting parallels to this and other scenes in 'The Steam Excursion' are to be found in an earlier essay by John Poole entitled 'Preparations for Pleasure; or, A Pic-Nic.' See Appendix D for details.

['] Well, Mr. Willis,' continued [Walker], addressing the young man with the cigar, 'you seem rather down to-day – floored, as one may say. What's the matter, Sir? Never say die, you know.'

'Oh! I'm all right,' replied the smoker. 'I shall be bailed out to-morrow.'

'Shall you though?' enquired the other. 'Damme, I wish I could say the same. I am as regularly over head and ears as the Royal George; and stand about as much chance of being *bailed out*. Ha! ha! ha!'

'Why,' said the young man, stopping short, and speaking in a very loud key, 'Look at me. What d'ye think I've stopped here two days for?'

''Cause you couldn't get out, I suppose,' interrupted Mr. Walker, winking at the company. 'Not that you're exactly obliged to stop here, only you can't help it. No compulsion, you know, only you must – eh?'

'A'n't he a rum'un?' inquired the delighted individual, who had offered the gin-and-water, of his wife.

'Oh, he just is!' replied the lady, who was quite overcome by these flashes of imagination.

'Why, my case,' frowned the victim, throwing the end of his cigar into the fire, and illustrating his argument by knocking the bottom of the pot on the table, at intervals – 'my case is a very singular one: my father's a man of large property, and I am his son.'

'That's a very strange circumstance,' interrupted the jocose Mr. Walker, *en passant*.

' – I am his son, and have received a liberal education. I don't owe no man nothing – not the value of a farthing, but I was induced, you see, to put my name to some bills for a friend – bills to a large amount. I may say a very large amount, for which I didn't receive no consideration. What's the consequence?'

'Why, I suppose the bills went out, and you came in. The acceptances were'nt taken up, and you were, eh?' inquired Walker.

(Monthly Magazine, N.S. 19, 124–25)

The concrete details, the highly colloquial and self-characterizing speech, the easy and sometimes biting banter between the characters, the choric effect provided by the amused man and his wife, the bravado and prevarication of Willis, and the assurance and cleverness of Walker provide in large part the freshness and gusto of the scene. There are a few moments of stilted writing, but the dialogue generally reflects consistency of characterization and produces a reasonably subtle mixture of the comic and, a bit later in the scene, the pathetic.

★

Fully dramatized scenes in a novel require a number of ingredients in addition to structural unity and inner continuity of action and dialogue. One such ingredient is a setting that reflects or reinforces the author's view of human nature, of society, and of life itself. Considering Dickens's genius in creating such settings – the slums of *Oliver Twist*, the street riots of *Barnaby Rudge*, the storm at sea in *David Copperfield*, Krook's shop and the oppressive fog of *Bleak House*, and, even in *Pickwick Papers*, the idyllic country scenes, the inns and law offices, Dingley Dell, and the Fleet environment – it is surprising to find so little description of this kind in the *Monthly Magazine* tales. Yet, again, what there is reveals Dickens's slowly developing concern for colorfully detailed settings and his increasing use of them to reinforce at least incidental if not overall mood, tone, or thesis. In his second tale, 'Mrs. Joseph Porter, "Over the Way"' (January 1834), the description of the preparations for the amateur production of *Othello* only generally refers to 'a strange jumble of flats, flies, wings, lamps, bridges, clouds, thunder and lightning, festoons and flowers, daggers and foil, and all the other messes which in theatrical slang are included under the comprehensive name of "properties"' (*Monthly Magazine*, N.S. 17, 11). Quantity is here, but not color or the unique perception. However, later descriptions, such as the following from 'Sentiment!' where Dickens gives a promising glimpse of a 'finishing establishment for young ladies,' are somewhat more colorful and original:

> The house was a white one, a little removed from the road-side, with close palings in front. The bedroom windows were always left partly open to afford a bird's-eye view of numerous little bedsteads, with very white dimity furniture, and thereby impress the passer-by with a due sense of the luxuries of the establishment; and there was a front parlour hung round with highly-varnished maps, which nobody ever looked at, and filled with books which no one ever read, appropriated exclusively to the reception of parents, who whenever they called, could not fail to be struck with the very knowledge-imparting appearance of the place.
>
> (*Sketches by Boz*, First Series, II, 320)

In his comments about the open windows and the maps no one ever touches, Dickens makes some use of the physical characteristics of Minerva House to supply information about his characters and to suggest his attitude toward them. Certainly we learn much about the intellectual pretensions and interests of students, teachers, and parents.

It is, however, in 'The Steam Excursion,' that we find more positive evidence of Dickens's developing powers of description, though even here descriptive passages are still not numerous; we get only a glimpse of Percy Noakes's chambers, for example, none whatever of the Tauntons' apartment, and very little of the excursion boat on which much of the action takes place. It is not essential that we be provided with detailed settings in these instances, but Dickens could have used them to characterize and satirize several of his main characters as well as to afford additional opportunities for incidental humor. On the other hand, a description of London streets early in the morning is well done, the details of the setting furnished mainly by people rather than by buildings and other inanimate objects:

The streets looked as lonely and deserted as if they had been crowded over-night for the last time. Here and there an early apprentice, with quenched-looking, sleepy eyes, was taking down the shutters of a shop; and a policeman or milk-woman might occasionally be seen pacing slowly along; the servants had not yet begun to clean the doors, or light the fires, and London looked the picture of desolation. At the corner of a bye-street, near Temple Bar, was stationed a 'street breakfast.' The coffee was boiling over a charcoal fire, and large slices of bread and butter were piled one upon the other, like deals in a timber-yard. The company were seated on a form, which, with a view both to security and comfort, was placed against a neighbouring wall. Two young men, whose uproarious mirth and disordered dress bespoke the conviviality of the preceding evening, were treating three 'ladies' and an Irish labourer. A little sweep was standing at a short distance, casting a longing eye at the tempt-ing delicacies; and a policeman was watching the group from the opposite side of the street. The wan looks, and gaudy finery of the wretched, thinly clad females, contrasted as strangely with the gay sun-light, as did their forced merriment with the boisterous hilarity of the two young men, who now and then varied their amusements by 'bonneting' the proprietor of this itinerant coffee house.

(*Monthly Magazine*, N.S. 18, 365–66)

At the same time, this setting is quite extraneous to the forward movement of the tale and contradictory to its general satiric tone. In calling attention to what is little more than a transitional scene, Dickens momentarily distorts the structure and intent of his tale.

On the other hand, the description of the storm that arises on the steam-boat's return trip contributes greatly to the humor of the tale's final scene. The description of the interior of the cabin and of the articles on the banquet table beautifully characterizes the storm outside – and its effect on the excursion party:

The throbbing motion of the engine was but too perceptible. There was a large substantial cold boiled leg of mutton at the bottom of the table, shaking like blanc-mange; a hearty sirloin of beef looked as if it had been suddenly seized with the palsy; and some tongues, which were placed on dishes rather too large for them, were going through the most surprising evolutions, darting from side to side and from end to end, like a fly in an inverted wine-glass. Then the sweets shook and trembled till it was quite impossible to help them, and people gave up the attempt in despair; and the pigeon-pies looked as if the birds, whose legs were stuck outside, were trying to get them in. The table vibrated and started like a feverish pulse, and the very legs were slightly convulsed – every thing was shaking and jarring. The beams in the roof of the cabin seemed as if they were put there for the sole purpose of giving people head-aches, and several elderly gentlemen became ill-tempered in consequence. As fast as the steward put the fire-irons up, they would fall down again; and the more the ladies and gentlemen tried to sit comfortably on their seats, the more the seats seemed to slide away from the ladies and gentlemen. Several ominous demands were made for small glasses of brandy, the countenances of the company gradually underwent the most extraordinary changes; and one gentleman was observed suddenly to rush from table without the slightest ostensible reason, and dart up the steps with incredible swiftness, thereby greatly damaging both himself and the steward, who happened to be coming down at the same moment.

(Monthly Magazine, N.S. 18, 373–74)

This passage contains virtues of the later Dickens: the animation of inanimate objects, here for the purpose of humor; the pseudo-innocence of the narrator, who presumably cannot for the life of himself imagine why the gentleman should dash madly from the cabin; the inconsequential, unreasonable, and therefore humorous action of the steward's constant putting-up of the fire-irons; and the realism lying behind the colorfully exaggerated descriptions.

★

While Dickens developed some understanding of the function of setting in a tale and improved his descriptive techniques, the results are not as satisfying in the matter of characterization. Most characters lack the sparkle of originality, probably because the models that he imitated so obsequiously while writing the *Monthly Magazine* tales were of inferior quality. Not until he abandoned the style of farcical tales and plays and came under the more edifying influence of descriptive essays and the eighteenth-century novel would his characters become more imaginative. The popular farcical tale required much narration simply to get itself told. As a result the characters had to be easily recognizable comic types. While the truly creative artist is always able to give dramatic life to such stereotypes, Dickens was still too much of a novice for such an achievement. Nor did his strong reliance on the stage farce serve him well. The stories contain the dialogue of a script but too often lack the details of the successful performance. Allardyce Nicoll points out that most of the farces of the period 'were written for low-comedy actors who could "put across" almost anything, and consequently there is generally evident a carelessness on the part of the authors both as regards plot and form.'[17] These playwrights were equally lax with characterization, again relying upon the actors to provide details of speech, appearance, mannerism, and stage movement – the very details that made audiences laugh. The actors themselves were obviously not slow to accept such flattering challenges to their abilities. After examining scripts by such turn-of-the-century writers of farces as Frederick Reynolds and Charles Dibden, Leigh Hunt concluded that while the actors were excellent, the 'phrases, the sentiments, the fancies' of the playwrights appeared 'very monotonous and inefficient, when separated from the grins

---

[17] Allardyce Nicoll, *A History of English Drama, 1660–1900*, Vol. IV: *Early Nineteenth Century Drama, 1800–1850*, 2nd ed. (Cambridge: Cambridge University Press, 1955), p. 133.

of [JOSEPH] MUNDEN and the chatterings of [JOHN] FAWCETT.'[18] Elsewhere, to illustrate the 'great power' a fine comic actor had of 'filling up the paltriest sketches,' Hunt described Munden's actions in connection with a single line from Thomas Knight's *The Turnpike Gate*, a musical farce first performed in 1799:

> [He] comes in and hovers about a pot of ale which he sees standing on a table, looking about him with ludicrous caution as he makes his advances, half-afraid and half-simpering when he has got near it, and then after circumventing it with his eyes and feelings over and over again, with some more cautious lookings about, heaving a sudden look into it in the most ludicrous manner imaginable and exclaiming, in an under voice of affected indifference and real chuckling, 'Some gentleman has left his ale.'[19]

It is precisely the comic mannerisms, gestures, and actions contributed by Munden to give body to this role that the characters in Dickens's early tales too often lack. They do not have the life, not even the artificial life of caricature, that the actors were apparently able to give to the crude, stereotyped characters of their playwrights. Dickens's early stories contain a superfluity of bachelors – old, young, romantic, misanthropic, many resembling the types that he later described in *Sketches of Young Gentlemen* (1838), a pedestrian work hurriedly written. His young ladies are generally silly and romantic, insipid and simpering, painted in the worst tradition of the very sentimental novels that they dote upon, the satire tired and pallid. Couples, old and young, usually resemble those in *Sketches of Young Couples* (1840). Families are almost solely occupied in social climbing, with the mothers tediously restricted to backbiting and gossip, the sons to stupid remarks, the daughters to romantic nonsense, the fathers to thoughts of their clubs and to stolid, sanctimonious commonplaces, and other relatives to embarrassing but tired eccentricities. Sarcastic cabmen, servants, tiresome children, and foolish old men and women virtually complete the lifeless gallery of characters in Dickens's early tales.

That most can be so quickly summarized reveals the shallow conception of characterization underlying them. The effect on the plots of these tales is

---

[18] From the Preface to Hunt's *Critical Essays on the Performers of the London Theatres, Including General Observations on the Practise and Genius of the Stage* (London: John Hunt, 1807), pp. vi–vii.

[19] Lawrence Huston Houtchens and Carolyn Washburn Houtchens, eds., *Leigh Hunt's Dramatic Criticism, 1808–1831* (New York: Columbia University Press, 1949), pp. 101–102. The quotation is from an essay on comic actors originally published in the *Examiner*, 29 January 1815. If Dickens's early tales lacked such 'characterizing' action, his later sketches did not (see Ch. iii below), nor did *Pickwick Papers*, as this description of Pickwick on the ice slide at Dingley Dell illustrates: 'Mr. Pickwick paused, considered, pulled off his gloves and put them in his hat, took two or three short runs, baulked himself as often, and at last took another run and went slowly and gravely down the slide, with his feet about a yard and a quarter apart, amidst the gratified shouts of all the spectators' (Ch. xxix, p. 313 – Ch. xxx in later editions).

all too evident. Such characters can only engage in limited and predetermined actions, carry on stilted conversations, and have only the most
superficial thoughts.

Besides dealing too exclusively with general, commonplace types,
Dickens also fails with his early characters because the techniques he uses are
primitive. When the reader is more aware of the device than of the
character, the author's limitations are evident. To mention two particularly
disturbing characteristics, Dickens usually summarizes the distinguishing
traits of his characters rather than revealing them or before revealing them
through speech, mannerisms, and actions, and he indulges in a continual
flow of obtrusive stage directions and unnecessary explanations. These
techniques may be an aid to the swift movement needed in a short comic
tale, but when the result is not brilliantly comic, the story falters. For
example, in 'Horatio Sparkins,' a page before Mr. Jacob Barton's
entrance, Dickens has Mr. Malderton say of his brother-in-law, that
'insufferable' tradesman: 'I wouldn't care if he had the good sense to conceal
the disgrace he is to the family; but he's so cursedly fond of his horrible
business, that he will let people know what he is.' The omniscient
narrator adds: 'Mr. Jacob Barton, the individual alluded to, was a large
grocer; so vulgar, and so lost to all sense of feeling, that he actually never
scrupled to avow that he wasn't above his business; "he'd made his money
by it, and he didn't care who know'd it"' (*Monthly Magazine*, N.S. 17,
156). Although the narrator is being satiric of Malderton's snobbery, he is
equally critical of the grocer. When Barton does arrive at the dinner party,
virtually every speech he makes contains at least one reference to his having
made his money in business 'and he didn't care who know'd it.' The only
other aspect of his character is his lower-class manner of speaking.

Sparkins himself is characterized largely through the narrator's stage
directions and explanatory remarks, as in the following passage:

> The first object that met the anxious eyes of the expectant family, on their
> entrance into the ball-room, was the interesting Horatio, with his hair brushed
> off his forehead, and his eyes fixed on the ceiling, reclining in a contemplative
> attitude on one of the seats. . . .
> The elegant Sparkins attitudinized with admirable effect until the family had
> crossed the room. He then started up with the most natural appearance of
> surprise and delight: accosted Mrs. Malderton with the utmost cordiality,
> saluted the young ladies in the most enchanting manner; bowed to, and shook
> hands with Mr. Malderton, with a degree of respect amounting almost to
> veneration, and returned the greetings of the two young men in a half-
> gratified, half-patronizing manner, which fully convinced them that he must
> be an important and, at the same time, condescending personage.
> (*Monthly Magazine*, N.S. 17, 153–54)

Although all authors occasionally use such shortcuts to characterization,
Dickens's reliance upon them in his early writings was unusually heavy;

not until he was about one-third of the way through *Pickwick Papers* did he drop them from his repertory.

Dickens is much more successful in these early tales with his minor characters – those presented in a single paragraph or even sentence, for that matter – who are sometimes simply part of the background of action. The nurse carrying the Kitterbell infant in 'The Bloomsbury Christening' is one example. On hearing Dumps compare the baby to 'one of those little interesting carved representations that one sometimes sees blowing a trumpet on a tombstone!' she '*stooped down over the child, and with great difficulty prevented an explosion of mirth,*' while the proud parents stand aghast at the funereal allusion (*Monthly Magazine*, N.S. 17, 381. Emphasis added). The nurse obviously understands both Dumps and the Kitterbells, has a most enlightened comprehension of the situation, and directs our response to the scene. Other such characters include the members of the amateur orchestra in 'Mrs. Joseph Porter, "Over the Way,"' particularly the deaf flute player who loses the race through the overture; the guests and musicians – 'the harp, in a state of intoxication,' for example – in 'Sentiment!'; various members of the excursion party in 'The Steam Excursion'; and in particular the inhabitants of the sponging house social room in 'Passage in the Life of Mr. Watkins Tottle.' But minor characters do not make a short story, and even less so do those from a short story make a novel, where they fade immediately into the background. Not until Dickens discards the commonplace protagonists of these early tales, expands his minor characters into either major characters or into minor characters suitable to a novel, and allows himself to be more directly influenced by the best eighteenth-century novelists, will he be ready to write even *Pickwick Papers*.

But perhaps the most significant development in characterization in these early tales is to be found in Watkins Tottle, the one major character who stands out as something of an exception to the generally low level of character creation and who dimly foreshadows some of the virtues of the great comic figures in the novels. Tottle, another aging bachelor, is a stock character, certainly, but he exhibits, to begin with, a greater variety of emotion than do Minns and Dumps, his predecessors in the role. He has more susceptible than misanthropy to humorous treatment. Although situation more effectively. But then, Tottle thinks he is in love, a subject more susceptible than misanthropy to humorous treatment. Although the humor in chapter one of his story gives Tottle life, he is by no means portrayed there as a sympathetic character. And yet, in chapter two, this is exactly what he becomes – a comic character, likeable in a way Dickens's earlier protagonists had not been, as much because of his shortcomings as despite them. The change is partly effected by our corresponding rejection of Gabriel Parsons, who becomes mercenary and selfish in chapter two. We find ourselves turning to Tottle, who is, at least, less vicious. The unpleasant reality of the sponging house to which Tottle is taken at the suit of his creditors also modifies our view of the man and his situation. We really had not thought he was so desperately in want of money when he agreed to pay court to the wealthy Miss Lillerton.

It also seems very likely that at this point in his story Dickens began to realize what he had in hand – his first character with some suggestion of the roundness of human nature. Chapter two seems to proceed quite tangentially to expectations aroused in chapter one. Tottle is now described as acting valorously, resolutely, intelligently, bashfully, and mildly. His nobler emotions are revealed: 'Mr. Watkins Tottle expressed a hope that the Parsons family never would make a stranger of him, and wished internally that his bashfulness would allow him to feel a little less like a stranger himself' (*Monthly Magazine*, N.S. 19, 130). Moreover, now for the first time in any of his tales, Dickens reveals the thoughts and feelings of a character in some detail. He shows us Tottle's embarrassment on spilling and breaking a water tumbler, his bashfulness in proposing to Miss Lillerton, and his feelings of foolishness on learning that she has accepted Timson's marriage proposal. Here in Tottle is at least the promise if not yet the realization of the great comic figures who romp through the pages of Dickens's novels, beginning with Pickwick himself. Indeed, Tottle bears something of a resemblance to Pickwick, who, in the early numbers of *Pickwick Papers*, undergoes a similar metamorphosis at the hands of his author.[20]

But Tottle also takes his own life at the end of the story, an action that detracts from the genuinely comic elements of his character and throws the story once again out of alignment. Nevertheless, we have had a momentary glimpse of true artistic promise.

★

Why was Dickens attracted to the kind of story that he wrote in 1833 and 1834? One answer is that it was a popular form that editors would pay money for, even though Dickens eventually abandoned the *Monthly Magazine* as an outlet because it was not coming through with the 'needful.'[21] He must have seen being published in the journal as necessary if unremunerative experience. Certainly he also wanted to amuse his readers with his writings. There is sufficient indication in his background that he was more likely to turn first to comic pieces than to writing of a more serious nature. The multitude of farcical situations and characters and the abundance of puns and other verbal witticisms that fill the pages of these

---

[20] A passage that Dickens excised from the original version of 'Passage in the Life of Mr. Watkins Tottle' when he collected the story in the First Series of *Sketches by Boz* suggests that his plans for further stories about Tottle may very likely have been incorporated into *Pickwick Papers*: '[Upon his death, Mr. Tottle] left a variety of papers in the hands of his landlady – the materials collected in his wanderings among different classes of society – which that lady has determined to publish, to defray the unpaid expenses of his board and lodging. They will be carefully arranged, and presented to the public from time to time, with all due humility, by BOZ' (*Monthly Magazine*, N.S. 19, 137). Tottle also bore some resemblance to Pickwick: he was about fifty years old, 'stood four feet six inches and three-quarters in his socks,' and was 'plump, clean, and rosy' (N.S. 19, 15).

[21] *Pilgrim Letters*, I, 33, to H. W. Kolle, [?10 December 1833].

early stories were clearly intended to amuse readers and display the author's cleverness.

But he must also have been attracted to the farcical tale because of the opportunities for satire – of his fellow human beings and his society. Sometimes Dickens does little more than parody after-dinner speeches (in 'A Dinner at Poplar Walk' and 'The Bloomsbury Christening') and sentimental novels and political oratory (in 'Sentiment!'). At other times, however, as in 'The Bloomsbury Christening,' 'The Boarding House,' and 'Passage in the Life of Mr. Watkins Tottle,' he seems to be developing a relatively dark view of human beings and their motivations, one not entirely suitable to a farcical production. At least two or three of his early tales have noticeably bitter, ironic, and distinctly *un*-humorous endings. It is possible, I suppose, to see this disparity in tone between the ending and the rest of the tale as simply an indication that the young author did not understand the genre in which he was working or underestimated the force of the endings. On the other hand, Dickens may have had good reasons for using these particular endings. He was, after all, thoroughly familiar with the genre of farce; he would surely have known by instinct and experience as a playgoer, if not by intellectual analysis, when an ending was drastically inconsistent with the rest of the story. In part one of 'The Boarding House,' Dickens concludes one of the three love affairs with a breach of promise suit, but he allows the two remaining couples to marry. A farce might have ended at this point, with some effect. But 'The Boarding House' continues on: Mr. Hicks deserts his bride, Mrs. Simpson elopes with an army officer when her husband of six weeks is carried off to debtors' prison, and Mrs. Tibbs, the manager of the boarding house, banishes her husband to the kitchen for the part he played in marrying off her boarders and thereby losing their patronage. In part two, the Tibbses themselves separate.

Perhaps Dickens wanted to do more than write imaginative but totally unreal farces whose clever, beautiful, and comic characters belonged to a century and a class different from his own and who worked out their comic destinies in an unreal world governed by artificial laws of nature that permitted relatively happy endings for a number of unbelievable, flawed but loveable 'people.' Instead, he was more likely than not to inject small doses of reality into his tales by dealing in part (though by no means as fully as in the descriptive essays he would write for the *Morning Chronicle* in late 1834 and for the *Evening Chronicle* in 1835–36) with people, places, and events familiar to him from his daily life – and always for satiric effect. Scholars believe that Mrs. Joseph Porter, for example, bears the 'malicious tongue' of Mrs. Leigh, the mother of Maria Beadnell's closest friend, and that Mr. Bagshaw is really Mr. Leigh.[22] The theatrical entertainment in 'Mrs.

---

[22] John Harrison Stonehouse, *Green Leaves: New Chapters in the Life of Charles Dickens*, rev. and enl. ed. (London: Piccadilly Fountain Press, 1931), pp. 12–13. Johnson (I, 91–92) accepts these identifications. The Leighs were the parents of Marianne Leigh, Maria Beadnell's closest friend.

Joseph Porter, "Over the Way"' seems to be modeled upon the amateur productions in the Dickens home. The young author also served as god-father to Henry Kolle's son, a fact he alludes to in a letter to Kolle that closes with 'Have you seen "The Bloomsbury Christening"? If not I'll send it you,'[23] a suggestion possibly of the source of the setting, several characters, and perhaps a satirical incident or two in the story. In another letter to Kolle, Dickens takes great care to point out that as 'neither you or yours have the most remote connexion with the Boarding House of which I am the Proprietor, I cannot have the least objection to (indeed I shall feel flattered by) your perusing it.'[24] Isn't there at least a suggestion here that he was not averse from including occasional cutting sketches of friends and acquaint-ances in his tales?

At times the satire is bitter; Dickens may indeed, as Monroe Engel sug-gests, have been consciously attempting to delineate 'the striving preten-sions of the insecure lower middle class; and the brutalization of those just beneath them; and the callousness of those above.'[25] 'Horatio Sparkins' contains such satiric elements, as do other tales. But again, the crudity of technique is evident when one compares these tales to the brilliant scenes connected with Mr. Pickwick's visits to Eatanswill and Bath, for example, particularly Sam's attendance at the footmen's 'swarry' (*Pickwick Papers*, Ch. xxxvi, pp. 392–401 – Ch. xxxvii in later editions). In several of the early stories the deliberate inversions of typically happy endings suggest that Dickens saw the representation of an unpleasant rather than a comic reality as one of his purposes as a serious writer. These endings do give a satiric twist to the stories, but they are generally far less effective than the equally satiric but more comic endings to scenes in *Pickwick Papers*, the Bardell *vs.* Pickwick trial, for instance. At the end, Tony Weller's 'Oh Sammy, Sammy, vy worn't there a alleybi!' is rich with satire of the individuals involved as well as of legal precedent and procedure (see Ch. xxxiii, p. 370 – Ch. xxxiv in later editions). Unfortunately, in order to shock the reader with an unexpected ending to what seemed a pleasant farce, Dickens had to distort the structure of his stories, thus failing to achieve a consistent farcical, realistic, or satiric effect. In reading the first part of 'The Boarding House,' for example, one has no reason to believe that any of the couples is incompatible. And in 'Passage in the Life of Mr. Watkins Tottle,' the protagonist, a bachelor looking for a rich wife, certainly a suit-able if over-used subject for a farce, scarcely seems destined for suicide. While such endings are not false to life itself, which does not operate by the laws of fiction, they do conflict with the expectations aroused in the

---

[23] *Pilgrim Letters*, I, 39, to H. W. Kolle, [Spring 1834].
[24] *Pilgrim Letters*, I, 38, to H. W. Kolle, [April 1834].
[25] Monroe Engel, *The Maturity of Dickens* (Cambridge: Harvard University Press, 1959), p. 78. Engel is speaking of the collected *Sketches by Boz* rather than just the early farcical tales, and he adds that Dickens at this time lacked 'the literary force to make much of it.'

reader. They force him to reappraise what he has read, but with little hope of resolving the conflicts between tone and theme.

Whether Dickens's purpose in these early tales was to amuse the reader with farcical characters and situations, to paint a bitterly satirical picture of human nature, or perhaps to do both cannot be clearly ascertained; probably he himself was not entirely clear about his intentions. If one critic holds that the endings reinforce, though somewhat belatedly, a comic view of life, another could just as well believe – as I sometimes do – that the use of unexpectedly unhappy endings is a clever technique of literary parody, used to reinforce a view of the relationship of literature to life; that is, Dickens may be bringing his stories to such conclusions not because the conclusions are what he would necessarily expect to occur in real life but because typically happy endings are so grossly unreal. As does C. B. Cox, a critic might also explain away the apparent conflict of purpose by insisting that Dickens is already working with a comic view of life as a paradox of human existence: man is a fool (Cox uses Percy Noakes of 'The Steam Excursion' and Watkins Tottle as his examples), 'a creature whose attempts to take himself seriously are worthy only of ridicule; yet, on the other hand, the vigour with which such characters pursue their activities redeems them from futility.'[26] However, these tales come too early in Dickens's life and literary career, it seems to me, to admit of such an interpretation. At least it is not one that Dickens would have recognized.

*

By February 1835, when his last tale was published in the *Monthly Magazine*, Dickens had written eight tales (in ten parts) in each of which he had mixed characters, plots, setting, and a way of looking at life into a series of scenes that produced a complete story – if in every instance an imperfect one. The precise technical means to perfect the product were just beginning to manifest themselves to the young author. We can see him, I think, making tentative movements in the right direction, but still often holding back, content for the moment in the security of imitating his flawed models with some success, failing to follow through in a tale with a technique that was particularly effective in the preceding one. He has yet but the shakiest conception of structure. He achieved, it is true, a certain unity in 'The Bloomsbury Christening,' and 'The Steam Excursion' contains at least a progression of events that completes itself in a satisfactory if not striking way, but the other *Monthly Magazine* tales are woefully lacking in effective structure. In characterization, too, the promise that one would like to find is not evident – except suddenly in 'Passage in the Life of Watkins Tottle,' the last story in this group. More promising is Dickens's improvement in constructing scenes within stories and his increasingly intelligent and artistic if still too infrequent use of setting, particularly for humorous and

---

[26] Cox, 'Comic Viewpoints in *Sketches by Boz*,' p. 135.

satiric effect. His style of writing also exhibits improvement, almost impossible to trace from one tale to the next, but evident if 'Passage in the Life of Watkins Tottle' is read after the original version of 'A Dinner at Poplar Walk.' Finally, a fairly conscious satiric intent, present in characterization, setting, and narrative tone of voice, if not so clearly in the plotting of the stories, holds out promise for the future. But Dickens will need to embody in his works a much more conscious, grander, and certainly more focused literary vision – and become more proficient in the techniques by which a writer conveys this vision in words.

The learning process during 1833 and 1834 was slow but valuable; of this there cannot, I trust, be any doubt. For the most part the *Monthly Magazine* tales justify Dickens's own later estimate of them as 'often being extremely crude and ill-considered, and bearing obvious marks of haste and inexperience.'[27] But they are no worse than much of the fiction that Dickens read in the magazines of the 1830's. If we are still surprised upon reading the first few installments of *Pickwick Papers* to see the amazing improvement in the quality of Dickens's writing over that in these early tales, we must remember that he turned out thirty-seven sketches for the *Morning Chronicle*, the *Evening Chronicle*, and *Bell's Life in London, and Sporting Chronicle* between late 1834 and the publication of the first number of *Pickwick* in March 1836, and thirteen additional sketches in 1836 (three of which were originally published in the First Series of *Sketches by Boz*), to produce the sixty (as fifty-six) pieces that comprise all editions of *Sketches by Boz* from the 1837–39 edition on. It is to these that we must turn for further enlightenment about Dickens's early development as a writer of fiction.

---

[27] Preface to the Cheap Edition of *Sketches by Boz*, p. [vii].

CHAPTER THREE

'Street Sketches' and 'Sketches of London'

EVEN before most of the *Monthly Magazine* tales had been published, Dickens was looking for a more remunerative outlet for his writing and was at that time considering the *Metropolitan Magazine* as a possibility. Several months later, however, in August 1834, his fortunes took a turn upward when he was hired as a Parliamentary reporter for the *Morning Chronicle*. It was here during the last three months of the year, running concurrently with the last *Monthly Magazine* tales, that his first five essays appeared as 'Street Sketches' by 'Boz,' his recently acquired pseudonym.[1] Then in January 1835 George Hogarth, the newly appointed co-editor of the forthcoming *Evening Chronicle* and Dickens's future father-in-law, asked the young man to write a sketch for the opening number of this thrice-weekly offshoot of the *Morning Chronicle*. Dickens agreed to do so and suggested that he write an entire series of 'light papers in the style of my "street sketches"' under 'some attractive title' for the paper, possibly for a sum of money beyond his salary from the *Morning Chronicle*. He was granted an additional two guineas per week. The evening paper proved a success, and so did the twenty 'Sketches of London' that he wrote for it.[2]

Even in their later, slightly revised state, these two sets of essays exhibit at times what Edgar Johnson refers to as 'polysyllabic turgidness,' 'showy and cocksure jibing,' 'flip puns,' and 'knowing word-plays,'[3] their inheritance from the *Monthly Magazine* tales. Yet often theme, tone, content, and style merge in imaginative sketches that reviewers praised when they were republished in 1836 and that, as Lionel Stevenson states, 'stood out

---

[1] Dickens first used 'Boz' as his pseudonym at the end of 'The Boarding-House. – No. II,' in the *Monthly Magazine*, N.S. 18 (August 1834), 192.

[2] *Pilgrim Letters*, I, 55, to George Hogarth, 20 January [1835]. See Appendix A, below, for a listing of the 'Street Sketches' and the 'Sketches of London.'

[3] Johnson, I, 112. Nevertheless, the confidence underlying such pretentious stylistic infelicities may possibly explain Dickens's rapid and certain rise as a creative writer almost as much as do the years of practice, experimentation, and revision.

conspicuously among the writings of 1834–35.'[4] The finest sketches also reveal the favorable influence not only of the best contemporary journalism but also of the best essay writing of the eighteenth- and early nineteenth-century. What is particularly significant, I think, is that the 'Street Sketches' and the 'Sketches of London' – rich with narrative and descriptive passages, colorful scenes, and brief character sketches, and heavily dependent upon a witty, obtrusive narrative point of view and tone of voice for their effect – served Dickens admirably well as exercises in the craft of fiction. As a result, he not only developed at this time some of the characteristics that would later define his novels and his unique style of writing (those 'Dickensian' touches) but also got valuable practice at a relatively simple level in techniques of fiction he had by no means mastered in the *Monthly Magazine* pieces. When he returned to fiction in some of his contributions to *Bell's Life in London, and Sporting Chronicle*, the improvement, as we shall see, was great indeed.

As essays the 'Street Sketches' and the 'Sketches of London' are striking because they lack the lengthy philosophical ruminations, elaborate analogies, scholarly allusions, and predominantly classical literary quotations that adorn not only the essays of Addison, Steele, Johnson, and Goldsmith, but those of Hunt, Lamb, Washington Irving, and even the more journalistic and inferior pieces of John Poole. But more than this, in Dickens's sketches we are always close to the young man's object-packed, people-filled world: the middle-class society of the Beadnell family to which he aspired; the classless life of his financially impoverished family that led the boy from the pleasant surroundings of Chatham to the slums, blacking factories, and debtors' prisons of London; the world of his early initiation into manhood – the London of lawyers' chambers, law courts, newspaper offices, the reporters' gallery in Parliament, public dinners, theaters, concert halls, Greenwich fair, Astley's Circus, private theaters, public gardens, inns, gin shops, pawn shops, coach stands, the streets at morning, noon, and night – all subjects of these essays.

A passage selected virtually at random, from 'The Streets – Morning,' sufficiently illustrates the straight-forwardness of the style and the profusion of obviously realistic, carefully observed and recorded detail:

> An hour wears away; the spires of the churches and roofs of the principal buildings are faintly tinged with the light of the rising sun, and the streets, by almost imperceptible degrees, begin to resume their bustle and animation. Market carts roll slowly along, the sleepy waggoner impatiently urging on his tired horses, or vainly endeavouring to awaken the boy, who, luxuriously stretched on the top of the fruit baskets, forgets in happy oblivion his long cherished curiosity to behold the wonders of London. . . . Here and there a bricklayer's labourer, with the day's dinner tied up in a handkerchief, walks

---

[4] Lionel Stevenson, 'An Introduction to Young Mr. Dickens,' *Dickensian*, 29 (1932/33), 112.

briskly to his work, and occasionally a little knot of three or four school-boys on a stolen bathing expedition, rattle merrily over the pavement; their boisterous mirth contrasting forcibly with the demeanour of the little sweep, who, having knocked and rung till his arm aches, and being interdicted by a merciful Legislature from endangering his lungs by calling out, sits patiently down on the door step until the house maid may happen to wake. Covent-garden Market, and the avenues leading to it, are thronged with carts of all sorts, sizes, and descriptions, from the heavy lumbering waggon with its four stout horses, to the jingling costermonger's cart with its consumptive donkey. The pavement is already strewed with decayed cabbage leaves, broken hay-bands, and all the indescribable litter of a vegetable market and the numerous noises are almost as multifarious. Men shouting, carts backing, horses neighing, boys fighting, basket-women talking, piemen expatiating on the excellence of their pastry, donkeys braying, and a hundred other sounds, form a compound discordant enough even to a Londoner's ears, and remarkably disagreeable to those of country gentlemen. . . .

(Evening Chronicle, 21 July 1835)

'Things are painted literally as they are,' claims Forster (and he may have been referring to this passage as to a hundred others), 'and, whatever the picture, whether of every-day vulgar, shabby genteel, or downright low, with neither the condescending air which is affectation, nor the too familiar one which is slang.'[5] When *Sketches by Boz* was published in 1836, most reviewers, like the one in the *Morning Post*, found that the 'graphic descriptions of "Boz" invest all he describes with amazing reality,' though a few commented disparagingly on the unsuitability of its lower class elements as subjects for essays with any pretension to literary quality.[6] But this 'unusually truthful observation of a sort of life between the middle class and the low,' Forster knew, was the book's novelty and value (p. 77).

The emphasis on reality comes most directly from what Dickens himself referred to much later as 'the wholesome training of severe newspaper work.'[7] While Parliament was in session, Dickens spent most of his working hours recording the debate in shorthand from the uncomfortable gallery seats. When Parliament was not sitting, he was occasionally assigned to review plays at the London theaters or was sent out of town to report on various political, social, and charitable events.[8] In the latter case, he again transcribed invariably lengthy speeches, but he also reported the details of

---

[5] Forster, pp. 76–77. He is speaking of *Sketches by Boz* in general, but his comments are appropriate to the 'Street Sketches' and 'Sketches of London.'

[6] The *Morning Post*, 12 March 1836. Quoted (p. 48), along with excerpts from other contemporary reviews, in D[exter], 'The Reception of Dickens's First Book,' pp. 43–50.

[7] Stated by Dickens at a banquet in his honor given by the New York press, 18 April 1868. In Fielding, ed., *The Speeches of Charles Dickens*, p. 379.

[8] Besides the banquet given to Earl Grey and the benefit promenade in Edinburgh referred to in the footnote following, Dickens also covered, in 1834–35, a Liberal party pre-election meeting at Birmingham (28 November 1834); a meeting of the Southwark parish to discuss Reform measures (4 December 1834); possibly a West Kent Conservative party dinner (19 December 1834); a series of General Election nominations in Essex and

the occasion; it is this more descriptive, more creative aspect of his report-ing that directly influenced the texture and tone of his essays. One of Dickens's earliest pieces of such descriptive writing is the introductory paragraph to a lengthy report by himself and Thomas Beard of the Edin-burgh banquet honoring Lord Grey on his retirement as Prime Minister. It might, with minor revisions, have come from one of the sketches:

It had been announced that the dinner would take place at five o'clock precisely; but Earl Grey, and the other principal visitors, as might have been expected, did not arrive until shortly after six. Previous to their arrival, some slight confusion, and much merriment, was excited by the following circum-stance: – A gentleman who, we presume, had entered with one of the first sections, having sat with exemplary patience for some time in the immediate vicinity of cold fowls, roast beef, lobsters, and other tempting delicacies (for the dinner was a cold one), appeared to think that the best thing he could pos-sibly do, would be to eat his dinner, while there was anything to eat. He accordingly laid about him with right good-will, the example was contagious, and the clatter of knives and forks became general. Hereupon, several gentle-men, who were not hungry, cried out 'Shame!' and looked very indignant; and several gentlemen who were hungry, cried 'Shame!' too, eating, neverthe-less, all the while, as fast as they possibly could. In this dilemma, one of the stewards mounted a bench, and feelingly represented to the delinquents the enormity of their conduct, imploring them, for decency's sake, to defer the process of mastication until the arrival of Earl Grey. This address was loudly cheered, but totally unheeded; and this is, perhaps, one of the few instances on record of a dinner having been virtually concluded before it began.[9]

Suffolk that took him to Colchester, Braintree, Chelmsford, Sudbury, and Bury St. Edmunds (8–16 January 1835); Lord John Russell's nomination speech for South Devon at Exeter (1 May 1835); Lord Russell's speech at a dinner given in his honor by the Bristol Reformers in that city (10 November 1835); a dinner given to General Palmer and J. A. Roebuck, members for Bath, in that city (11 November 1835); the tragic fire at Hatfield House, Hatfield, in which the Dowager Marchioness of Salisbury lost her life (27 Novem-ber and succeeding days); and the North Northamptonshire by-election (14–19 December 1835). See *Pilgrim Letters*, I, 41, n. 1; 46–47; 49, n. 1; 51, n. 2; 52–54; 58–60; 88–93; 101–102; and 105–11. For further details of his reportorial activities and for information about his play-reviewing for the *Morning Chronicle*, see *Pilgrim Letters*, I, *passim*, and Carlton, 'Charles Dickens, Dramatic Critic,' pp. 11–27, which contains excerpts from several of the reviews.

[9] Carlton, *Charles Dickens, Shorthand Writer*, pp. 107–108. The article covered eleven closely-printed columns in the 18 September 1834 issue of the *Morning Chronicle*, Carlton reports (p. 106). Dickens's earliest bit of descriptive journalism, a report of a 'promenade' for the benefit of the Blind Asylum, the Deaf and Dumb Institution, and the House of Refuge in Edinburgh, is reprinted in Walter Dexter, 'Charles Dickens: Journalist,' *Nine-teenth Century and After*, 115 (1934), 709. The article appeared in the *Morning Chronicle* on 17 September 1834, datelined 13 September. See 'Dickens's First Contribution to "The Morning Chronicle"': Now Identified and Republished for the First Time,' *Dickensian*, 31 (1934/35), 5–10, for fuller details and a more complete reprinting of these two lengthy reports. In 'The Steam Excursion' (*Monthly Magazine*, October 1834), Mr. Hardy is identified as the person at the Edinburgh dinner 'to whose eager appetite on that occasion we find allusion made in *The Morning Chronicle* of a few days since,' a passage canceled for *Sketches by Boz*, First Series. See Alain de Suzannet, 'How Mr. Hardy of Steam Excursion Fame Made His Mark at the Great Edinburgh Dinner to Lord Grey,' *Dickensian*, 36 (1939/40), 89.

This early sample of Dickens's reportorial writing already contains what would later be called characteristic 'Dickensian' touches – the absurd situation, the contrast between what a man professes and what he does, the conflict between natural behavior and social mannerisms, and the verbal cleverness. Yet the scene, the people, and the place described were certainly factual. While Dickens had not yet developed what George Gissing called his 'liking for the grotesque, the extravagant,'[10] even the later grotesque and extravagant elements in his writing would have the spark of reality and realistic details at their core. The descriptive essays are important to the fiction because they gave Dickens a second start, a better one certainly than his imitation of the popular, artificial farces had afforded him. His next attempts at fiction would rise from the stronger base of realistic detail and the general air of veracity that the newspaper reporting and essay writing provided.

Upon the thick body of realistic details, Dickens imposed a more obtrusive, more varied, and therefore more complex narrative tone of voice than he had used in the tales. It is basically that of the detached, superior, slightly satirical observer of the passing scene recording his impressions and responses for an audience of his peers. The influence of the eighteenth-century essayist and novelist (Goldsmith, Smollett, and Fielding in particular, I suspect) is evident, but so also may be a more natural source, to be found in what G. K. Chesterton termed 'all the peculiar hardness of youth; a hardness which in those who have in any way been unfairly treated reaches even to impudence.' The resulting 'smartness' Chesterton found sometimes irritating.[11] The eighteenth-century satirical detachment and at least traces of youthful impudence and offensive smartness are certainly present in passages such as this from 'Shops, and Their Tenants':

> One of our principal amusements is to watch the gradual progress – the rise or fall – of particular shops. We have formed an intimate acquaintance with several, in different parts of town, and are perfectly acquainted with their whole history. We could name, off-hand, twenty at least, which we are quite sure have paid no taxes for the last six years. They are never inhabited for more than two months consecutively, and we verily believe have witnessed every retail trade in the directory. There is one, whose history is a sample of the rest, in whose fate we have taken especial interest, having had the pleasure of knowing it ever since it has been a shop. . . . It was, originally, a substantial good-looking private house enough; the landlord got into difficulties; the house got into Chancery; the tenant went away; and the house went into ruin. At this period our acquaintance with it commenced. . . .
>
> (*Morning Chronicle*, 10 October 1834)

---

[10] George Gissing, *Charles Dickens: A Critical Study* (London: Blackie & Son, 1898), p. 41. Gissing is speaking of *Sketches by Boz* generally.

[11] G. K. Chesterton, *Appreciations and Criticisms of the Works of Charles Dickens* (London: Dent; New York: Dutton, 1911), pp. 6–7.

On the other hand, Dickens's occasional melancholic reflections on the effects of time passing, on the pathos of the human condition, and on the picturesque though dirty sights of London more closely mirror the influence of the Pre-Romantics and the Romantic essayists than of the mid-eighteenth-century writers. Obviously, this influence, too, contributes to the tone of the above passage. And the absence of stylistic elaborations, the rapidity with which the prose moves, the verbal economy with which Dickens presents his ideas and illustrations, and the vividness produced by these and (in passages more descriptive than the one above) the color of the writing, suggest the influence of journalism circa 1834.

Whether intended or not, a more individual and more consistent way of looking at life than was evident in the *Monthly Magazine* tales emerges. This is also evident in the personal letters that Dickens wrote at this time, as illustrated by the following passage from a letter to a friend written while Dickens was covering a provincial election in 1835:

> Owing to the slippery state of the roads on the morning I started, I magnanimously declined the honor of driving myself, and hid my dignity in the Inside of a Stage Coach. As the Election here had not commenced, I went on to Colchester (which is a very nice town) and returned here on the following morning. Yesterday I had to start at 8 OClock, for Braintree – a place 12 miles off; and being unable to get a Saddle Horse, I actually ventured on a gig, – and what is more, I actually did the four and twenty miles without upsetting it. I wish to God you could have seen me tooling in and out of the banners, drums, conservative Emblems, horsemen, and go-carts with which every little Green was filled as the processions were waiting for Sir John Tyrell and Baring. Every time the horse heard a drum he bounded into the hedge, on the left side of the road; and every time I got him out of that, he bounded into the hedge on the right side. When he *did* go however, he went along admirably. The road was clear when I returned, and with the trifling exception of breaking my Whip, I flatter myself I did the whole thing in something like style.[12]

The tone of this passage is more personal than that of the essays, but the stylist is obviously at work here, too. It is not so much the ride itself that makes the description exciting as it is the verbal and descriptive coloring, the exaggeration of the horse's movement, the unexpected detail of the broken whip, and the partly comic, partly egotistical portrait that Dickens paints of himself. The result, in this letter, in his essays, and ultimately in his fiction, is a heightened picture of reality, a detailed *impression* rather than simply a statistical record. It is the tone, created by the stylist, that provides the significant communication here. The passage is filled with promises of

---

[12] *Pilgrim Letters*, I, 53, to Thomas Beard, [11 January 1835]. This letter was written from the Black Boy Hotel, Chelmsford, where Dickens had been sent to cover the election for the *Morning Chronicle*.

the comic exuberance of *Pickwick Papers*,[13] but it also illustrates what Dickens was achieving in his writing with greater consistency and aware-ness in late 1834 and 1835.

It is perhaps in the development of a definite and consciously determined point of view towards people, situations, and social conditions that Dickens most effectively molds a style and tone more characteristic of the author of *Pickwick Papers* than of the novice who wrote 'A Dinner at Poplar Walk.' Occasionally, as in the concluding paragraph from 'Gin Shops,' Dickens's attitude is stated all too clearly:

> We have sketched this subject very slightly, not only because our limits compel us to do so, but because if it were pursued further it would be painful and repulsive. Well-disposed gentlemen and charitable ladies would alike turn with coldness and disgust from a description of the drunken, besotted men, and wretched, broken-down, miserable women, who form no incon-siderable portion of the frequenters of these haunts; – forgetting, in the pleasant consciousness of their own high rectitude, the poverty of the one, and the temptation of the other. Gin-drinking is a great vice in England, but poverty is a greater; and until you can cure it, or persuade a half-famished wretch, not to seek relief in the temporary oblivion of his own misery, with the pittance which, divided among his family, would just furnish a morsel of bread for each, gin-shops will increase in number and splendour. If Temperance Societies could suggest an antidote against hunger and distress, or establish dispensaries for the gratuitous distribution of bottles of Lethe water, gin-palaces would be numbered among the things that were. Until then, we almost despair of their decrease.
>
> (*Evening Chronicle*, 7 February 1835)

However, most of the 'Street Sketches' and 'Sketches of London' are not so dependent upon irony and invective as is the conclusion of 'Gin Shops,' for Dickens's intent (as evident in the passage from 'Shops, and Their Tenants') is more to 'amuse' his readers than to 'reform' their manners or morals. This intent is constantly evident in the essays. 'It is very generally allowed that public conveyances afford an extensive field for amusement and observation,' Dickens begins in 'Omnibuses' (*Morning Chronicle*, 26 September 1834), establishing in his opening sentence the form and emphasis of the sketch. He will present his observations in more or less organized fashion with an occasional, clearly indicated digression, attempt-

---

[13] As the editors of *Pilgrims Letters* indicate (I, 53, n. 5), the behavior of Winkle's horse in Ch. v of *Pickwick Papers* bears striking similarities to that of Dickens's beast. For other views on the relationship between reality and imagination, particularly in Dickens's comic writing, see Robert Browning, 'Sketches by Boz,' in *Dickens and the Twentieth Century*, ed. John Gross and Gabriel Pearson (Toronto: University of Toronto Press, 1962), pp. 19–34; Margaret Ganz, 'Humor's Alchemy: The Lessons of *Sketches by Boz*,' *Genre*, 1 (1968), 290–306; and J. Hillis Miller, 'The Fiction of Realism: *Sketches by Boz*, *Oliver Twist*, and Cruikshank's Illustrations,' in Miller and David Borowitz, *Charles Dickens and George Cruikshank: Papers Read at a Clark Library Seminar on May 9, 1970* (Los Angeles: William Andrews Clark Memorial Library, University of California, 1971), pp. 1–69.

ing in the process to amuse his readers. This effort will virtually require him to fill each essay with descriptive passages, with narrative and dramatic scenes, with plotted anecdotes, and with colorful characterizations. While 'Omnibuses' consists mainly of a lengthy scene, 'Shops, and Their Tenants' and 'Brokers' and Marine Store Shops' (*Morning Chronicle*, 15 December 1834) – to limit ourselves to the 'Street Sketches' – are developed through series of descriptions, and 'The Old Bailey' (*Morning Chronicle*, 23 October 1834; retitled 'Criminal Courts' in *Sketches by Boz*, Second Series) unfolds in a sequence of scenes. 'Shabby-Genteel People' (*Morning Chronicle*, 5 November 1834) supports the statement, 'There are certain descriptions of people, who, oddly enough, appear to appertain exclusively to this metropolis,' and is developed through a series of descriptive characterizations followed by a detailed portrait of a 'shabby-genteel' man whom Dickens apparently knew from the reading room of the British Museum.

In emphasizing amusement as his goal, Dickens was writing much in a tradition of 'amiable humor,' as Stuart Tave recently characterized it. Although such humor can range from satire to sentimentality, Tave indicates, in practice it 'measured reality not, as the satirist tends, by an ideal against which reality is terribly wanting, nor did it, in the manner of the sentimentalist, deny or falsify the gap between the real and the ideal. It accepted the difference with a liberal tolerance, or unlike both satirist and sentimentalist, it found the ideal in the varied fulness of the real with all its imperfections.'[14] It is Sterne's conception of the hobbyhorse not Jonson's 'ruling passion' that determines the emphasis – the hobbyhorse being 'a peculiarity loved for its own sake and for the part it plays in fulfilling the endlessly prolific scheme of things.'[15]

'Hackney-Coach Stands' (*Evening Chronicle*, 31 January 1835) is an excellent illustration of the 'amiability' of Dickens's humor. The essay's structure is simple. Following four paragraphs of commentary on his acquaintance with hackney-coaches, 'Boz,' the narrator, describes one such vehicle standing beneath the very window at which he is writing. A daughter, four grandchildren, and a servant-girl are packing a grandmother and her baggage into it with great ceremony and affection. In the latter part of the essay, he describes a wedding-party taking another such coach to church.

The early portion of the essay is dominated by the assumed superiority with which the narrator views the passing scene:

> Take a regular, ponderous, ricketty, London hackney-coach of the old school, and let any man have the boldness to assert, if he can, that he ever

---

[14] Stuart M. Tave, *The Amiable Humorist: A Study in the Comic Theory and Criticism of the Eighteenth and Early Nineteenth Centuries* (Chicago: University of Chicago Press, 1960), pp. 166–67.
[15] Tave, p. 167. Uncle Toby is the 'brightest name in this galaxy' before Pickwick, says Tave (p. 148).

beheld any object on the face of the earth which at all resembled it – unless, indeed, it were another hackney-coach of the same date. We have recently observed on certain stands – and we say it with deep regret – rather dapper-green chariots, and coaches of polished yellow, with four wheels of the same colour as the coach; whereas it is perfectly notorious to everyone who has studied the subject, that every wheel ought to be of a different colour, and a different size. These are innovations; and, like other mis-called improvements, awful signs of the restlessness of the public mind, and the little respect paid to our time honoured institutions. Why should hackney-coaches be clean? – our ancestors found them dirty, and left them so. Why should we, with a feverish wish to 'keep moving,' desire to roll along at the rate of six miles an hour, while they were content to rumble over the stones at four? These are solemn considerations. Hackney-coaches are part and parcel of the law of the land – they were settled by the Legislature – plated and numbered by the wisdom of Parliament. Then why have they been swamped by cabs, and omnibuses? – or why should people be allowed to ride quickly for eight-pence a mile, after Parliament had come to the solemn decision that they should pay a shilling a mile for riding slowly? We pause for a reply; – and, having no chance of getting one, begin a fresh paragraph.

The note of satire in this passage is partly dependent upon the pseudo-patriotic tone with which Dickens invests the paragraph, partly upon a young man's underlying exasperation with the institutions and social appurtenances of earlier generations, and partly upon the obvious eccentricity of his support of run-down, dirty, and slow hackney-coaches.

Yet, as the essay progresses, the satire becomes modified by an apparent love of humanity that 'Boz,' man-of-the-world, sophisticate, and observer of life, finds difficult to disguise in this essay. Here C. B. Cox's interpretation of the nature of Dickens's comic perception of man does make sense, I believe. While Dickens sees man as a fool, he also, Cox states, sees that man's love of life and man's exuberant and unhypocritical acceptance of life are what at the same time redeem him from utter futility.[16] This love of life is evident in both the characters and the narrator himself in the scene of the grandmother's leavetaking:

> The smart servant-girl, with the pink ribbons, at No. 5, opposite, suddenly opens the street-door, and four small children forthwith rush out, and scream 'coach!' with all their might and main. The waterman darts from the pump, seizes the horses by their respective bridles, and drags them, and the coach too, round to the house, shouting all the time for the coachman at the very top, or rather bottom of his voice – for it is a deep base growl. A response is heard from the tap-room – the coachman, in his wooden-soled shoes, makes the street echo again as he runs across it – and then there is such a struggling, and backing, and grating of the kennel, to get the coach-door opposite the house-door, that the children are in perfect extasies of delight. What a commotion!

---

[16] Cox, 'Comic Viewpoints in *Sketches by Boz*,' p. 135.

After the children and their mother have seen the grandmother into the coach, along with 'a little basket, which we could almost swear contains a small black bottle and a paper of sandwiches,' Dickens concludes the scene with more of the same:

> Up go the steps – bang goes the door – 'Golden-cross, Charing-cross, Tom,' says the waterman – 'Good bye, Grandma,' cry the children – off jingles the coach at the rate of three miles an hour – and the mamma and children retire into the house, with the exception of one little villain, who runs up the street at the top of his speed, pursued by the smart servant, not ill-pleased to have such an opportunity of displaying her attractions. She brings him back, and, after casting two or three gracious glances across the way, which are either intended for us or the pot-boy (we are not quite certain which), shuts the door – and the hackney-coach stand is again at a stand still.

It is, in the end, the picture of the 'little villain' pursued by the flirtatious servant-girl with the pink ribbons that establishes the tone and the authorial attitude in the passage. Despite the humor in the exaggeration, we see that the specific and carefully selected details give the scene the color of reality and the characters a touch of human nature as we know it from our own experiences with life. We see human weaknesses, but they are so amusingly presented, in such an 'amiable' tone of voice, that we smile in delight not derision.

In the last section of the essay, Dickens describes a wedding party, appropriately dressed for the occasion, that stops at the corner to call, 'with an air of indescribable dignity,' for a coach. Once in, the bridesmaid throws a red shawl, which, the narrator tells us, she had probably brought on purpose, over the number on the door of the coach, 'evidently to delude pedestrians into the belief that the hackney-coach was a private-carriage,' quite unaware that 'there was a great, staring number stuck up behind, on a plate as large as a schoolboy's slate.' To this point the scene is mildly satirical; a few additional touches could easily make it a sharp exposé of human pretentiousness. But in keeping with his purpose to amuse his readers, Dickens must not let the satire predominate. A touch of Sternean sentiment puts the entire scene into proper focus: 'A shilling a mile! – the ride was worth five, at least, to them.' This highly effective combination of satire with sentiment is, certainly, characteristic of the later more famous works of Dickens, where one finds it used for characterizations as well as for mood. We see signs of it in Watkins Tottle, as pointed out earlier, whose two-part story was appearing at just this time (January–February 1835) in the *Monthly Magazine*. In the essays, it blossoms forth, particularly in the dominant tone, as an important element of Dickens's approach to life. It will later be modified by a bitterer view of man, his institutions, and his society, but never will the happy combination of satire and sentiment entirely disappear from Dickens's writing.

In somewhat more specialized aspects of fiction, Dickens also showed significant improvement: in description and narration, in techniques and theory of characterization, and, in the case of several sketches published under the general title of 'Our Parish,' in the creation of an environment of people, place, and time seen through the obtrusive, focusing eye of a fictional narrator.

To begin with, because the 'Street Sketches' and the 'Sketches of London' are, after all, predominantly descriptive essays, Dickens worked far more extensively with the techniques of description to set and to develop scenes in these essays than he had earlier in the *Monthly Magazine* tales. It is true that his descriptions are sometimes little more than lists. In 'The Pawnbroker's Shop' (*Evening Chronicle*, 30 June 1835), for example, his depiction of the exterior and interior of the shop is simply an itemization of the articles displayed in the window or behind the counter. But in the earlier 'Brokers' and Marine Store Shops,' he not only described but also humanized the articles in the shop by relating them to the lives of the people who once owned them. Most of the descriptions in his essays are at least equal to the best passages in the *Monthly Magazine* tales and not inferior to many of the descriptive passages in *Pickwick Papers*. The following paragraph from 'Hackney-Coach Stands' might very well have begun a scene in which Mr. Pickwick and his company set out for a new destination and new adventures. Specific details, a certain amount of exaggeration for effect, striking imagery, and even a bit of pathetic fallacy characterize the passage, as do Dickens's concern with the sounds, colors, and pictures created by certain words ('lumbering,' for instance) and his fascination with various rhetorical devices:

> There is a hackney-coach stand under the very window at which we are writing; there is only one coach on it now, but it is a fair specimen of the class of vehicles to which we have alluded – a great, lumbering, square concern, of a dingy-yellow colour (like a bilious brunette), with very small glasses, but very large frames; the pannels are ornamented with a faded coat of arms, in shape something like a dissected bat; the axle-tree is red, and the majority of the wheels are green. The box is partially covered by an old great-coat, with a multiplicity of capes, and some extraordinary-looking cloths; and the straw, with which the canvas cushion is stuffed, is sticking up in several places, as if in rivalry of the hay which is peeping through the chinks in the boot. The horses, with drooping heads, and each with a mane and tail as scanty and straggling as those of a worn-out rocking-horse, are standing patiently on some damp straw, occasionally wincing, and rattling the harness; and, now and then, one of them lifts his mouth to the ear of his companion, as if he were saying, in a whisper, that he should like to assassinate the coachman.

A number of the essays, such as 'The Streets – Morning' and 'Greenwich Fair' (*Evening Chronicle*, 16 April 1835) are almost completely descriptive. In the former, Dickens recreates the changing scenes and moods of the streets of London at various hours and half-hours of the morning. The details are effective if conventional – the drunken man staggering home, a policeman, market carts, laborers on their way to work, the confusion in Covent Garden market, the servants and apprentices beginning another day of work, the opening of the shops, stage coaches arriving and departing. But occasionally we are given a more imaginative detail, as that of the 'rakish-looking' cat that 'runs stealthily across the road, and descends his own area with as much caution and slyness – bounding first on the water-butt, then on the dust-hole, and then alighting on the flag-stones – as if he were conscious that his character depended on his gallantries of the pre-ceding night escaping public observation.'

Here Dickens isolates and individualizes a minor detail in order to establish a mood; elsewhere, as in the following passage from 'Greenwich Fair,' his details imaginatively convey a general impression of mass and movement, but even here the specificity of detail is responsible for creating the mood of bustle and gaiety that pervades the entire sketch:

> The road to Greenwich during the whole of Easter Monday presents a scene of animated bustle, which cannot fail to amuse the most indifferent observer. Cabs, hackney-coaches, 'shay' carts, coal-waggons, stages, omni-buses, sociables, gigs, donkey-chaises – all crammed with people (for the question never is what the horse can draw, but what the vehicle will hold), roll along at their utmost speed – the dust flies in clouds – ginger-beer corks go off in vollies – the balcony of every public-house is crowded with people smoking and drinking – half the private-houses are turned into tea-shops – fiddles are in great request – every little fruit-shop displays its stall of gilt gingerbread and penny toys – turnpike-men are in despair – horses won't go on, and wheels will come off – ladies in 'carawans' scream with fright at every fresh concussion, and their admirers find it necessary to sit remarkably close to them, by way of encouragement – servants of all work who are not allowed to have followers, and have got a holiday for the day, make the most of their time with the faithful admirer who waits for a stolen interview at the corner of the street every night, when they go to fetch the beer – apprentices grow sentimental, and straw-bonnet makers kind; every body is anxious to get on, and actuated by the common wish to be at the fair or in the park as soon as possible.

Frequently Dickens mixes description and action to produce the effect described by Percy Lubbock in *The Craft of Fiction* as 'pictorial' – that is, 'the reflection of events in the mirror of somebody's receptive conscious-ness' rather than 'a scene which might be put upon the stage' (which Lub-bock terms 'dramatic').[17] In the novels Dickens naturally will use the pictorial method to move his story rapidly through time or space from one 'dramatic' scene to another or to speed up time slightly within such a

---

[17] Percy Lubbock, *The Craft of Fiction* (New York: Viking Press, 1957), pp. 69–70. I am obviously more indebted to Lubbock's classic work (originally published London: J. Cape, 1921) than my footnotes indicate.

scene. He will also use it for humor, to present minor and particularly comic characters, and to describe comic and melodramatic action.

His use of the pictorial mode is illustrated by 'Early Coaches' (*Evening Chronicle*, 19 February 1835). In this essay, the narrator describes his preparations for a trip out of town: his visit to the booking-office to purchase a place on the six a.m. coach, the difficulty of getting to sleep the night before, the inconvenience of arising at five o'clock on a frosty morning, the trek through the streets of London at that ungodly hour, the wait for the coach, and, finally, the departure itself. The method used is pictorial, for though Dickens's intention is essentially dramatic in nature, his approach is more naturally descriptive since he is writing an essay, not a tale. Yet action seems to be taking place in the sketch, as in this description of the streets as seen from the window of 'Boz' at five in the morning:

> A thaw, by all that's miserable! The frost is completely broken up. You look down the long perspective of Oxford-street, the gas-lights mournfully reflected on the wet pavement, and can discern no speck in the road to encourage the belief that there is a cab or a coach to be had – the very coachmen have gone home in despair. The cold sleet is drizzling down with that gentle regularity which betokens a duration of four-and-twenty hours at least; the damp hangs upon the house-tops, and lamp-posts, and clings to you like an invisible cloak. The water is 'coming in' in every area – the pipes have burst – the water butts are running over – the kennels seem to be doing matches against time – pump-handles descend of their own accord – horses in market-carts fall down, and there's no one to help them up again – policemen look as if they had been carefully sprinkled with powdered glass – here and there a milk woman trudges slowly along, with a bit of list round each foot to keep her from slipping – boys who 'don't sleep in the house,' and an't allowed much sleep out of it, can't wake their masters by thundering at the shop-door, and cry with the cold – the compound of ice, snow, and water on the pavement is a couple of inches thick – nobody ventures to walk fast to keep himself warm, and nobody could succeed in keeping himself warm if he did.

The vividness of the description, intensified by Dickens's use of the present tense and the 'you' who is not exactly the narrator and not exactly the reader, gives this passage the immediacy of a dramatically conceived scene. The active, highly descriptive verbs also contribute to this effect: the sleet 'drizzling down,' the water 'running,' the horses falling down, the milk woman trudging slowly along, the apprentices 'thundering' and crying at the doors. The paragraph still remains basically descriptive, and therefore pictorial, however. An earlier passage, which describes the trip to the booking-office, though again technically still pictorial, is even more dramatic in effect:

> You enter a mouldy-looking room, ornamented with large posting bills, the greater part of the place enclosed behind a huge lumbering rough counter, and fitted up with recesses that look like the dens of the smaller animals in a

travelling menagerie, without the bars. Some half dozen people are 'booking' brown paper parcels, which one of the clerks flings into the aforesaid recesses with an air of recklessness, which you, remembering the new carpet-bag you bought in the morning, feel considerably annoyed at; porters, looking like so many Atlas's, keep rushing in and out with large packages on their shoulders; and while you are waiting to make the necessary inquiries, you wonder what on earth the booking office clerks can have been before they were booking office clerks; one of them with his pen behind his ear, and his hands behind him, is standing in front of the fire, like a full-length portrait of Napoleon; the other fellow with his hat half off his head, enters the passengers' names in the books with a coolness which is inexpressibly provoking; and the villain whistles – actually whistles – while a man asks him what the fare is outside, all the way to Holyhead! In frosty weather too! They are clearly an isolated race, evidently possessing no sympathies or feelings in common with the rest of mankind. Your turn comes at last, and having paid the fare, you tremblingly inquire – 'What time will it be necessary for me to be here in the morning?' 'Six o'clock,' replies the whistler, carelessly pitching the sovereign you have just parted with into a wooden bowl on the desk. 'Rather before than arter,' adds the man with the semi-roasted unmentionables, with just as much ease and complacency as if the whole world got out of bed at five. You turn into the street, ruminating, as you bend your steps homewards, on the extent to which men become hardened in cruelty by custom.

There is, obviously, very little need for a dramatically conceived scene at this point in the essay; thus, the pictorial approach is highly effective. In addition, because the narrator is speaking directly to the reader, he can comment humorously on the action or the characters, and he can economically summarize at any one point action, such as the booking-clerk's whistling, that is apparently continuous throughout the scene. He is himself the strongest dramatic element present. Whether tending toward the descriptive or toward the dramatic, the pictorial technique is one that Dickens always found exceedingly useful and effective for the obviously necessary foreshortening of action but also as a means of achieving comic and sentimental effects.[18]

In addition to developing in his ability to construct narrative and pictorial scenes, Dickens made important advances in both his concept of characterization and his creation of characters. Some of the characters who appear in the 'Street Sketches' and the 'Sketches of London' might, as quite minor figures, have fit comfortably into *Pickwick Papers* and would certainly have made the *Monthly Magazine* tales sparkle with life.

The characters in the essays have the advantage of being based more fully upon people whom Dickens knew or had at least observed in his travels about London and the countryside. When he sees them through the filter

---

[18] An interesting parallel to the last passage quoted from 'Early Coaches' is to be found in an earlier essay by John Poole entitled 'Early Rising: "I'll Pack My Portmanteau."' See Appendix D for details.

of his imagination and shapes them to suit his creative, expository demands, he combines characteristics of one person with those of another; exaggerates speech peculiarities, mannerisms, or physical traits; and even generalizes their characteristics sufficiently to make them representative individuals. The effect is infinitely more rewarding than that produced in the *Monthly Magazine* tales by wholesale imitation of the stock, artificial types in the farces of the day. His new characters, it is true, were easier to create because they are merely examples in an expository essay, not fully conceived personages interacting with others within a scene and busily working out a predetermined fictional plot. They are at best minor characters, not protagonists in a tale. If dealt with to the same length in a novel, they would merely be people who inhabit a landscape through which a group of principal or, more likely, secondary characters might move. In a short story they would not play roles of much greater importance. Yet because they do serve primarily as illustrations of the expository ideas in the essays – Boz's generalizations about life, society, and the times – they were created with careful attention to details supportive of the author's observations. Sometimes a quick physical description is all that an essay requires; at other times, often within a sentence or two, Dickens must begin to create a mood, add a touch of humor, relate the characterization to the theme, establish one character's attitude toward another, tone down a satirical portrait with a touch of humor or sentiment, or give the final twist to the developing picture of a disgusting human being. He early learned the value of such quick, characterizing description, and his later works are memorable at least partly because even the most minor characters there – equivalent to the ones he requires for these essays (Trabb's boy in *Great Expectations*, for example, or Mrs. Smallweed in *Bleak House*) – are just as carefully created. Because of the extremely limited space (most of the essays are only about 2000 words long) and the expository emphasis, Dickens's accomplishments are not sensational, but they are substantial. The style and substance of the essays written about the middle of 1835 would have seemed reasonably familiar to a reader of *Pickwick Papers*.

Particularly noticeable is Dickens's much greater use of mannerisms and action, dialogue and dialect to delineate his characters, what Walter Bagehot referred to as the '*vivification* of character, or rather of characteristics,' the process by which Dickens 'expands traits into people.'[19] The servant girl with the pink ribbons running down the street in 'Hackney-Coach Stands' and the whistling booking-clerk in 'Early Coaches,' already mentioned, are two good examples. A cleverly handled scene in 'Gin Shops' between one of the female gin dispensers and an impudent young man in a 'brown-coat and bright buttons,' as he is succinctly de-

---

[19] Walter Bagehot, 'Charles Dickens (1858),' in his *Literary Studies* (London: Longmans, Green, 1879), II, 197, 202. The essay was originally published in *National Review*, 7 (1858), 458–86.

scribed, illustrates a growing facility with dialogue and dialect. The combination of realistic speech patterns with characterizing mannerisms not only creates a humorous incident but also, despite the sparsity of physical description, brings two characters to life in about one hundred words:

> The two old washerwomen . . . are quite astonished at the impudent air of the young fellow in the brown-coat and bright buttons, who ushering in his two companions, and walking up to the bar in as careless a manner as if he had been used to green and gold ornaments all his life, winks at one of the young ladies with singular coolness, and calls for 'a kervorten and a three-out glass,' just as if the place were his own. 'Gin for you sir,' says the young lady when she has drawn it, carefully looking every way but the right one to show that the wink had no effect upon her. 'For me, Mary, my dear,' replies the gentleman in brown. 'My name an't Mary as it happens,' says the young girl in a most insinuating manner as she delivers the change. 'Vell, if it an't, it ought to be,' responds the irresistible one; 'all the Marys as ever I see was handsome gals.'

The young man is one of several characters originally created simply to illustrate Dickens's remark at the beginning of the long paragraph in which they make their brief appearance: 'Look at the groups of customers, and observe the different air with which they call for what they want, as they are more or less struck by the grandeur of the establishment.'[20]

Occasionally, as in 'Astley's' (*Evening Chronicle*, 9 May 1835), somewhat more fully developed scenes enable Dickens to do greater justice to his characters. The description of a family consisting of father, mother, nine or ten children, and a governess (admittedly a large cast of characters) is notable for its delicate touches of humor, its minute details, and, despite the essayist's claim that he is describing 'our *beau ideal* of a group of Astley's visitors,' its individualized characterizations. Here we find 'a child in a braided frock and high state of astonishment, with very large round eyes, opened to their utmost width,' who is lifted over the seats, 'a process which occasioned a considerable display of little pink legs,' and an eldest son, 'a boy of about fourteen years old, who was evidently trying to look as if he didn't belong to the family.' The entire group is effectively captured in the following passage:

> The play began, and the interest of the little boys knew no bounds; Pa was clearly interested too, although he very unsuccessfully endeavoured to look as if he wasn't. As for Ma, she was perfectly overcome by the drollery of the principal comedian, and laughed till every one of the immense bows on her ample cap trembled, at which the governess peeped out from behind the pillar again; and whenever she could catch Ma's eye, put her handkerchief to her mouth, and appeared, as in duty bound, to be in convulsions of laughter also.

---

[20] When he excised this opening sentence, in the 1837–39 edition of *Sketches by Boz*, Dickens gave the scene greater immediacy by making it important in itself rather than using it, as he had originally, merely to illustrate an uninspired expository idea.

Then when the man in the splendid armour vowed to rescue the lady, or perish in the attempt, the little boys applauded vehemently, especially one little fellow who was apparently on a visit to the family, and had been carrying on a child's flirtation the whole evening with a small coquette of twelve years old, who looked like a model of her Mama on a reduced scale; and who in common with the other little girls (who generally speaking have even more coquettishness about them than much older ones) looked very properly shocked when the knight's squire kissed the princess's confidential chambermaid.

In addition to creating the new richness that we find in the characters who appear in the 'Street Sketches' and the 'Sketches of London,' Dickens seems to be more consciously working to produce a predetermined effect, a combination of tone and attitude, that requires a more consistent concept of characterization than he had hitherto managed. A good many of his characters, the 'people' he describes to illustrate the expository themes of his essays, are defined by the 'amiable' humor he uses to 'amuse' his readers. He forces us to laugh at the family in Astley's audience and, in doing so, perhaps to laugh at ourselves. At the same time, however, the joyous outing of the family leaves us with a refreshing sense of the occasional splendor of the human condition. Dickens's attitude toward such characters is reflected in his remark in 'Thoughts about People' (*Evening Chronicle*, 23 April 1835) that he admires his 'very particular friends,' the hackney-coachmen, cabmen, and omnibus conductors of London, 'in proportion to the extent of their cool impudence and perfect self-possession.' He was certainly conscious by the end of 1835 of the effect that he wanted his description of such characters to have upon his readers, as is evident in the revised ending that he wrote at that time for 'Thoughts about People' for the First Series of *Sketches by Boz*. Referring to a group of London apprentices with a touch of satirical humor, a certain sentimental affection, and perhaps a remembrance of his own recent past as a clerk with Ellis and Blackmore, Dickens had concluded the original version of the essay with what Butt and Tillotson characterize as a 'much more clearly partisan' and less urbane conclusion, with 'the glare of the propagandist' rather than, as in the revised version of 1836, 'the bland smile of the periodical essayist' about it.[21] Compare the two endings:

Original Version

It may be urged that if London apprentices continue to pursue these freaks [the silly fashions and behavior of upper-class fops], they will no longer be the distinct class which we shall attempt to show they now are, by tracing them through the different scenes we propose to sketch. We feel the whole force of the objection; and we see no reason why the same gentleman of enlarged and comprehensive views who proposes to Parliament a measure for preserving the amusements of the upper classes of society, and abolishing

---

[21] Butt and Tillotson, p. 46, where the excised passage is quoted in part.

those of the lower, may not with equal wisdom preserve the former more completely, and mark the distinction between the two more effectually, by bringing in a Bill 'to limit to certain members of the hereditary peerage of this country and their families, the privilege of making fools of themselves as often and as egregiously as to them shall seem meet.' Precedent is a great thing in these cases, and Heaven knows he will have precedent enough to plead.

There are so many classes of people in London, each one so different from the other, and each so peculiar in itself, that we find it time to bring our paper to a close before we have well brought our subject to a beginning. We are, therefore, induced to hope that we may calculate upon the permission of our readers to think about people again at some future time.

Revised Version

We may smile at such people as these, but they can never excite our anger. They are usually on the best terms with themselves, and it follows almost as a matter of course, in good humour with every one about them. And if they do display a little occasional foolery in their own proper persons, it is surely more tolerable than the precocious puppyism of the Quadrant, the whiskered dandyism of Regent-street and Pall-mall, or gallantry in its dotage any where.

(*Sketches by Boz*, First Series, I, 106)

The original version is heavy with criticism of society and human beings, conveyed in a tone verging on righteous indignation. In the revised version, Dickens considerably tones down the criticism and emphasizes a more understanding attitude toward the people he has been describing. The emphasis on amiability was in the description of the apprentices to begin with; the revision points up Dickens's fuller awareness of what I believe to be the concept of characterization underlying many of the personages whom he creates in the essays.

Two concluding paragraphs that Dickens omitted in the First Series of *Sketches by Boz* contain other examples of a young man's indignation; by removing them, he considerably modified the tone of the essays. The first was originally the concluding paragraph to 'Astley's':

It is to us matter of positive wonder and astonishment that the infectious disease commonly known by the name of 'stage-struck,' has never been eradicated, unless people really believe that the privilege of wearing velvet and feathers for an hour or two at night, is sufficient compensation for a life of wretchedness and misery. It is stranger still, that the denizens of attorneys' offices, merchants' counting-houses, haberdashers' shops, and coal sheds, should squander their own resources to enrich some wily vagabond by paying – actually paying, and dearly too – to make unmitigated and unqualified asses of themselves at a Private Theatre. Private Theatres, so far as we know, are peculiar to London; they flourish just now, for we have half a dozen at our fingers' ends. We will take an early opportunity of introducing our readers to the Managers of one or two, and of sketching the interior of a Private Theatre, both before the curtain and behind it.[22]

With this paragraph removed, the essay ends on a much milder note, more humorous than satirical. Describing the circus performers in their shabby street clothing, 'Boz' refuses to believe that these are the same magnificently costumed 'gods and sylphs' that he applauded in the arena. 'With the exception of Ducrow, who can scarcely be classed among them,' he concludes, 'who ever knew a rider at Astley's, or saw him, but on horseback? Can our friend in the military uniform ever appear in threadbare attire, or descend to the comparatively un-wadded costume of every-day life? Impossible! We cannot – we will not – believe it' (*Sketches by Boz*, First Series, I, 312–13).

The other canceled passage originally concluded 'London Recreations':

> There are many other classes who regularly pursue the same round of recreation. The better description of clerks form rowing clubs, and dress themselves like sailors at fancy balls; others resort to the billiard table. Some people think the greatest enjoyment of existence is to stew in an unwholesome vault for a whole night, drinking bad spirits and hearing worse singing; and others go half-price to the theatre regularly every evening. A certain class of donkeys think the chief happiness of human existence is to knock at doors and run away again; and there are other men whose only recreation is leaning against the posts at street-corners, and not moving at all. Whatever be the class, or whatever the recreation, so long as it does not render a man absurd himself, or offensive to others, we hope it will never be interfered with, either by a misdirected feeling of propriety on the one hand, or detestable cant on the other.
>
> (*Evening Chronicle*, 17 March 1835)

The concluding sentence does modify the earlier anger, but by removing the entire paragraph, Dickens left himself with a much more dramatic, more amiable, certainly more effective, and yet unsentimental conclusion about rural tea-gardens to which Londoners resorted:

> It's getting dark, and the people begin to move; the field leading to town is quite full of them; the little hand-chaises are dragged wearily along; the children are tired, and amuse themselves and the company generally by crying, or resort to the much more pleasant expedient of going to sleep – the mothers begin to wish they were at home again – sweethearts grow more sentimental than ever, as the time for parting arrives – the gardens look mournful enough by the light of the two lanterns which hang against the trees for the convenience of smokers – and the waiters, who have been running about incessantly for the last six hours, think they feel a little tired, as they count their glasses and their gains.
>
> (*Sketches by Boz*, First Series, I, 145–46)

---

[22] Dickens did not write the promised sketch, 'Private Theatres' (*Evening Chronicle*, 11 August 1835), until three months later, but it is one of the more strongly satirical essays in the series.

Dickens was obviously not so consistent a practitioner of 'amiable humor' at this point in his early development as a reading of the revised versions of less than a year later would lead one to believe. But such examples of indignation are relatively rare in the 'Street Sketches' and the 'Sketches of London.' Certainly by the end of 1835, when the First Series of *Sketches by Boz* was ready for the press, he had a firmer grasp of the overall tone he wanted the collection of essays, the *literary* work, to have.

But a few of the essays are consciously products of a more condemnatory view, such as 'The Pawnbroker's Shop,' where the satirical treatment of the pawnbroker, his clerks, an old 'sallow-looking' woman, a 'slip-shod' woman, and an unshaven, dirty, 'sottish-looking' fellow is unrelieved by the least hint of good-humor. But here, too, the characters are strikingly developed:

'What do you strike the boy for, you brute?' exclaims a slip-shod woman, with two flat-irons in a little basket. 'Do you think he's your wife you willin?' 'Go and hang yourself,' replies the gentleman addressed, with a drunken look of savage stupidity, aiming at the same time a blow at the woman, which fortunately misses its object. 'Go and hang yourself; and wait there till I come and cut you down.' 'Cut you down,' rejoins the woman, 'I wish I had the cutting of you up, you wagabond (loud), – oh! you precious wagabond (rather louder), – where's your wife, you willin (louder still; women of this class are always sympathetic, and work themselves up into a tremendous passion in no time)? Your poor dear wife as you uses worser nor a dog – strike a wo-man –you a man! (very shrill); I wish I had you – I'd murder you, I would, if I died for it.' 'Now be civil,' retorts the man fiercely. 'Be civil, you wiper!' ejaculates the woman contemptuously – 'An't it shocking,' she continues, turning round and appealing to an old woman who is peeping out of one of the little closets we have before described, and who has not the slightest objection to join in the attack possessing, as she does, the comfortable conviction that she's bolted in. 'An't it shocking ma'am ("Dreadful" says the old woman in a parenthesis, not exactly knowing what the question refers to); he's got a wife, ma'am, as takes in mangling, and is as 'dustrious and hard working a young ooman as can be, (very fast) as lives in the back parlour of our 'ous, which my husband and me lives in the front one (with great rapidity) – and we hears him a beaten' on her sometimes when he comes home drunk, the whole night through, and not only a beaten' her, but beaten his own child too, to make her more miserable – ugh, you beast – and she, poor creetur won't swear the peace agin him. nor do nothin', because she likes the wretch arter all – worse luck.'

The satire succeeds in reinforcing the picture of pawnshops that Dickens had initially proposed in the sketch: 'Of all the numerous receptacles for misery and distress with which the streets of London unhappily abound, there are, perhaps, none which present such striking scenes of vice and poverty as the pawnbrokers' shops.'[23]

---

[23] Dickens canceled the phrase 'of vice and poverty' in the Cheap Edition of *Sketches by Boz* (1850).

Another manifestation of this less optimistic view of human nature is to be found in 'Thoughts about People,' which plays upon the theme of man's inhumanity to his fellow man. ''Tis strange,' Dickens begins, 'with how little notice, good, bad, or indifferent, a man may live and die in London. He awakens no sympathy in the breast of any single person; his existence is a matter of interest to no one save himself, and he cannot be said to be forgotten when he dies, for no one remembered him when he was alive.' Admittedly, much of this gloom may be a narrative pose, imitative of the sentimental melancholy of Irving, Lamb, Hunt, and even Goldsmith; no doubt the tone is a complex, inseparable mixture of assumed and genuinely felt responses to life. But it is equally true that Dickens's major example in the essay, the friendless office clerk, a product (as the narrator sees him, at any rate) of man's indifference to other men, will appear over and over again in the later works. Other examples may be found in 'Gin Shops,' 'London Recreations,' 'The Pawnbroker's Shop,' 'Shabby-Genteel People,' and one or two of the 'Our Parish' sketches. In *Pickwick Papers* the interpolated tales and the chapters devoted to Mr. Pickwick's incarceration in the Fleet abound with such creatures. The sentimental tone with which Dickens surrounds them at times disguises, perhaps even thereby modifies, the underlying bitterness of the narrator's view of man; in such later works as *Little Dorrit* and *Our Mutual Friend*, while the characters are more complex (Mr. Dorrit and Bradley Headstone, for example), much of the sentimental mood is gone.

But perhaps more significant is the method by which Dickens develops the character of the clerk, illustrative surely of the process by which many other characters were conceived in his mind. Beginning with the idea, already stated, that many Londoners live and die unnoticed, Dickens – through his narrative persona – searches for examples from life itself to illustrate the idea: 'We were seated in the inclosure in St. James' Park the other day, when our attention was attracted by a man whom we immediately set down in our own mind as one of this class.' Having selected his model, Dickens describes the man's appearance, which of necessity reinforces the initial concept: the external man, at least, must indeed be one of the unfortunate, unnoticed people of London. But Dickens is no longer satisfied, as he was in the *Monthly Magazine* tales, to allow broad surface details and a few generalities to create a character; 'there was something,' he continues, 'in his manner and appearance which told us, we fancied, his whole life, or rather his whole day, for a man of this sort has no variety.' At this point, then, Dickens calls his imagination into full play. Speculating about the man's life, he projects in great realistic detail a day in it that, in various ways – through the man's actions, his occupation, his behavior, his mannerisms, his thoughts, all the minutiae of his life – reveals the essence of an individual as well as a type. Although this may be only a rough approximation of how Dickens built his characters, it is, I think, close enough to show the necessarily realistic expository requirements and the imaginative urgings that develop the friendless office clerk into more than a stick figure or a simple farcical, satiric, or melodramatic type. The very process by which, as a child, he colored reality with his own imagination to make it more palatable, lies at the heart of his creation of character as an author. The boy who made up stories about the Marshalsea prisoners filing in to sign his father's petition was using the same techniques as the author of 'Thoughts about People.'

By 20 August 1835, when the last of his 'Sketches of London' appeared, Dickens had come a long way in his understanding of the needs of effective characterization and his ability to use at least the important basic techniques to achieve such characterizations. How unimaginative the figures of the early farcical tales are can easily be seen by contrasting them with those Dickens created to illustrate his descriptive essays. He has not as yet, it is true, produced a character approaching the scope and depth of a Pickwick or Sam Weller, say, or even an Alfred Jingle or a Fat Boy; for such an achievement he would need the space that only a novel or at least a single installment of one could provide. Yet in the 'Street Sketches' and the 'Sketches of London,' he is at least beginning to exhibit a better under- standing of what genuinely comic, more bitterly satiric, and more sentimentally conceived characters require if they are to transcend the stick figures and stock types in his earliest writing. Minor though they still are, he is beginning to breathe some life into them. In the tales and character studies that he will shortly write for *Bell's Life in London* and in the some- what longer tales he will write for the First Series of *Sketches by Boz* and for the *Library of Fiction*, he will have an opportunity at least to use the length of a short story in which to develop his characters more fully. Obviously the very nature of a descriptive essay rigidly limited what he could accomplish with characterization at this point. And yet it also forced him to base his characterizations on real persons and provided him with a philo- sophy and a technique. In addition, the opportunity to practice using tech- niques of characterization without having to manipulate the other elements of fiction at the same time enabled him to initiate certain basic improve- ments that would make his next tales superior to the earlier ones and pro- duce characters approaching the vividness of those that would make *Pickwick Papers* a success.

Finally, in the six 'Sketches of London' entitled 'Our Parish,'[24] Dickens combined several techniques of fiction, in slight imitation, one suspects, of Mary Russell Mitford's *Our Village: Sketches of Rural Character*

---

[24] Dickens added a seventh sketch, 'Our Next-Door Neighbour,' to the 'Our Parish' group in the 1837–39 edition of *Sketches by Boz*, but this was not a new sketch. It had origin- ally been published as 'Our Next Door Neighbours' in the Second Series of *Sketches by Boz*, with no indication that it belonged to the 'Our Parish' group. Although it is set in the parish, it is not about any of the characters, concerns, or incidents in the six original sketches.

and Scenery,[25] with excellent results. Long before the first 'Our Parish' sketch appeared in the *Evening Chronicle*, Dickens intended to create a series with this title;[26] had he written it then, it could have been nowhere near as successful as he was able to make it in 1835. As a group, the essays form a setting – a background of buildings, people, action, and attitudes, seen through a limited and dramatized point of view (the editorial 'we' of 'Boz'). The essence and the details of life in a suburban parish provide an environment in which the main characters of a novel could function adequately, akin, say, to the Dingley Dell setting in *Pickwick*, the Yarmouth scenes in *David Copperfield*, the precincts of the Court of Chancery in *Bleak House*, and the Bleeding Heart Yard buildings and inhabitants in *Little Dorrit*.

The first sketch in the group, 'The Beadle – The Parish Engine – The Schoolmaster,'[27] was No. IV of the 'Sketches of London' (28 February 1835). At the end of the essay, in a passage he removed when preparing the First Series of *Sketches by Boz* for publication, Dickens reveals something of his scheme:

> It was our original intention to have sketched, in a few words more, such fragments of the little history of some other of our parishioners as have happened to come under our observation. Our space, however, is limited; and, as an editor's mandate is a wholesome check upon an author's garrulity, we have no wish to occupy more than the space usually assigned to us. It is generally allowed that parochial affairs possess little beyond local interest. But, should we be induced to imagine that the favour of our readers disposes them to make an exception of the present case, we shall vary our future numbers [of the 'Sketches of London'], by seeking materials for another sketch in 'our parish.'

At the beginning of the second 'Our Parish' sketch, 'The Curate – The

---

[25] Published in five volumes, 1824–32. Butt and Tillotson (p. 41, n. 2) suggest that Dickens's series was 'probably intended as a novel variation' on Mitford's. Like *Our Village* it is fragmentary in nature and uses recurring characters and a narrator who is both observer and occasional participant in the action. 'Our Next Door Neighbours' is structured similarly to 'Rosedale,' and two or three other sketches, 'The Election' and 'The Two Sisters' in particular, may have suggested topics to Dickens for his own series (all three Mitford sketches mentioned are in Vol. IV of *Our Village*). But the differences between the two works are great. Mrs. Mitford's work, concerned with a country village and pastoral subjects rather than a suburban parish and its interests, is discursive in style and leisurely in its approach to its subjects; Dickens's narration is always tight and economical. Mitford indulges in sentimentality and pathos; Dickens is noticeably more satiric.

[26] See *Pilgrim Letters*, I, 33–34, to H. W. Kolle, [?10 December 1833].

[27] All but the first of the six essays in the *Evening Chronicle* series were published under the title 'Our Parish' (the first was titled 'The Parish'), but for purposes of identification, I shall refer to them by the individual chapter titles that Dickens gave them in the First Series of *Sketches by Boz*, where he grouped them under the general heading of 'The Parish.' He also numbered the chapters in the order of their original publication. In the 1837–39 edition, he changed the general heading back to 'Our Parish' and in this and the Cheap Edition (1850) made minor modifications in two of the chapter titles.

Old Lady – The Captain,'[28] No. XII of the 'Sketches of London' (19 May 1835), 'Boz' reminds his readers of his promise of nearly three months before. 'The promise,' he states, 'escaped our attention until a few days ago; but we now hasten to redeem it with a due sense of contrition for our negligence in not having done so before.' At the end of the number, he proposes more papers in the same vein:

> We have attained our usual limits, and must conclude our paper. We are not sufficiently acquainted with the details of the recent alteration in the Poor-laws, to know whether we have a legal settlement anywhere or not; but we hope our readers will not object, when subjects are scarce,, and we distressed, to our deriving assistance from the parochial funds. We are perfectly willing to work for their amusement; but we openly avow our determination, on some future occasions, to throw ourselves again upon – 'Our Parish.'[29]

From this point to the end of the series of 'Sketches of London,' the 'Our Parish' essays – No. XIV, 'The Four Sisters' (18 June); No. XVI, 'The Election for Beadle' (14 July); No. XVIII, 'The Broker's Man' (28 July); and No. XX, 'The Ladies' Societies' (20 August 1835) – alternated with other essays in the larger series, a publication plan that Dickens officially announced to his readers at the end of No. XIV, adding that 'from this time forward we shall make no further apology for an abrupt conclusion to an article under the title of "Our Parish," than is contained in the words "To be continued,"' a phrase with which the last three 'Our Parish' sketches are concluded.[30]

The setting seems to be a mixture of places. On the one hand it is clearly a suburban London parish, for the essays are 'Sketches of London' first of all, and Dickens describes the parish as 'suburban' in 'The Curate – The Old Lady – The Captain.' A reference in 'The Ladies' Societies' to Exeter Hall, a building in the Strand where concerts, various entertainments, and undenominational religious meetings were held,[31] clearly places the parish within the vicinity of London, as do allusions in 'Our Next Door Neighbours.'[32] But according to Robert Langton and, later, William J. Carlton, the old lady in 'The Curate – The Old Lady – The Captain' is unquestionably modeled on a Mrs. Mary Ellen Newnham, a resident of Chatham, who dates back to Dickens's childhood. 'There are good

---

[28] The title was expanded in the 1837–39 edition of *Sketches by Boz* to 'The Curate – The Old Lady – The Half-Pay Captain.'

[29] Dickens omitted these two quotations from 'The Curate – The Old Lady – The Captain' in the First Series of *Sketches by Boz*.

[30] Dickens also omitted these announcements in the First Series of *Sketches by Boz*.

[31] T. W. Hill, 'Notes on *Sketches by Boz*,' *Dickensian*, 46 (1949/50), 209.

[32] In 'Our Next Door Neighbours,' the narrator walks from the parish toward Eaton Square and elsewhere alludes to one of his neighbors as having 'settled in London' (*Sketches by Boz*, Second Series, pp. 119 and 127). But, as mentioned, the connection of this seventh sketch to the 'Our Parish' group is tenuous.

reasons,' states Carlton, 'for believing that the parish was St. Mary's, Chatham, and the neat row of houses [in the sketches] Ordnance Terrace,'[33] where the Dickens family lived from 1817 to 1821. In any case, Dickens relocated St. Mary's in London, and the mixture reveals the presence of more fictional content in these sketches than their expository emphasis would at first indicate. And who knows to what extent the various parishes in which Dickens lived while growing up in London also provided materials for the 'Our Parish' pieces?

Even more important, as an examination of the content and structure of the six essays will reveal, again we see Dickens working with the techniques of fiction individually but also in relatively simple combinations in a unified series of essays. It is a more complex exercise in the craft of fiction than is any of the individual 'Street Sketches' or 'Sketches of London.'

The first 'Our Parish' essay begins abruptly with a series of character sketches, with very little by way of an introduction to the series; only at the end does Dickens suggest that this is to be the first of a series. Indeed, the opening paragraph simply indicates that 'The Beadle – The Parish Engine – The Schoolmaster' is likely to be one of the rare censorious 'Sketches of London':

> How much is conveyed in those two short words – the parish; and with how many tales of distress and misery; of broken fortune and ruined hopes – too often of unrelieved wretchedness and successful knavery – are they associated! A poor man, with small earnings and a large family, just manages to live on from hand to mouth, and to procure food from day to day; he has barely enough for the present, and can take no heed of the future. . . . What can he do? To whom is he to apply for relief? To private charity? To benevolent individuals? Certain not; hasn't he – the parish?

As a parish official associated with the workhouse, the beadle is treated to a lengthy description, but his other functions, including the more comic ones of church disciplinarian and official custodian of the parish fire-engine, also come into the picture. The essay concludes with a brief description of the master of the workhouse and a sentimentalized portrait of the local schoolmaster. These are more detailed descriptions than one finds in many of the other 'Sketches of London'; the description of the schoolmaster, though shorter than that of the beadle, is actually a summary of the man's entire life.

---

[33] William J. Carlton, '"The Old Lady" in *Sketches by Boz*,' *Dickensian*, 49 (1952/53), 149. Also see Langton, p. 23. In a letter to Catherine Hogarth (probably of 20 March 1836, thirteen days before their marriage), describing tentative plans for their forthcoming marriage and wedding trip, Dickens writes: 'I have been thinking the matter over; and it strikes me, the best plan will be, when we are married, for us to go straight to Rochester. Mother can write to the "old Lady's" Servant: and she, I have no doubt, will procure us comfortable Lodgings there' (*Pilgrim Letters*, I, 141). Obviously, as Carlton indicates (p. 152), the connection between the old lady in the second 'Our Parish' sketch, the Rochester–Chatham area, and Mrs. Newnham was clear in Dickens's mind.

The character sketches continue in the second 'Our Parish' sketch, with the more comic descriptions of the curate, the old lady, and the half-pay captain. Dickens has now modified what seemed to be his original intention. He is not writing a series of angry essays on the injustices and inhumanities of the Poor Laws after all but rather, in the tradition of the familiar essay, examining with humane amusement the fallible, comic, pathetic body of humanity around him. But significantly for his continuing exercises in the craft of fiction, he is also creating more than simply a series of character sketches. Since the curate is largely depicted through the responses (amorous, sentimental, matrimonial, maternal) of his female parishioners to his 'prepossessing appearance,' 'fascinating manners,' 'deep sepulchral voice,' and consumptive cough, description crosses over into narration – and the narration has something of a plot to it, as the women first vie for the curate's attentions and then abandon him for the new clergyman at the parish chapel of ease, a 'pale, thin, cadaverous man, with large black eyes, and long straggling black hair,' slovenly dress, ungainly manner, and start-ling doctrines. The old lady is presented in more conventional fashion, through relatively straightforward description of her person, her home, and her activities. But her next-door neighbor, the half-pay captain, is characterized largely in terms of his relationship with the old lady:

> In the first place he *will* smoke cigars in the front court; and when he wants something to drink with them – which is by no means an uncommon circum-stance – he lifts up the old lady's knocker with his walking-stick, and demands to have a glass of table ale handed over the rails. In addition to this cool pro-ceeding he is a bit of a Jack of all trades, or to use his own words, 'A regular Robinson Crusoe,' and nothing delights him better than to experimentalize on the old lady's property. One morning he got up early and planted three or four roots of full-blown marygolds in every bed of her front garden to the inconceivable astonishment of the old lady, who actually thought when she got up and looked out of the window, that it was some strange eruption which had come out in the night.

He also managed to put her clock together, after taking it apart for cleaning, we are told, so that 'the large hand has done nothing but trip up the little one ever since.' And, while raising silkworms, he left a virtual path of the creatures behind him in her house, forcing her to flee for a time to the seaside. But despite these and other less desirable characteristics, the captain is 'a charitable, open-handed old fellow at bottom after all; so, although he puts the old lady a little out occasionally, they agree very well in the main; and she laughs as much at each feat of his handy-work when it's all over as anybody else.' The captain is a multi-sided man, an intriguing combination of brusqueness, impetuosity, male egotism, eccentricity, and amiability. Again we see characterization turning or about to turn into rudimentary plotting. We want to know more about the relationship of these two people, for we suspect that a story is lurking somewhere about. But since the sketch concludes a paragraph or so later, the story, obviously, never gets told.

'The Four Sisters,' the third 'Our Parish' sketch, is also to be a character study, we assume, for Dickens begins:

> The row of houses in which our friends the old lady and her troublesome neighbour reside, contains, we think, within its circumscribed limits, a greater number of characters than all the rest of our parish put together. When we say that we live in the row ourselves, we have not the slightest intention to insinuate that we can lay claim to any peculiar characteristics. We merely mention the fact, in order that the statement may have the authority of our own personal observation and experience; and we present our readers occasionally with a slight sketch of the materials we have collected from this source, in the hope that an attempted delineation of character now and then will vary the numerous scenes we undertook to describe when we entitled these papers, 'Sketches of London.'[34]

But it is nothing like the first two sketches. The Miss Willises live in Gordon-place, as do the old lady, the captain, and the narrator. While the first two play no part in this sketch, the narrator himself becomes part of a developing drama that makes it more a plotted tale than a familiar essay. The story is told as a flashback. The aging Miss Willises moved into the row thirteen years ago; three years later a Mr. Robinson appeared on the scene as a suitor to one of the sisters. But it is not clear to the narrator and the other neighbors which sister is being courted. At least this is the naïve point of view with which the narrator, as editorial 'we,' credits himself: '(we are in a state of bachelorship),' he adds apologetically as well as parenthetically.[35] The sisters do not clarify the situation – '*We*,' says the eldest Miss Willis, contributing to the confusion, 'are going to marry Mr. Robinson.' Even at the marriage ceremony, all four women kneel down at the communion table, repeat the responses, and go into hysterics. The drama in the story, unfolding itself in the narrator's response to the events involving the Willises, moves to a forceful, comic conclusion, an ending of

---

[34] Dickens left the first sentence (considerably modified) of this passage in the First Series of *Sketches of Boz* and added to it a sentence explaining why the series ended abruptly with 'The Ladies' Societies,' the sixth piece: 'The row of houses in which the old lady and her troublesome neighbour reside, comprises, beyond all doubt, a greater number of characters in its circumscribed limits than all the rest of our parish put together. As we cannot, consistently with our present plan, however, extend the number of our parochial sketches beyond six, it will be better perhaps to select the most peculiar, and to introduce them at once without further preface' (I, 24). Surprisingly, when he added the seventh sketch in the 1837–39 edition, he did not make a corresponding correction in this passage, nor did he make it later, though in the 1837–39 edition and the Cheap Edition (1850) he identifies the seven as 'Seven Sketches from Our Parish' in the table of contents.

[35] For the 1837–39 edition of *Sketches by Boz*, Dickens, by then married for over a year, changed this passage to '(we were in a state of bachelorship then),' to reflect his actual situation. But in doing so, he slightly altered the meaning of the original; the married narrator obviously has a perspicacity that the bachelor narrator of 1835 did not have.

a higher quality than Dickens had found for any of the *Monthly Magazine* tales. Time passes; and, as the narrator points out, 'Coming events cast their shadows before, and events like that at which we hint with becoming delicacy and diffidence *will* happen occasionally in the best regulated families – indeed the best regulated are usually supposed to be the most subject to such occurrences.'[36] Mrs. Robinson – that is, the youngest sister, it is now evident – has become pregnant, come to term, and been delivered of a daughter before 'Boz,' our apparent man of the world, is fully enlightened about these *new* strange comings and goings at No. 25. 'And then,' he continues, 'in common with the rest of the row, our curiosity was satisfied, and we began to wonder it had never occurred to us what the matter was before.'

Although the story of the Miss Willises completes itself by the end of the sketch, in a concluding paragraph (omitted in the First Series of *Sketches by Boz*) Dickens promises not only to alternate 'Our Parish' sketches with the other 'Sketches of London' but also to give a further account of the sisters at another opportunity.[37] Certainly his account of the parish is not expanding as it would in an admitted work of fiction, but I think we do see the young author becoming aware of the potential of his subject as fiction and half-consciously testing this potential while still maintaining the mode of the familiar essay, stretching a subject here, continuing it as a sequel there, elsewhere developing a character with some roundness, merging descriptive detail with action, interrelating characters, reintroducing them in later sketches in the series, involving himself (as a member of the parish) in their activities, even dramatizing his difficulties *as* a narrator with the variety and quantity of materials to be presented in a series of essays – and all at much greater length than previously.

Such dramatization continues and intensifies in the remaining sketches. 'The Election for Beadle,' is not only dramatic in itself, as suggested by the title Dickens gave it later, but continues the drama in which the narrator is involved. 'An event has recently occurred in our parish,' 'Boz' states at

---

[36] Dickens canceled most of this passage in the First Series of *Sketches by Boz*, referring there only vaguely to 'a circumstance of the most gratifying description, which *will* happen occasionally in the best-regulated families' (I, 31), thereby removing, Butt and Tillotson indicate, one of the 'touches of indelicacy' in the original essays (p. 48).

[37] The canceled passage follows:

Official parish registers of marriages, births, christenings, and deaths, are not generally considered to possess any amusement or much interest, except for those who are personally connected with some individual record contained within their musty leaves. *Our* parish register will have, at least, three advantages – it will be easy of access, it will be faithfully entered up from time to time, and it will at least be penned with a humble desire to amuse those who may consult it. As we dare not occupy any greater space at this busy period, we have only to add that we must defer any further account of the four Miss Willises until another opportunity; that we propose in future publishing a parochial sketch alternately with one coming more immediately under our first heading ['Sketches of London']; and that from this time forward we shall make no further apology for an abrupt conclusion to an article under the title of 'Our Parish,' than is contained in the words 'To be continued.'

the beginning, 'which for the moment completely absorbs every other consideration, and throws even the Miss Willises entirely into the shade. We have had an election – an election for beadle; a contest of paramount interest has just terminated; a parochial convulsion has taken place.'[38] The narrator's very plan of writing has been disrupted. He must put aside his intention of continuing the character sketch (which is no longer merely that, as we have seen) of the four sisters and deal with matters of the moment in the parish. The beadle whom he described in the first sketch in this series, has died, prompting the occasion for the election. The drama has extended itself over the larger arena of several 'Our Parish' sketches. The leader of the official political party, another resident of Gordon-place, it turns out, 'a tall, thin, bony man, with an interrogative nose, and little restless perking eyes, which appear to have been given him for the sole purpose of peeping into other people's affairs with,' is a new character. But the leader of the reform party turns out to be none other than the half-pay captain, now identified as Captain Purday; his aggressive (and suspect) behavior in support of his candidate, Mr. Bung, against Mr. Spruggins is quite consistent with his earlier characterization. The battle rages, and is as much a satire on political campaigning, campaign speeches, and corrupt voting practices as the Eatanswill election campaign in *Pickwick Papers* (see Ch. xiii), though it is nowhere near as comic:

> On the following day the polling began. . . . The Captain engaged two hackney coaches and a cab for Bung's people – the cab for the drunken voters, and the two coaches for the old ladies, the greater portion of whom, owing to the Captain's impetuosity, were driven up to the poll and home again, before they recovered from their flurry sufficiently to know with any degree of clearness what they had been doing; the opposite party wholly neglected these precautions, and the consequence was, that a great many ladies who were walking leisurely up to the church – for it was a very hot day – to vote for Spruggins, were artfully decoyed into the coaches, and voted for Bung. The Captain's arguments, too, had produced considerable effect; the attempted influence of the vestry produced a greater. A threat of exclusive dealing was clearly established against the vestry-clerk – a case of heartless and profligate atrocity. It appeared that the delinquent had been in the habit of purchasing six penn'orth of muffins weekly from an old woman who rents a small house in our parish, and resides among the original settlers; on her last weekly visit

---

[38] For the First Series of *Sketches by Boz*, Dickens revised these opening sentences as follows: 'A great event has recently occurred in our parish. A contest of paramount interest has just terminated; a parochial convulsion has taken place. It has been succeeded by a glorious triumph which the country – or at least the parish, it's all the same – will long remember. We have had an election – an election for beadle' (I, 35). But in omitting the reference to the Miss Willises, he canceled much of the drama concerning the narrator's editorial difficulties that gives a unity to the 'Our Parish' series. It is easy to see why he removed most of the introductory and concluding remarks that I have quoted in the last few pages; in most cases proximity was a sufficient link. Nevertheless, necessary though the cuts were, the loss of the Shandian approach can only be regretted.

a message was conveyed to her through the medium of the cook, couched in mysterious terms, but indicating with sufficient clearness, that the vestry-clerk's appetite for muffins in future depended entirely on her vote on the beadleship. This was sufficient; the stream had been turning previously, and the impulse thus administered directed its final course. The Bung party ordered one shillingsworth of muffins weekly for the remainder of the old woman's natural life; the parishioners were loud in their exclamations; and the fate of Spruggins was sealed.

In the fifth 'Our Parish' sketch, 'The Broker's Man,' the excitement has subsided; the parish is 'again restored to a state of comparative tranquillity,' thus enabling 'Boz,' as he promptly informs us, 'to continue our sketches of individual parishioners who take no share in our party contests, or in the turmoil and bustle of public life.' But he does not return to the Miss Willises, as he had promised. (Is there a slight suggestion of Shandyism here?) Instead, Mr. Bung, who has just won the election for beadle, has helped him 'in collecting materials for this task,' by providing him with 'one or two professional anecdotes' from his previous occupation as a broker's man. Following a generalized description of Bung's 'chequered' past, 'Boz' retells the man's 'anecdotes' in 'nearly his own words,' a lower-class dialect. Bung describes three incidents from his career as a broker's man – one basically comic ('the bright side of the picture,' he calls it), the other two with varying degrees of attendant pathos, the same sort of mixture that 'Boz' himself used in 'The Beadle – The Parish Engine – The School-master.' This new Bung is not really the minor character to whom we were introduced in 'The Election for Beadle,' but the revelation of his new char-acter through the dialect, the details he selects, and the attitudes he expresses toward individual characters and situations in his story is richly detailed through the man's own narrative. As 'Boz' relates just prior to Bung's narrative, 'his fluctuations have been between poverty in the extreme & poverty modified, or, to use his own emphatic language, between nothing to eat and just half enough. He is not as he forcibly remarks, "One of those fortunate men who if they were to dive under one side of a barge stark-naked, would come up on the other, with a new suit of clothes on, and a ticket for soup in the waistcoat pocket;" neither is he one of those, whose spirit has been broken beyond redemption by misfortune and want.'

In the sixth sketch, 'The Ladies' Societies,' Dickens returns to the women of the parish whom he introduced in the second. Apparently he intended the various charitable societies to represent the force of women in the community, just as the electioneering activity for the office of beadle represented that of the men. The curate and Mr. Bung (in his role as a pro-vider of material for 'Boz') reappear briefly, but the Miss Browns, merely mentioned in the second 'Our Parish' sketch, return as the leaders of one group of women, the Child's Examination Society. The others are new and relatively minor characters. Again, action is more important than character sketch, as the narrator, going back in time to the appearance of the popular curate on the parish scene, recounts the competition among the various ladies' societies for popularity in the parish and favor in the eyes of the unmarried curate. Having been nearly defeated in the contest by the Child's Examination Society, the Ladies' Bible and Prayer-Book Distribution Society, led by Mrs. Johnson Parker, conceives of the brilliant idea of sending 'a deputation of old ladies' to wait upon 'Mr. Somebody O' Something, a celebrated Catholic renegade and Protestant bigot,'[39] with a request for a speech, which is accepted. Wiping his eyes, blowing his nose, and quoting Latin, the orator speaks of 'green isles – other shores – vast Atlantic – bosom of the deep – Christian charity – blood and extermination – mercy in hearts – arms in hands – altars and homes – household gods' (a technique Dickens learned from Charles Mathews and perfected for Jingle in *Pickwick Papers*). The Child's Examination Society is completely defeated by the Irishman's popularity: 'Nobody knew exactly what it was about,' the narrator informs us, 'but everybody knew it must be affecting, because even the orator was overcome.' The plot is simple, and its resolution is not subtle, but there is a certain forcefulness in its very simplicity. Admittedly it is a simplicity that works better in a short expository essay, particularly in one of a closely related series, than in a short story or novel. However, as preparation for Dickens's future career as a writer of fiction, such basic plotting is clearly preferable to the artificiality and unnecessarily complicated structuring that caused the young author trouble in the *Monthly Magazine* tales.

Obviously Dickens meant to continue the 'Our Parish' sketches, for 'The Ladies' Societies' ends with '[To be continued],' as had 'The Election for Beadle' and 'The Broker's Man.' It must be time for the Miss Willises to reappear (Dickens had twice promised more of their story), as well as the old lady and the half-pay captain and possibly, from the first sketch, the schoolmaster. But 'The Ladies' Societies' was not only the last 'Our Parish' sketch but also the last 'Sketch of London' in the *Evening Chronicle*. The pressure of Dickens's reportorial duties for the *Morning Chronicle* may have forced the discontinuation of the series – his letters of August and September 1835

---

[39] In the First Series of *Sketches by Boz*, Dickens changed the speaker to 'Mr. Mortimer O'Silly-one,' dropping the descriptive appositives but sharpening his satire of a Reverend Mortimer O'Sullivan, 'an Irish controversialist,' Butt and Tillotson indicate, 'who had come to England on a deputation from the Irish Protestant clergy' and had spoken at Exeter Hall on 20 June and 11 July 1835. They also quote from a notice in the *Morning Chronicle* of 2 July to the effect that O'Sullivan had been 'going about this country like a showman,' addressing meetings 'in the most bombastic, frothy, nonsensical style' (p. 47, n. 1). In the second edition of the First Series (August 1836), the speaker loses his name to become more generally 'a celebrated oratorical pedlar' (I, 77), and in the 1837–39 edition, he is merely 'a celebrated orator' (p. 44), as first caution apparently and then the passage of time rendered the changes desirable. In every edition, he was clearly identified as an Irishman in the following sentence. For another interesting instance in which Dickens deliberately blurred realistic details, see Carlton's study, in 'Portraits in "A Parliamentary Sketch,"' pp. 100–109, of the revisions in 'The House' (*Evening Chronicle*, 7 March 1835) and 'Bellamy's' (*Ibid.*, 11 April 1835) when he combined them as 'A Parliamentary Sketch. With a few Portraits' in the Second Series of *Sketches by Boz*.

contain several references to the long, weary hours he was forced to devote to recording Parliamentary debate.[40] But it seems more likely that he received an offer to do a series of 'Scenes and Characters' for *Bell's Life in London, and Sporting Chronicle* from its editor, Vincent Dowling, that was more financially attractive, personally satisfying, and professionally rewarding.[41]

Although no more were forthcoming, the 'Sketches of London' – and the earlier 'Street Sketches' for the *Morning Chronicle* – had served Dickens well as exercises in the craft of fiction. Between 26 September 1834 and 20 August 1835, while writing essays rather than tales, Dickens came of necessity to place much greater reliance than earlier on a body of realistic details, culling his subject matter from the life he observed around him. He also developed, as a writer of familiar essays inevitably would, a more consistent attitude toward his subjects; in his efforts to 'amuse,' to 'interest,' and to 'entertain' his reading audience in the popular press, he found it necessary to trim away the verbal flowers that characterize the essays of his predecessors and even of his contemporaries, while cultivating

---

[40] See *Pilgrim Letters*, I, 71–74. But then, Dickens was also under such pressure during June and July, during which he wrote eight 'Sketches of London,' including the last four 'Our Parish' sketches (see *Pilgrim Letters*, I, 62–71). The effect on him may, of course, have been cumulative. Catherine Hogarth, to whom he had become engaged in May, was also making numerous demands upon his valuable time for writing.

[41] *Bell's Life in London* was a four-page weekly. According to James Grant in *The Great Metropolis* (New York: Saunders and Otley, 1837, II, 134, '. . . with the single exception of "The Dispatch," it is the largest of any paper, daily or weekly, in the United Kingdom' (noted in Butt and Tillotson, p. 41, n. 3). Dickens's 'Scenes and Characters' were featured in the left hand column of the first page, a prominent and surely flattering position; his 'Sketches of London' had often been relegated to other pages and less prominent positions in the *Evening Chronicle*. Dowling himself has been credited with being the first to recognize Dickens's genius for sketching characters – according to Charles Gruneisen, another Parliamentary reporter, as quoted in [John Camden Hotten and H. T. Taverner], *Charles Dickens, the Story of His Life* (London: John Camden Hotten, [1870]), p. 35. Perhaps all of these circumstances worked together to make a series for *Bell's Life in London* attractive to the young author. If the editors of the *Evening Chronicle* did not object to the discontinuation of the 'Sketches of London,' this may have been because Dickens was engaged to the daughter of George Hogarth, one of the co-editors. Hogarth had both a personal and paternal interest in forwarding the young man's career (see *Pilgrim Letters*, I, 54–55, n. 2; F. R. Dean, 'George Hogarth,' *Dickensian*, 43 (1946/47), 22; and Chapter V, below). He knows, Dickens explained to Macrone when he was preparing the First Series of *Sketches by Boz* for publication, 'all the sketches by heart, and takes an interest in the book in no way secondary to my own' – *Pilgrim Letters*, I, 108, [17 December 1835]. In any case, Dickens changed his pseudonym from 'Boz' to 'Tibbs' for the new series, perhaps at Hogarth's suggestion and very likely to avoid any apparent competition with the by then discontinued *Evening Chronicle* series. In 'The Genesis of *Sketches by Boz*,' *Dickensian*, 30 (1933/34), 110, Walter Dexter suggests that those 'who had been following Dickens's work would recognise this name as that of the proprietor of "The Boarding House."' Edgar Johnson suggests (I, 103) that it was 'probably derived from the character of Beau Tibbs, in Goldsmith's essays.' Yet it is difficult to see Dickens identifying himself in any way with the odd little married man of small means in *The Citizen of the World*, unless he means to allude to the man's frequent noting of memorandums in a notebook (Letter LV) or to Tibbs's statement there that 'when the world laughs at me, I laugh at the world, and so we are even.'

the style of the 'amiable humorist,' a complex tone of voice – witty, ob-trusive, yet sympathetic at times, at times descending to pathos, sometimes angry, sometimes condescending, but also understanding and – in its judgment of human frailties – lenient, and on occasion admiring. Both the greater emphasis on realistic detail and the more complex tone of voice would greatly change the nature of the tales Dickens would write in the next few months and prepare the way for the astonishing success of *Pickwick Papers*. Writing the twenty-five essays also provided Dickens with further opportunities to improve his handling of somewhat more specialized techniques of fiction, particularly those of narration, description, and characterization, as he used them incidentally in writing the essays. The scenes are more realistic and colorful, the characters fuller, more individualized, and more subject to a controlling narrative view of human nature. Moreover, in the 'Our Parish' sketches, Dickens successfully creates an entire environment involving people, place, and time, unified to a con-siderable extent by the point of view, the responding intellect of 'Boz,' his narrator. But more than this accomplishment, he also seems to be experi-menting with actions and forces on a scale more suitable to the long novel that was shortly to become a way of life for him. Characters never quite emerge from the parish background to dominate the scene as principals in a novel would; the plotted actions remain on a small scale, completing themselves within the individual essay rather than maintaining conflict or suspense from sketch to sketch; and although point of view and tone are sufficiently consistent within the individual sketch, the sequence of sketches is too fragmentary in nature to enable Dickens to work on the unity of tone and view of life essential to a major fictional work, a unity of which he may have been unaware in any case. But characters do reappear and do interact, there is great potential for one or another character to develop into a protagonist and engage in the larger action required to structure a novel, and the mild drama of the narrator's involvement in parish events and of his occasional references to his duty, as a writer to his readers, to provide a number of parish character studies gives a continuity to the series that is another requisite of a long work of fiction. Dickens is on the verge of breaking away from the short work to the long one.

As essays, the 'Street Sketches' and the 'Sketches of London' are often excellent; as exercises in the individual elements of fiction, they play a major role in Dickens's early development as a novelist by providing him with a second start, canceling out much of the unfavorable influence of the popular farcical tales and plays of the day and giving solid ground for building his future works of fiction. He is obviously much better prepared to return to fiction in some of the 'Scenes and Characters' he will write next for *Bell's Life in London*.

CHAPTER FOUR

'Scenes and Characters'

Dickens returned to the farcical tale in several of the twelve 'Scenes and Characters' that he contributed to *Bell's Life in London, and Sporting Chronicle* between 27 September 1835 and 17 January 1836.[1] The title of the series suggests that he wrote these sketches with two important aspects of the craft of fiction in mind. When he republished *Sketches by Boz* in monthly parts (1837–39), he grouped the contents for the first time under the headings that survived in all later editions: 'Our Parish' ('Seven Sketches from Our Parish' in the table of contents), 'Scenes,' 'Characters,' and 'Tales.' Three of the twelve sketches from *Bell's Life in London* – 'Seven Dials' (27 September 1835), 'Some Account of an Omnibus Cad' (1 November 1835), and 'The Streets at Night' (17 January 1836)[2] – appeared under 'Scenes' and the rest under 'Characters,' but five of the 'Characters' could justifiably have been placed under the heading of 'Tales.' These five conveniently provide us with an opportunity to observe Dickens again manipulating the several aspects of fiction within a single work.

The other seven essays, like those he wrote for the *Morning Chronicle* and *Evening Chronicle*, continued to serve Dickens as exercises in the individual aspects of fiction. 'Seven Dials' and 'The Streets at Night' are developed largely through descriptions of buildings, streets, shops, and people, and are endowed with perhaps even slightly more colorful, realistic, and imaginative details than were the earlier essays of 1834 and 1835, as this excerpt from 'The Streets at Night' illustrates:

> The streets in the vicinity of the Marsh-gate and Victoria Theatre present an appearance of dirt and discomfort on such a night, which the groups who lounge about them in no degree tend to diminish. Even the little block tin temple sacred to 'baked 'taturs,' surmounted by a splendid design in variegated lamps, looks less gay than usual; and as to the kidney-pie stand, its glory has

---

[1] See list in Appendix A.
[2] In the Second Series of *Sketches by Boz*, 'Some Account of an Omnibus Cad' was reprinted, with revisions, as the second half of 'The Last Cab Driver, and the First Omnibus Cad.' 'The Streets at Night' was reprinted as 'The Streets by Night' in the Second Series and as 'The Streets – Night' in the 1837–39 and later editions.

quite departed, for the candle in the transparent lamp, manufactured of oiled paper, embellished with 'characters,' has been blown out fifty times, so the kidney-pie merchant, tired with running backwards and forwards to the next wine-vaults to get a light, has given up the idea of illumination in despair, and the only signs of his whereabout are the bright sparks, of which, a long irregular train is whirled down the street every time he opens his portable oven to hand a hot kidney-pie to a customer. Flat-fish, oyster, and fruit-vendors linger hopelessly in the kennel, in vain endeavouring to attract customers; and the ragged boys who usually disport themselves about the street, stand crouched in little knots in some projecting door-way, or under the canvass window-blind of the cheesemonger's, where great flaring gas lights, unshaded by any glass, display huge piles of bright red, and pale yellow cheeses, mingled with little five penny dabs of dingy bacon, various tubs of weekly Dorset, and cloudy rolls of 'best fresh.'

'The Parlour' (13 December 1835; reprinted as 'The Parlour Orator' in *Sketches by Boz*, Second Series) and 'The Prisoners' Van' (29 November 1835) rely mainly on dramatic scenes and strong characterizations for their effect. The former contains an excellent satire of a disputatious, red-faced man who, though accustomed to having his own way on political topics, is put down by a little greengrocer using the orator's own favorite argumentative response of 'Prove it.'[3] 'The Prisoners' Van' is notable for what is surely a strong, realistic glimpse of two young prostitutes, sisters of fourteen and sixteen:

'How long are you for, Emily?' screamed a red-faced woman in the crowd. 'Six weeks, and labour;' replied the elder girl, with a flaunting laugh; 'and that's better than the Stone Jug any how; the mill's a d—d sight better than the

---

[3] Dickens's condemnation is particularly strong in the original version:

'Wonderful man!' said he of the sharp nose.
'Splendid speaker!' added the broker.
'Great power!' said everybody but the green-grocer.
'Great ass,' thought we – 'a very common character, and in no degree exaggerated. Empty-headed bullies, who by their ignorance and presumption bring into contempt whatever cause they are connected with; equally mischievous in any assembly from the highest to the lowest, and disgusting in all. There is a red-faced man in every "parlour." '

In the revision, Dickens canceled the last paragraph, added a sentence to the preceding one (in which the orator's listeners shake their heads 'mysteriously' and leave the narrator alone with the man), and wrote two new paragraphs of conclusion. In the first, 'Tibbs' muses about the 'ancient appearance' of the room, and discovering, as he explains, that he is not in 'a romantic humour,' his thoughts return to parlor orators. In the last paragraph, he points out that they are a numerous race of '[w]eak-pated dolts' who do much mischief to their cause, however good. 'So,' he concludes, 'just to hold a pattern one up, to know the others by, we took his likeness at once, and put him in here. And that is the reason why we have written this paper.'

Dickens also removed a long paragraph from the beginning of the original version in which he discussed varieties of parlors before turning (in the second, and in the revision the opening, paragraph) to the parlor referred to in the title of the essay. The canceled passage is reprinted in Appendix C, below.

Sessions; and here's Bella a-going too for the first time. Hold up your head, you chicken,' she continued, boisterously tearing the other girl's handkerchief away; 'Hold up your head, and show 'em your face. I an't jealous, but I'm blessed if I an't game.' – 'That's right, old girl,' exclaimed a man in a paper cap, who, in common with the greater part of the crowd, had been inexpressibly delighted with this little incident. – 'Right!' replied the girl; 'ah, to be sure; what's the odds so long as you're happy.' – 'Come, in with you,' interrupted the driver. – 'Don't you be in a hurry, Coachman,' replied the girl; 'and recollect I want to be set down in Cold-Bath Fields – large house with a high garden wall in front; you can't mistake it. Hallo, Bella, where are you going to – you'll pull my precious arm off?' This was addressed to the younger girl, who, in her anxiety to hide herself in the caravan, had ascended the steps first, and forgotten the strain upon the handcuff; 'Come down, and let's show you the way.' And after jerking the miserable girl down with a force which made her stagger on the pavement, she got into the vehicle, and was followed by her wretched companion.[4]

'The New Year' (3 January 1836) and 'Some Account of an Omnibus Cad' deal primarily with single characters, the former with a most sociable man with the Pickwickian-like name of Winkles in the original and Tupple in the revised version of 1836, and the latter with an omnibus conductor by the name of 'Bill Boorker' (William Barker). This roguish gentleman bears a strong resemblance to the cab driver whom Pickwick encounters in the opening number of *Pickwick Papers* and whom Butt and Tillotson rightly see as an undeveloped forerunner of Sam Weller.[5] A number of the characters in 'Christmas Festivities' (27 December 1835; retitled 'A Christmas Dinner' in *Sketches by Boz*, First Series) also turn up again with various modifications and in fuller detail at Dingley Dell.

In the earlier 'Street Sketches' and 'Sketches of London,' Dickens had begun, as 'Boz,' to assume the role of the superior, sophisticated observer of human behavior, but the requirements of the popular press, where, as Richard D. Altick points out, 'variety, simplicity, and brevity were the rule,'[6] prevented him from obtruding much as narrator. The essays that he wrote for *Bell's Life in London* are also very brief and, like the earlier ones, lack the stylistic ornaments that his contemporaries and predecessors alike favored highly. Nevertheless, they do seem to have been conceived by

---

[4] In revising 'The Prisoners' Van' for the Second Series of *Sketches by Boz*, Dickens excluded a long introductory paragraph (over 500 words), which, Butt and Tillotson state, 'no one who has read it would willingly lose.' It is a passage 'not only exceptionally racy and vivid, but providing the best early example of Dickens's trick (to be elaborated in *Oliver Twist*) of dealing with low life in a detached and whimsical style' (p. 44). Butt and Tillotson quote a portion of the passage; it will be found in its entirety in Appendix C, below.

[5] Butt and Tillotson, p. 70. But they also point out that the basic type is that of the stock comic servant of the eighteenth-century novel and play. For the original conclusion to the essay, see Butt and Tillotson, p. 54.

[6] Altick, *The English Common Reader*, p. 369.

Dickens as essays of greater 'literary' quality than the pieces of 1834–35. He was making arrangements with John Macrone as early as 22 October 1835 to publish by that Christmas a collection of his sketches in two volumes[7] and was no doubt thinking, even then, of a second series to be published at some later time, for most of the 'Scenes and Characters' were not included in the First Series. Probably from the beginning the pieces in *Bell's Life in London* were written with an eye to their publication in a volume of essays of high literary quality – a volume that would help to make the author's reputation. Influenced by his favorite eighteenth-century essayists in another respect, he made 'Tibbs,' his narrator, not only a recorder of what he saw but a presumably omniscient evaluator of it. 'Christmas time! That man must be a misanthrope indeed in whose breast something like a jovial feeling is not roused – in whose mind some pleasant associations are not awakened – by the recurrence of Christmas,' is how he begins 'Christmas Festivities.' He concludes his opening paragraph with an exhortation to his readers redolent with assumed patriarchal wisdom: 'Dwell not upon the past. . . . Reflect upon your present blessings – of which every man has many – not on your past misfortunes, of which all men have some. Fill your glass again, with a merry face and a contented heart. Our life on it but your Christmas shall be merry, and your new year a happy one.'[8] Clever – too clever, perhaps – is the disdainful 'Pooh!' to which he builds in the first paragraph of 'Seven Dials':

> We boldly aver that we doubt the veracity of the legend to which we have adverted. We *can* suppose a man rash enough to inquire at random – at a house with lodgers too – for a Mr. Thompson, with all but the certainty before his eyes, of finding at least two or three Thompsons in any house of moderate dimensions; but a Frenchman – a Frenchman – in Seven Dials! Pooh! He was an Irishman. Tom King's education had been neglected in his infancy, and as he couldn't understand half the man said, he took it for granted he was talking French.

---

[7] See *Pilgrim Letters*, I, 81–84, to John Macrone, [?27 October 1835], and I, 94, to John Macrone, [18 November 1835].

[8] Some of the immediacy of the original series of 'Scenes and Characters' is indicated in the concluding paragraphs to his two seasonal essays, conclusions that he canceled before reprinting the pieces:

> There are a hundred associations connected with Christmas which we should very much like to recall to the minds of our readers; there are a hundred comicalities insepar-able from the period, on which it would give us equal pleasure to dilate. We have attained our ordinary limits, however, and cannot better conclude than by wishing each and all of them, individually & collectively, 'a merry Christmas and a happy new year.'
> ('Christmas Festivities')

> But twelve has struck, and the bells ring merrily out which welcome the new year. Away with all gloomy reflections. We were happy and merry in the last one, and will be, please God, in this. So as we are alone, and can neither dance it in, nor sing it in, here goes our glass to our lips, and a hearty welcome to the year one thousand eight hundred and thirty-six say we.'
> ('The New Year')

While the narrator's archness is not always pleasing, we must remember that we are observing an author consciously developing a style, formulating an attitude toward his subject, and working with a predetermined point of view in his narrator. Dickens will abandon the flippant tone following *Oliver Twist*, but it will be an important characteristic of his writing until then, and *Pickwick Papers* and *Oliver Twist* are awash with it.

In these seven sketches from *Bell's Life in London*, we see Dickens continuing to develop, in his descriptive essays, as a conscious technician of the individual aspects of fiction. In the five remaining 'Scenes and Characters' – 'Miss Evans and "The Eagle"' (4 October 1835), 'The Dancing Academy' (11 October 1835), 'Making a Night of It' (18 October 1835), 'Love and Oysters' (25 October 1835; retitled 'Misplaced Attachment of Mr. John Dounce' in *Sketches by Boz*, Second Series), and 'The Vocal Dress-Maker' (22 November 1835; retitled 'The Mistaken Milliner. A Tale of Ambition' in *Sketches by Boz*, Second Series) – he takes up the farcical tale once again. These tales are much better written than the earlier *Monthly Magazine* stories, largely because of the experience Dickens had acquired in handling the techniques of fiction while writing the twenty-five essays for the *Morning Chronicle* and the *Evening Chronicle*.

His return to fiction did not indicate a mastery of effective plotting, however; his plots are still the weakest element in his tales, sometimes because these tales, too, lack that element of suspense created by the conflict inherent in the structure of an effective story, sometimes because that conflict is crudely developed and its resolution comes too abruptly. In 'Miss Evans and "The Eagle,"' for instance, Mr. Wilkins calls to escort Miss Evans to the Eagle, a pleasure garden. On their way, they encounter a couple known to Miss Evans with whom they stop for alcoholic refreshments. Following a few rounds, the happy group proceeds to the Eagle where, after still more intoxicants, the escorts become incensed by the attentions a gentleman with large whiskers and a second in a plaid waistcoat are paying to the not unwilling women. A verbal exchange gives way to fisticuffs, and Mr. Wilkins and his fellow beau are bested. Upon the shrieks of Miss Evans and her friend, the other gentlemen fade into the night, and the women are conveyed home by hackney-coach in 'a state of insensibility, compounded of shrub, sherry, and excitement.' The tale lacks the requisite structural conflict, for the one-sided fight that ends the tale is incidental, not really the inevitable or even necessarily plausible result of earlier established behavior or deliberate scheming. As readers, we recognize the lower class characteristics of the people Dickens has created by their dialect, and we know from the tone of the story that comic action will ensue, but these clues are no clear indication that the two women will be easy marks for the two rakish gentlemen, or that Mr. Wilkins and Co. will be aroused to violence by the behavior of the interlopers. As in most of the other tales, Dickens does not adequately prepare the reader for what is to come in the story. Events seem to occur more by accident than by plotted design.

Character does not lead to action; rather, action ultimately determines character. But this process does not produce an effectively plotted tale.

What is still missing in Dickens's plots can easily be shown by yet another reference to a scene from *Pickwick Papers*, the cleverly structured encounter of Pickwick and Sam with Jingle and Job Trotter at Eatanswill.[9] Sam and Pickwick are out for revenge of Jingle's elopement with Miss Wardle, but they have failed to keep in mind the devious cleverness of the men with whom they are dealing. As a result, Mr. Pickwick, our hero who, upon the 'confessions' of Job Trotter, and at great risk of limb, has gone to warn the young women at the Westgate House Establishment for Young Ladies about Mr. Jingle's reputation, finds himself in the extremely awkward position of having to explain his nocturnal presence in the school's back garden. He is finally rescued when his friends come to vouch for his character, but he and Sam realize that they have been duped again. Their final conversation before retiring for the night not only prepares us for the later incidents in the novel, but completes the structure of the story that Dickens has been telling in Chapter xvi:

> 'Jingle suspected my design, and set that fellow on you, with this story, I suppose?' said Mr. Pickwick, half choking.
> 'Just that, Sir,' replied Mr. Weller.
> 'It was all false, of course?'
> 'All, Sir,' replied Mr. Weller. 'Reg'lar do, Sir; artful dodge.'
> 'I don't think he'll escape us quite so easily the next time, Sam?' said Mr. Pickwick.
> 'I don't think he will, Sir.'
> 'Whenever I meet that Jingle again, wherever it is,' said Mr. Pickwick, raising himself in bed, and indenting his pillow with a tremendous blow, 'I'll inflict personal chastisement on him, in addition to the exposure he so richly merits. I will, or my name is not Pickwick.'
> 'And venever I catches hold o' that there melan-cholly chap with the black hair,' said Sam, 'if I don't bring some real water into his eyes, for once in a way, my name an't Weller. Good night, Sir.'
>
> (*Pickwick Papers*, p. 172)

Given the characters of the four men, the revenge planned by Sam and Pickwick has to end as ignominiously as it does. Besides, Dickens intends the innocence reflected in Pickwick to be ineffective when it comes up against men like Jingle who are wise to the ways of the world and direct their lives in conformity to this knowledge. Not even the experience of Sam Weller is always sufficient to save Pickwick. Yet, as a result of what happens in Chapter xvi, Pickwick and Sam have learned another lesson in life; it seems likely that the vows they make at the end of the chapter, if not utterly futile (and thus, temporarily at least, an appropriately satiric conclusion),

[9] In *Pickwick Papers*, Ch. xvi, pp. 158–72 (No. VI, September 1836).

will be fulfilled at some time later in the novel. And indeed they are, though not quite in the way one might have expected.

Nevertheless, the tales in *Bell's Life in London* are better than their predecessors. Despite structural problems, the episode described in 'Miss Evans and "The Eagle"' could, with little difficulty, be fit into an early Dickens novel and not seem completely out of place. But Dickens would need to do more by way of preparing us for Miss Evans's character, and more by way of making something more conclusive or at least something cleverer out of the sequence of events that form the tale. In addition, the ending would probably need to be more than simply a return home at the end of a rather unsuccessful evening out. These generalizations apply to the four other tales as well. Fortunately, their effectiveness as potential scenes or episodes in an early Dickens novel has little to do with plot. It is in the characterization, description, narration, point of view, and tone that these five tales are notable improvements over the *Monthly Magazine* pieces, and approach at least the vicinity of the quality of *Pickwick Papers*. Structurally, the tales hold up fairly well as gradual revelations of the true personalities of certain characters.[10] In 'Miss Evans and "The Eagle,"' we do at least see that Miss Evans and her female friend are flirtatious by nature (manifest after a few drinks) and are by no means the quiet, delicate, fragile creatures that the narrator archly pretends they are. In 'The Dancing Academy,' Dickens reveals the foolish behavior that results from a young man's social pretensions, but he also uncovers the disgusting motivations of Signor Billsmethi and his family, who, as one shortly discovers, play upon the vanities of foolish young men. In 'The Vocal Dress-Maker,' we make a nearly parallel discovery about the gullibility of Miss Amelia Martin, who is convinced by Mr. and Mrs. Rodolph that she sings well enough to be a professional entertainer. And we learn that the Rodolphs, who elevate their own reputations as judges of talent, while persuading Miss Martin, in gratitude for their attentions, to sew elegant costumes for Mrs. Rodolph, are the grossest of predators. 'Love and Oysters' is even more obviously a character study from the beginning; the opening paragraphs are even in the essay mode. Only after Dickens has generalized about old gentlemen, does he present Mr. Dounce as his example. The whole purpose of the piece is to illustrate the foolishness of 'old boys,' just as in 'Making a Night of It' the purpose is to show the comic foolishness of two 'younger boys' on their night off as counting-house clerks.

These characters may all be types, but they are superior to those in the earliest tales that Dickens wrote. For example, although his story is much briefer, Mr. Dounce is more thoroughly delineated than his predecessor, Watkins Tottle, whose story is rather too long and who, himself, as

---

[10] In this respect, at least, Dickens was justified in grouping them under the heading of 'Characters' in the 1837–39 edition of *Sketches by Boz*, as he had earlier grouped them under 'Scenes and Characters' on their first publication.

discussed earlier, is somewhat confusingly characterized by Dickens. Mr. Dounce is certainly not a 'round' character, but he does have the advantage over Tottle, at least in regard to comic action, of being motivated from the beginning by love alone, rather than by financial necessity. Even if it is merely the pretty face and the pleasing manner of the young lady in the oyster shop that attract Dounce, we readers at least sympathize with the aging gentleman's all too human foibles. Although we laugh at him, we are also aroused to sympathy by the lady's cruel treatment, by his loss of friends and daughters, and by his subsequent unfortunate marriage to his cook – obviously a grim punishment, although one not quite so drastic as that Dickens provided for Tottle.

In 'The Dancing Academy,' Mr. Augustus Cooper, one of many young men in Dickens's tales, is a new variety of character. Perhaps we get an earlier suggestion of him in the apprentices briefly glimpsed in 'Thoughts about People.' He may also bear a slight resemblance to the frustrated amateurs in 'Private Theatres,' one of the 'Sketches of London.' He is definitely a predecessor himself of Mr. Winkle. But he is not the typical young man of the *Monthly Magazine* tales – all the Percy Noakeses, Theodosius Butlers, and Horatio Sparkinses – who seem to have been attractive to Dickens earlier. Mr. Cooper, Mr. Wilkins of 'Miss Evans and "The Eagle,"' and Potter and Smithers of 'Making a Night of It' are not heroic figures. As such, they deserve Dickens's satire; they are defined as characters by it. And yet, there is also a certain vivacity in their actions that keeps them from being merely farcical creations. They benefit from the spirit of amiability with which Dickens in the essays of late 1834 and 1835 conceived and created his characters. We must not forget just how naïve, even foolish, Mr. Cooper is, but we must remember that, after all, he joined the dancing academy to show his independence of a domineering mother. His return to her care after the incident at the dancing school should merit at least some pity from us. Besides, the Billsmethi family – even the name is suspicious – has victimized him to the tune of some twenty pounds.

But even so, our sympathy for Mr. Cooper does not fully loose our disgust upon the Billsmethis. Like other rogues, among them Mr. Jingle, who will later strut through Dickens's novels, they have a certain *elan*:

After the practising was over Signor Billsmethi and Miss Billsmethi, and Master Billsmethi, and a young lady, and the two ladies and the two gentlemen, danced a quadrille – none of your slipping and sliding about, but regular warm work; flying into corners, and diving among chairs, and shooting out at the door, something like dancing. Signor Billsmethi in particular, notwithstanding his having a little fiddle to play all the time, was out on the landing every figure; and Master Billsmethi, when everybody else was breathless, danced a hornpipe with a cane in his hand, and a cheese-plate on his head, to the unqualified admiration of the whole company. Then Signor Billsmethi insisted as they were so happy, that they should all stay to supper; and proposed sending Master Billsmethi for the beer and spirits, whereupon the two gentlemen swore, 'strike 'em wulgar if they'd stand that;' and they were just going to quarrel who should pay for it, when Mr. Augustus Cooper said he would, if they'd have the kindness to allow him – and they *had* the kindness to allow him; and Master Billsmethi brought the beer in a can, and the rum in a quart-pot; they had a regular night of it; and Miss Billsmethi squeezed Mr. Augustus Cooper's hand under the table; and Mr. Augustus Cooper returned the squeeze, and returned home too, at something to six o'clock in the morning, when he was put to bed by main force by the apprentice, after repeatedly expressing an uncontroullable desire to pitch his reverend parent out of the second-floor window, and to throttle the apprentice with his own neck-handkerchief.[11]

Reinforcing his gradual movement away from the simple, stereotyped characters of the *Monthly Magazine* tales is the greater emphasis Dickens puts on realistic and sometimes exaggerated details of characterization. As discussed earlier, Dickens's use of colorful details was noticeable in the last two *Monthly Magazine* tales but particularly and much more emphatically in the necessarily descriptive 'Street Sketches' and 'Sketches of London,' where they gave the characters in his illustrations, minor though many of the characters are, usually simple but always striking physical features, mannerisms, speech patterns, and personalities. This approach, soon to become one of the qualities that tens of thousands of readers would adore in Dickens's novels, is used with the main characters of the tales in *Bell's Life in London*. In the *Monthly Magazine* tales Dickens had seldom taken space for such minute, particularizing details as we find, for example, in his description of Mr. Samuel Wilkins's face as 'round and shiny, & his hair carefully twisted into the outer corner of each eye, till it formed a variety of that description of semi-curls, usually known as "haggerawators,"' or in one of Miss Evans wearing 'a white muslin gown, carefully hook-and-eyed, and little red shawl plentifully pinned, and white straw bonnet trimmed with red ribbons, and a small necklace and large pair of bracelets, and Denmark satin shoes, and open-work stockings, white cotton gloves on her fingers, and a cambric pocket-handkerchief carefully folded up in her hand – all quite genteel and lady-like.'

But Dickens's techniques of characterization go beyond detailed physical description. As the quotations above show, he is already using such description to suggest rather than state what his characters are like inside. We know, certainly, that both Mr. Wilkins and Miss Evans – or 'Miss Ivins,' as her family calls her, and as the narrator revealingly insists on referring to her in the tale – are to be comic rather than heroic or romantic figures. Mr. Wilkins's size borders upon the 'dwarfish,' his 'sabbath waist-

---

[11] To examine the extent to which the more 'villainous' characters in this tale are given humorous rather than condemnatory treatment, one may wish to contrast them to the Rodolphs in 'The Vocal Dress-Maker.' Dickens uses little or nothing to mitigate the harshness of his characterization of the Rodolphs, nor does he, for that matter, do much to attract our sympathies to Miss Amelia Martin.

coats' are 'dazzling,' and he talks 'domestic economy' with Mrs. Evans while waiting for the daughter to dress; and when he leaves for the Eagle with his beloved 'J'mima,' they are, as the narrator puts it, accompanied by 'a dress cane, with a gilt knob at the top.' Mr Wilkins's self-satisfaction, condescension, and cheap ostentation are all suggested in these quick but characterizing descriptive touches, particularly in the seemingly self-propelled cane. These characteristics provide proper foreshadowing of the way Wilkins acts later in the tale. Simply rereading the earlier 'Horatio Sparkins' at this point will reveal instantly the progress that Dickens made as a writer between February 1834 and October 1835. An example of even more careful foreshadowing of behavior is Dickens's treatment of the young woman in the oyster shop in 'Love and Oysters.' We will not be surprised at the end when she flippantly rejects Dounce's proposal of marriage, for her character is carefully and subtly established at the beginning of their encounter:

> Behind . . . the barrels was a young lady of about five and twenty, all in blue, and all alone – splendid creature, charming face, and lovely figure! It is difficult to say whether Mr. John Dounce's red countenance, illuminated as it was by the flickering gas-light in the window before which he paused, excited the lady's risibility, or whether a natural exuberance of animal spirits proved too much for that staidness of demeanour which the forms of society rather dictatorially prescribe; certain it is that the lady smiled, then put her finger upon her lip, with a striking recollection of what was due to herself; and finally retired, in oyster-like bashfulness to the very back of the counter. The sad-dog sort of feeling came strongly upon John Dounce: he lingered – the lady in blue made no sign. He coughed – still she came not. He entered the shop. . . .

Dounce's own foolish behavior had likewise been established even earlier in the tale. It is not a plotted story, but the ending is nearly inevitable.

Sometimes these touches are exaggerated for the sake of more immediate characterization – as well as for the sake of humor, of course – as in the picture of the drunken Mr. Smithers 'embellishing the theatre by falling asleep with his head and both arms gracefully drooping over the front of the boxes' ('Making a Night of It'). At other times, the descriptions of mannerisms, speech, or gestures display significant personality traits. The following passage from 'The Vocal Dress-Maker' pinpoints the pretentiousness and self-delusion of the Rodolphs upon their first appearance:

> To hear them sing separately was perfectly divine, but when they went through the tragic duet of 'Red Ruffian, retire!' it was, as Miss Martin afterwards remarked, 'thrilling;' and why (as Mr. Jennings Rodolph observed) – why were they not engaged at one of the patent theatres? If he was to be told that their voices were not powerful enough to fill the house, his only reply was, that he'd back himself for any amount to fill Russell-square – a statement in which the company, after hearing the duet, expressed their full belief; so they all said it was shameful treatment; and both Mr. and Mrs. Jennings Rodolph

said it was shameful too, and Mr. Jennings Rodolph looked very serious, and said he knew who his malignant opponents were, but they had better take care how far they went, for if they irritated him too much, he had not quite made up his mind whether he wouldn't bring the subject before Parliament; and they all agreed that it ''ud serve 'em quite right, and it was very proper that such people should be made an example of;' and Mr. Jennings Rodolph said he'd think of it.

Certainly missing from the various passages quoted above and, in general, from the tales themselves are many of the crudities that earlier marred Dickens's characterizations. No longer does he invariably summarize in direct statement the impression that he wants a character to have upon his readers; suggestion, humor, tone, carefully selected details, and even the remarks of others now reveal this character to us. He does not, for example, force his characters to converse monotonously upon irrelevant topics. If, as mentioned below, there is far less dialogue, that now present is there for the purpose of significant characterization as well as for moving along what plot there is. Finally, Dickens uses fewer elaborate stage directions in conjunction with the speeches of his characters than he had earlier, relying more upon a careful selection of language and upon other characterizing devices (such as synecdoche in the following passage where he refers to the various members of the audience by the kind of beverage each is drinking) than upon the elaborate speech tags that fill the *Monthly Magazine* tales. In this fragment of a scene from 'The Vocal Dress-Maker,' depicting her first public appearance in a duet with Mr. Rodolph, Miss Amelia Martin has just revealed the lamentable weakness of her singing voice. The characterization, as well as the effectiveness of the scene, depends far more upon the speeches and the colorful descriptions than upon speech tags that smack of stage directions:

'Sing out' – shouted one gentleman in a white great coat. 'Don't be afraid to put the steam on, old gal,' exclaimed another. 'S–s–s–s–s–s' – went the five-and twenty bottled ales. 'Shame, shame!' remonstrated the ornamental painter's journeyman's party – 'S–s–s' went the bottled ales again, accompanied by all the gins and a majority of the brandies. – 'Turn them geese out,' cried the ornamental painter's journeyman's party, with great indignation. 'Sing out,' whispered Mr. Jennings Rodolph. – 'So I do,' responded Miss Amelia Martin. 'Sing louder,' said Mrs. Jennings Rodolph. – 'I can't,' replied Miss Amelia Martin – 'Off, off, off,' cried the rest of the audience. – 'Bray-vo!' shouted the painter's party. It wouldn't do – Miss Amelia Martin left the orchestra with much less ceremony than she had entered it, and as she couldn't sing out, never came out.

Obviously, in putting the kinds of characters he had created for the *Morning Chronicle* and *Evening Chronicle* essays into the tales he wrote shortly thereafter, Dickens retained all of the vitality, the color, and the individualizing traits that made them notable. Admittedly there are rough spots in the passage describing Miss Martin's disgrace, particularly in the outrageous word-play in the last sentence and in Dickens's love of repeating the full names of the characters over and over again for what he thinks is comic effect. But in expanding a character, in developing a portrait to greater descriptive and psychological fullness, Dickens moved another step closer to the kind and scope of character and to the variety of techniques of portrayal that he would need in order to write a novel.

Another striking feature of these five tales is Dickens's almost complete use of the pictorial rather than the dramatic scene, the latter of which predominated in the *Monthly Magazine* tales. The pieces in *Bell's Life in London* are shorter than the earlier ones, and their brevity must surely have contributed to Dickens's decision to summarize much of the action in them. But the influence of the essayists upon whose writings he modeled his own must surely be important, too. And, then, he did not spend as much time at the theater as previously, for a good many of his evenings were now given over to writing in his rooms, covering a Parliamentary session, or journeying out of town on some reportorial mission.[12] Any lessening of the theatrical influence under which he had developed almost every scene dramatically through action and tedious, forced, and stilted dialogue, even when there was no structural necessity for such scenes, must surely be looked upon as a favorable occurrence. It is true that he comes close to the other extreme in the five tales; one occasionally wishes for more dialogue and less authorial wit and word-play. He had after all developed his ear for natural speech rhythms while writing his essays for the two *Chronicles*. But obviously Dickens is becoming aware that this method of narration suits the requirements of both the comic and pathetic moods, where the author often needs tighter control over his materials than a dramatically presented scene can give him. A pictorially conceived scene enables him to use not only direct statement and irony produced by obvious contrasts but also subtle forms of moralizing and social criticism and satire through the observing presence and directing tone of the narrator. Certainly Dickens was capable of constructing a fairly well-written dramatic scene – there is a fine one in 'The Parlour' as seen through the point of view of a narrator present in the scene but not an active participant in it. And I have already quoted one from 'The Prisoners' Van.' Yet the technical ability evident in Dickens's pictorial scenes makes more frequent dramatic ones not only unnecessary but often undesirable.

When a dramatic moment or scene is required to maintain the complex movement or rhythm of a story, Dickens writes it. In the admirable 'Making a Night of It,' the best tale in this series, he does not need to develop the opening scene in the inn dramatically. There his purpose is to show Smithers and Potter gradually getting drunk enough to commit with

[12] See *Pilgrim Letters*, I, 34–115, for glimpses of Dickens's activities in 1834–35.

imperturbability and impunity the outrageous acts they perform later in the evening. He can achieve this initial goal more humorously through a tongue-in-cheek description of their behavior than through what they might say to each other, to a waiter, or to other patrons of the inn. Such conversation could quickly become monotonous or humorous only for its own sake rather than for the effect of the whole story. And, as the young men become more vociferous, it might even make them less sympathetic characters than Dickens wishes. In the following description of their behavior in the inn, Dickens uses verbal humor that he could not have employed had the scene been dramatic. This verbal humor is important, for, while it points up the silly behavior of the men, it also encourages us to smile at them with the narrator. They are so comically amusing that we are incapable of condemning them:

When the cloth was removed, Mr. Thomas Potter ordered the waiter to bring two goes of his best Scotch whiskey, with warm water and sugar, and a couple of his very mildest Havannahs, which the waiter did. Mr. Thomas Potter mixed his grog, and lit his cigar; Mr. Robert Smithers did the same; and then Mr. Thomas Potter jocularly proposed as the first toast, 'the abolition of all offices whatsomever' (not sinecures, but counting-houses), which was immediately drank by Mr. Robert Smithers, with enthusiastic applause; and then they went on talking politics, puffing cigars, and sipping whiskey and water, till the 'goes' – most appropriately so called – were both gone, which Mr. Robert Smithers forthwith perceiving, immediately ordered in two more goes of the best Scotch whiskey, and two more of the very mildest Havannahs; and the goes kept coming in, and the mild Havannahs kept going out, until what with the drinking, and lighting, and puffing, and the stale ashes on the table, and the tallow-grease on the cigars, Mr. Robert Smithers began to doubt the mildness of the Havannahs, and to feel very much as if he'd been sitting in a hackney-coach, with his back to the horses. As to Mr. Thomas Potter, he would keep laughing out loud, and volunteering inarticulate declarations that he was 'all right,' in proof of which he feebly bespoke the evening paper after the next gentleman, but finding it a matter of some difficulty to discover any news in its columns, or to ascertain distinctly whether it had any columns at all, he walked slowly out to look for the comet, and after coming back quite pale with looking up at the sky so long, and attempting to express mirth at Mr. Robert Smithers having fallen asleep, by various galvanic chuckles, he laid his head on his arm, and went to sleep also. . . .[13]

Smithers and Potter, adamant upon 'making a night of it,' eventually proceed to the theater. Both are still considerably under the influence of the pots of stout and the glasses of whiskey-and-water. Smithers promptly falls asleep again over the front of the box, but Potter is ripe for action.

---

[13] To keep Dickens's achievements in 1835 in proper perspective, compare this scene with the one in Ch. xx of *Bleak House*, in which Guppy and Smallweed attend to the feeding – and for Guppy the manipulating – of Jobling. It is surely one of Dickens's great comic scenes. The comet referred to was Halley's comet, which reappeared in 1835.

At this point, the narrative, rising to its comic climax, moves momentarily and almost imperceptibly into a dramatic scene as Potter stirs up the audience:

On his first entry he contented himself by earnestly calling upon the gentlemen in the gallery to flare up, accompanying the demand with another request expressive of his wish that they would instantaneously form a union, both of which requisitions were responded to in the manner most in vogue on such occasions. 'Give that dog a bone,' cried one gentleman in his shirt sleeves. 'Vere have you been having half a pint of intermediate?' cried a second. 'Tailor!' screamed a third. 'Barber's clerk,' shouted a fourth. 'Throw him o-ver,' roared a fifth, while numerous voices concurred in desiring Mr. Thomas Potter to return to the arms of his maternal parent, or in common parlance to 'go home to his mother.' All these taunts Mr. Thomas Potter received with supreme contempt, cocking the low-crowned hat a little more on one side, whenever any reference was made to his personal appearance; and standing up with his arms a-kimbo, expressing defiance most melo-dramatically.

The scene is brief, quickly moving back into the pictorial mode in a brilliantly comic passage that not only describes the performance but also Potter's comments upon it, the audience's reactions to the comments, and the post-haste removal of Potter and Smithers from the theater:

The overture – to which these various sounds had been an *ad libitum* accompani-ment – concluded: the second piece began, and Mr. Thomas Potter emboldened by impunity, proceeded to behave in a most unprecedented and outrageous manner. First of all he imitated the shake of the principal female singer; then groaned at the blue fire, then affected to be frightened into convulsions of terror at the appearance of the ghost; and lastly, not only made a running commentary in an audible voice upon the dialogue on the stage, but actually woke Mr. Robert Smithers, who hearing his companion making a noise, and having a very indistinct notion of where he was, or what was required of him, immediately by way of imitating a good example, set up the most unearthly, unremitting, and appalling howling that ever audience heard. It was too much. 'Turn 'em out,' was the general cry. A noise as of shuffling of feet, and men being knocked up with violence against wainscotting, was heard: a hurried dialogue of 'come out' – 'I won't' – 'You shall' – 'I shan't' – 'Give me your card Sir' – 'Punch his head,' and so forth succeeded; a round of applause betokened the approbation of the audience; and Mr. Robert Smithers and Mr. Thomas Potter found themselves shot with astonishing swiftness into the road without having had the trouble of once putting foot to ground during the whole progress of their rapid descent.

Having attained a rhythmic peak of movement, the tale concludes in one long paragraph of action even more selectively summarized as, under the impetus of their experiences in the theater, Potter and Smithers continue to look for trouble, find it, are packed off by the police, spend the night in jail, and are found guilty of drunken assault, reprimanded, and fined in Police Court the following morning.[14]

If we regard these five tales as equivalent to small fragments of a twenty-part novel, rather than as full-scale short stories (their brevity alone perhaps disqualifies them from consideration as such), Dickens is obviously justified in using the pictorial approach almost exclusively. Such character-defining episodes would not be important scenes in a novel, so that developing them dramatically would distort the emphasis of the novels in which they might appear. Besides, since much of the humor in these five tales is more dependent upon what the characters do and how it is described than upon what they say, the comic mood is most effectively achieved through descriptive narrative liberally sprinkled with verbal witticisms and elaborate attention-attracting rhetorical devices, as amply illustrated in the paragraphs quoted from 'Making a Night of It.' There is, I think, a good possibility that Dickens had some inkling of what he was doing. Certainly the pictorial approach enabled him to present a wider range of details and actions with more economy, more humor, and, therefore, greater effectiveness.

Dickens's heavy reliance upon the pictorial method in these five tales contributes also to his attainment of a greater consistency between tone and purpose than he had achieved in the *Monthly Magazine* tales. Though perhaps somewhat more unobtrusively in the tales than in the sketches that he wrote for *Bell's Life in London*, he continues the role of narrator that he had assumed in his newspaper sketches. Thus, the stories are presented from a controlling point of view just as the contents of the essays among the 'Scenes and Characters' had been. This point of view combines objectivity with sentiment, humor with pathos, and worldly amusement at the foibles of man with a kind of naïve but pleasant enjoyment of the genuinely comic. The result, in both the essays and the tales, is a sketch or a story that amuses the reader, that frequently satirizes human behavior, and that almost as often, in the tradition of true amiable humor, softens the satire by making the faults of the characters pre-eminently human. The less bitter endings obviously contribute to this more characteristically Dickensian approach to reality. Miss Evans may be carried home drunk at the end of an exciting evening, but she will certainly live to flirt again. Mr. Cooper may return to

---

[14] For sheer comic brilliance, the following paragraph from *Pickwick Papers* illustrates what later use Dickens makes of summarized action. At Bath, Mr. Dowler, certain that Mr. Winkle is having an affair with Mrs. Dowler – a mistake on Dowler's part, obviously – takes out after Winkle with a 'small supper-knife':

But Mr. Winkle didn't wait for him. He no sooner heard the horrible threat of the valorous Dowler, than he bounced out of the sedan quite as quickly as he had bounced in, and throwing off his slippers into the road, took to his heels and tore round the Crescent, hotly pursued by Dowler and the watchman. He kept ahead; the door was open as he came round the second time, he rushed in, slammed it in Dowler's face, mounted to his bed-room, locked the door, piled a wash-hand stand, chest of drawers and table against it, and packed up a few necessaries ready for flight with the first light of morning' (Ch. xxxv, pp. 391–92 – corrected to Ch. xxxvi in later editions).

his mother, Potter and Smithers may be heavily fined after a night in jail and vow never to make another 'night of it,' Mr. Dounce may be taken in marriage by his cook and live 'a hen-pecked husband, a melancholy monument of antiquated misery, and a living warning to all uxorious old boys,' and Miss Martin may find it convenient to give up her hope for a singing career with some abruptness. But these are all relatively harmless punishments, or at least ones meted out with some cleverly but not harshly satiric justice – just what one might have expected from a story whose main purpose was to be humorous and entertaining. Certainly no one commits suicide, as Mr. Tottle had done, or gets involved in a marriage that leads to disgust, desertion, or debtors' prison. It is true that, like Calton in part one of 'The Boarding House,' and later like Pickwick, Augustus Cooper is sued for breach of promise, but a comic rather than a bitterly ironic effect is intended, as is also true in Mr. Dounce's case.

The relatively complex brand of humor that Dickens works into the five tales in *Bell's Life in London* is quite evidently more of an inheritance from the essays for the *Morning Chronicle* and *Evening Chronicle* than from the *Monthly Magazine* tales. This humor achieves in a subtler and more craftsmanlike and successful way the effect that Dickens may earlier have been trying quite unsuccessfully to achieve. These endings are more genuinely clever, and may indicate that he was finally capable of achieving the effect he had earlier been merely fumbling for. But the humor of amiability does more than characterize the dominant tone of Dickens's writings of late 1834 and 1835. It also contributes to the impression the reader receives of the tales' intimate associations with reality, an impression not produced more than incidentally and occasionally in the *Monthly Magazine* tales. In making us laugh and even momentarily sneer at the behavior of his characters and then sympathize with them at the moment of their downfall, Dickens forces us to an awareness of the fallibility of human nature, *our* human nature. He makes us see that Miss Evans, Mr. Cooper, Smithers and Potter, Mr. Dounce, and Miss Martin are each, as Northrop Frye would put it, 'one of us,' Frye's major criterion for realistic fiction.[15] Combined with this awareness of the plausibility of the characters is the sheer volume of details with which Dickens describes characters, actions, and setting. The more specific and detailed the writing becomes, the more we suspect (even though our logic may be faulty) that Dickens is frequently describing people, places, and events that are related in some way to his personal observation in the streets and inns, the playhouses and oyster bars of London, as well as in the homes of his family and friends. The observations involve an accuracy of perception that can only come, we

---

[15] Northrop Frye, *Anatomy of Criticism: Four Essays* (Princeton, New Jersey: Princeton University Press, 1957): 'If superior neither to other men nor to his environment, the hero is one of us: we respond to a sense of his common humanity, and demand from the poet the same canons of probability that we find in our own experience. This gives us the hero of the *low mimetic* mode, of most comedy and of realistic fiction' (p. 34).

suspect, from his actually having been there at the time. In the same way, our perception of the *human* behavior behind the artistic creation tells us that the author is sensitive to nuances of speech and gestures, to mannerisms, and to the comic and pathetic in the human condition. The vividness and sheer wit of much of the description, the colorful and often exaggerated personalities of the characters, and even the exuberance and vitality of the actions themselves lend a sense of joyous heightened life to these stories and sketches. Finally, the personality of the narrator himself, who seems to be the author (that is, 'Tibbs,' and ultimately Charles Dickens) also adds a sense of reality to these tales. If the characters may not always ring true to individual readers, the narrator himself invariably does. He is a never-tiring observer of men and events, sometimes a crusader in their behalf against the inhumanity of other men and institutions (particularly in the essays), frequently an exposer of their shortcomings, but always a supporter of their participation in the fullness of life.

By 17 January 1836, when the last of his 'Scenes and Characters' appeared in *Bell's Life in London*, Dickens was ripe for more important literary work. Since the time of his *Monthly Magazine* tales, and mainly as a result of the twenty-five essays he had written for the *Morning Chronicle* and *Evening Chronicle*, he had shown considerable improvement in the arts of description and narration, of tone, mood, and point of view, of characterization, and of thematic consistency. His writing of the 'Street Sketches,' the 'Sketches of London,' and some of the 'Scenes and Characters' enabled him to work with these various elements of fiction at the relatively simple level provided by the descriptive essay, as in a descriptive illustration, an anecdote, or a brief character study. When he did return once again, in five of the 'Scenes and Characters,' to character studies that bear a strong resemblance to the episodic *Monthly Magazine* tales, he was much better equipped technically to produce tales that had a heady air of reality about them and a sustained tone that often combined satire with sentiment, and was sometimes genuinely comic. Obviously, Dickens was now almost ready to write a novel. His final preparations, conscious and unconscious, filled the last months of 1835 and most of 1836, and form the subject of the following chapters.

CHAPTER FIVE

'A Visit to Newgate' and Three Tales

It was in the year 1836, upon being appointed by my kind friend John Black, the editor of the *Morning Chronicle*, to the office of assistant sub-editor of that influential journal, in conjunction with Mr. George Hogarth, that I first made the acquaintance of Charles Dickens. I was then in my twenty-second year, and Mr. Dickens was two years my senior. We were both of us comparatively unknown in literature, but Dickens had acquired some reputation as the author of some lively sketches which he contributed to the *Evening Chronicle* . . . under the celebrated signature of 'Boz.' He was one of the twelve parliamentary reporters of the *Chronicle*, and had the reputation of being the most rapid, the most accurate, and the most trustworthy reporter then engaged on the London press, and was consequently in high favour with his employers. . . .

It was part of my duty as sub-editor to confer with Mr. Hogarth and Mr. Black on the employment of the Parliamentary reporters during the recess, when Parliament was not in session, and to utilize their services in the general work of the paper, – such as attendance at public meetings, reviews of books, or notices of new plays at the theatres. Mr. Black desired to spare Mr. Dickens as much as possible from all work of this kind, having the highest opinion of his original genius, and a consequent dislike to employ him on what he considered the very inferior work of criticism. 'Any fool,' he said, in his usual broad Scotch, 'can pass judgment, more or less just or unjust, on a book or a play – but "Boz" can do better things; he can create works for other people to criticize. Besides, he has never been a great reader of books or plays, and knows but little of them, but has spent his time in studying life. Keep "Boz" in reserve for great occasions. He will *aye* be ready for them.'

– Charles Mackay[1]

While Black was mistaken about the extent of Dickens's reading, his praise indicates the reputation Dickens had gained among his colleagues. And, as F. J. H. Darton points out, by the autumn of 1835 Dickens 'must

---

[1] A recollection of Charles Mackay, quoted in Kitton, *Charles Dickens by Pen and Pencil*, pp. 133–34.

have begun to take himself a little more seriously as an original writer, or to think more clearly of prospects in that capacity.'[2] He had not yet written a novel but had certainly been developing as a writer in the sketches and tales for the *Monthly Magazine*, the *Morning Chronicle*, the *Evening Chronicle*, and *Bell's Life in London*. He wrote thirteen more pieces between late 1835 and the end of 1836, some while he was finishing the 'Scenes and Characters' for *Bell's Life in London*. Of these, all but 'The Tuggs's at Ramsgate' were reprinted or first printed in the two series of *Sketches by Boz*.[3]

Two of the thirteen – 'A Visit to Newgate' and 'The Black Veil' – were longer pieces specifically written for the First Series of *Sketches by Boz*. 'The Great Winglebury Duel,' intended for the *Monthly Magazine*, also first appeared in the initial series of the *Sketches*.[4] These and 'The Tuggs's at Ramsgate,' which was published in the April 1836 issue of the *Library of Fiction* but not included in the collected work until the combined edition in parts (1837–39), form a convenient and climactic group of compositions written by or about 8 February, the publication date of the First Series.[5] Only two days later, on the 10th, Chapman and Hall were to make Dickens the offer to write the text to accompany a series of comic sporting plates by Robert Seymour, the well-known illustrator. Under the title of *The Posthumous Papers of the Pickwick Club, Containing a Faithful Record of the Perambulations, Perils, Travels, Adventures and Sporting Transactions of the Corresponding Members*, edited by 'Boz,' this work, as we know, was to produce significant changes in the young author's life and career. Although I shall touch upon them in the last chapter, the nine shorter essays written in 1836, excellent though they are, would pale into insignificance in the shadow of the great comic work. But the four longer pieces were published earlier and were seen by Dickens and his literary friends – John Macrone, George Hogarth, John Black, and William Ainsworth – as the young author's most important literary achievements to date.

---

[2] Darton, 'Dickens the Beginner: 1833–1836,' p. 65.

[3] See Appendix A for a detailed listing.

[4] Dickens finished 'The Great Winglebury Duel' on 20 October and submitted it to the *Monthly Magazine*, where it was scheduled for publication in the December issue – see *Pilgrim Letters*, I, 79, to Catherine Hogarth, [?20 October 1835], and I, 83, to John Macrone, [?27 October 1835]. But it was not published there – perhaps because the *Monthly Magazine* was having its usual financial difficulties, perhaps because Dickens saved the piece to bolster the quality of the selections in the First Series of *Sketches by Boz*, perhaps, as Butt and Tillotson suggest (p. 42), because Dickens decided to dramatize it as *The Strange Gentleman*. His earlier concern over Buckstone's dramatization of 'The Bloomsbury Christening' may indeed have prompted him to such caution. He apparently completed the script of *The Strange Gentleman* by 18 February, when he offered the refusal of publishing it to Chapman and Hall – see *Pilgrim Letters*, I, 132, to Messrs. Chapman & Hall, [18 February 1836]. The play was first performed at the St. James's Theatre on 29 September 1836.

[5] 'A Visit to Newgate' was completed on 26 November 1835 (see text, below). 'The Black Veil' was probably written in late November, too, just after Dickens had finished 'A Visit to Newgate' and 'The Prisoners' Van' (*Bell's Life in London*, 29 November) – see Butt and Tillotson, p. 42, and *Pilgrim Letters*, I, 98, to Catherine Hogarth, [?27 November 1835]. Dickens apparently began 'The Tuggs's at Ramsgate' early in February 1836 and completed it by the 11th (see *Pilgrim Letters*, I, 128, to Catherine Hogarth, [10 February 1836]).

About 'A Visit to Newgate' the literary advisors were particularly enthusiastic. In late October 1835, while contemplating a tour of Newgate prison to acquire material for an additional sketch for the First Series, Dickens confidently told Macrone that the subject would 'tell extremely well.'[6] After finishing the essay on the evening of 26 November, he immediately showed it to George Hogarth. Hogarth, Dickens informed Macrone the following day, 'perused it very carefully last night, and bid me tell you that it would "make" any book – an opinion which Black more than confirms.'[7] Although he apparently suggested certain revisions and additions, Macrone, who had accompanied Dickens to Newgate, in turn, also praised the work, as did Ainsworth.[8] Not surprisingly, when Hogarth came to review the First Series of the *Sketches* for the *Morning Chronicle*, he singled out 'A Visit to Newgate' as the 'most remarkable paper in the book' and compared it favorably to Victor Hugo's *Le Dernier Jour d'un condamné*.[9]

Dickens had long intended to describe the interior of the prison; it was on a relatively long list of proposed topics for sketches.[10] He went over both Newgate and the House of Correction, at Coldbath Fields, Clerkenwell, on 5 November, with Macrone and Nathaniel Parker Willis, an American journalist.[11] But Dickens did not begin the piece that was to 'make' the two little volumes of sketches until 25 November. He was required to leave early on the 7th to report a dinner in honor of Lord John Russell at Bristol and did not return until late on the 13th. Among other matters, he was fully occupied during the next few days with the details of getting his collection of essays into print, including speaking with George Cruikshank, who had agreed to do the illustrations for the work. On the 19th he finished a tale ('The Vocal Dress-Maker') for *Bell's Life in London*, and on the 23rd spent his evening reviewing J. B. Buckstone's new burletta, *The Dream at Sea*, for the *Morning Chronicle*.[12] When he did finally settle

---

[6] *Pilgrim Letters*, I, 83, to John Macrone, [?27 October 1835].

[7] *Pilgrim Letters*, I, 98, to John Macrone, [?27 November 1835]. Since the letter is dated 'Friday Morning,' Dickens or, more likely, Hogarth showed the sketch to Black either Thursday night or that morning.

[8] *Pilgrim Letters*, I, 103, to John Macrone, [9 December 1835]; I, 115, to John Macrone, [7 January 1836]. Ainsworth, as Dickens states in the letter of 7 January, had taken a 'very kind interest . . . in our proceedings' (I, 116).

[9] In the *Morning Chronicle*, 11 February 1836. Quoted in D[exter], 'The Reception of Dickens's First Book,' p. 44.

[10] See *Pilgrim Letters*, I, 83, to John Macrone, [?27 October 1835]. Others in the list included 'The Cook's Shop,' 'Bedlam,' 'The Prisoners' Van,' 'The Streets – Noon and Night,' 'Banking-Houses,' 'Fancy Lounges,' 'Covent Garden,' 'Hospitals,' and 'Lodging Houses,' only three of which Dickens ever developed into essays, the third and fourth as 'The Prisoners' Van' and 'The Streets at Night' in *Bell's Life in London*, 29 November 1835 and 17 January 1836, respectively, and the next to last apparently as 'The Hospital Patient' in the *Carlton Chronicle*, 6 August 1836.

[11] For details and the identification of Willis as one of the party, see William J. Carlton, 'The Third Man at Newgate,' *Review of English Studies*, N.S. 8 (1957), 402–07.

[12] These details are to be found in *Pilgrim Letters*, I, 88–97, *passim*.

down to work on 'A Visit to Newgate,' he found, understandably enough, that he did not recall the prison as vividly and as fully as he would have liked. Macrone was urging him 'most imperatively and pressingly to "get on,"' and while he had made 'considerable progress' with the sketch, the subject, as he wrote to Catherine Hogarth on the evening of the 25th, 'is such a very difficult one to do justice to, and I have so much difficulty in remembering the place, and arranging my materials, that I really have no alternative but to remain at home to-night, and "get on" in good earnest.' However, the main reason for his slow progress was what he called his 'peculiar' method of composition. 'I never can write with effect,' he continued, ' – especially in the serious way – until I have got my steam up, or in other words until I have become so excited with my subject that I cannot leave off.'[13] The evening at his writing table was obviously productive, for he completed the 5000-word sketch in about two days.[14]

'A Visit to Newgate' is at least twice as long as Dickens's earlier essays and, as the letters to Macrone reveal, was a conscious attempt to produce a work of definite literary merit. As it had been in previous sketches, Dickens's purpose was certainly to 'amuse.' Some years later, in describing the visit to Newgate, N. P. Willis reported: 'We were there an hour or two, and were shown some of the celebrated murderers confined for life, and one young soldier waiting for execution. . . . Though interested in Dickens's face, I forgot him naturally enough after we entered the prison, and I do not think I heard him speak during the two hours.'[15] Dickens was equally absorbed with what he saw there. Immediately after returning to his chambers in Furnivals Inn, he wrote Catherine that he had 'lots of anecdotes to tell' her of both places he had visited, some of which he found 'rather amusing: at least to me, for I was intensely interested in everything I saw.'[16] This interest is indicated in the paper itself: having determined to visit Newgate, 'in an amateur capacity, of course,' Dickens states, 'and, having carried our intention into effect, we proceed to lay its results before our readers, in the hope – founded more upon the nature of the subject than on any presumptuous confidence in our own descriptive powers – that this

---

[13] *Pilgrim Letters*, I, 97, to Catherine Hogarth, [25 November 1835]. Although Catherine seems never to have been happy to have Dickens postpone his evening visits, she was certainly accustomed to such treatment from her ambitious suitor.

[14] *Pilgrim Letters*, I, 98, to John Macrone, [?27 November 1835]. Dickens was not a slow writer in these early days of his career. 'A day's time,' he had written Macrone a month earlier, 'is a handsome allowance for me – much [more] than I frequently had when I was writing for The Chronicle' – *Pilgrim Letters*, I, 83, [?27 October 1835]. He was, of course, referring to the 'Street Sketches' and the 'Sketches of London,' but there is evidence that some of the 'Scenes and Characters' for *Bell's Life in London* were written as fast – see *Pilgrim Letters*, I, 77, 80, 104, 111.

[15] Nathaniel P. Willis, *Dashes at Life with a Free Pencil*, The American Short Story Series, Vol. 30 (New York: Garrett Press, 1969), Part IV ('Ephemera'), p. 88 – originally published New York: Burgess, Stringer, & Co., 1845. Also quoted in Carlton, 'The Third Man at Newgate,' p. 404.

[16] *Pilgrim Letters*, I, 88, to Catherine Hogarth, [5 November 1835].

paper may not be found wholly devoid of interest' (*Sketches by Boz*, First Series, I, 109).

But the 'interest' that the prison had for Dickens and that, in turn, he hoped the subject would have for his readers, reveals another reason for writing the paper. Later in his career we might expect a strong plea for prison reform, but we find very little in 'A Visit to Newgate.' In *Dickens and Crime*, Philip Collins states that though some of Dickens's phrases 'suggest that he had more reserves about Newgate than he actually expresses, his account of the prison is in fact the least critical of any that I have seen from this period.'[17] One reason for this, Collins believes, is that Dickens's interest in Newgate in 1835 was that of 'a casual observer, or a journalist, not of a penologist' (p. 33). But Dickens also went, I think, as an author collecting material for what he intended to be a serious *literary* effort. Despite his modest disclaimer of having gone 'in an amateur capacity of course,' Dickens meant this essay to be the high point of *Sketches by Boz* and wrote it at virtually the last minute when he had more than enough essays to fill the two volumes of the First Series. It was to be descriptive and impressionistic, not didactic. Naturally, as Collins points out, the young journalist making his first visit to a prison since childhood 'failed to see any of the features which excited the wrath of the Prison Inspectors' (p. 36). But it is just this tone of a man observing the repulsiveness and horror of prison life for the first time, of the *naif*, that gives this essay its literary distinction. Dickens had, after all, used direct social criticism in such earlier sketches as 'Gin-Shops' and 'The Prisoners' Van,' and in other pieces he was, at this time, editing out some of the cruder criticism of this sort in preparing them for the First Series of the *Sketches*. It seems obvious, then, that the absence or presence of such in the First Series was in most cases a matter of conscious artistic choice. Perhaps some of the social criticism was canceled to give greater force to those essays in which such passages were allowed to stand, for much the same reason, that is, that Dickens decided not to include a second prison piece in the volume. 'Hogarth,' he wrote Macrone, ' – whose judgment in these matters from long experience is not to be despised – says that he thinks the insertion of another Prison Paper would decidedly detract from the "hit" of the first.'[18] Obviously Dickens agreed.

That his purpose was simply not didactic is evident in a few of the comments that he made about 'A Visit to Newgate.' Replying in the same letter to Macrone's query about the omission of some description of the prison kitchen, evidently concerning the appalling sanitary conditions there, Dickens wrote: 'I know no place in which I could introduce the fact without weakening my subsequent description, and I left it out lest scrupulous ninnies who do not see these things as you and I do, should

---

[17] Philip Collins, *Dickens and Crime*, Cambridge Studies in Criminology, ed. L. Radzinowicz, Vol. 17, 2nd ed. (London: Macmillan; New York: St Martin's, 1965), p. 36.
[18] *Pilgrim Letters*, I, 103, to John Macrone, [9 December 1835].

think there was something disgusting in the idea, and repulsive' (I, 103). Do we not see the literary craftsman at work here, less concerned about thorough, accurate description than about the exact effect a part of the work will have upon his readers? He particularly wants to avoid disgusting the reader with blunt rhetoric and repulsive detail. Nevertheless, something of a moral viewpoint is to be found in the work. Dickens seems to be aware that the techniques necessary to the development of this viewpoint must be subtle or at least unobtrusive. His explanation for omitting a section about the House of Correction at Coldbath Fields reinforces this. 'You cannot,' he writes, 'throw the interest over a years [sic] imprisonment, however severe, that you can cast around the punishment of death. The Tread-Mill will not take the hold on men's feelings that the Gallows does. . . .'[19]

It is just such an emphasis that George Hogarth noted in his review of *Sketches by Boz*. In unrecorded conversations with Dickens, he himself may well have contributed to the end effect. 'A Visit to Newgate,' he stated in the *Morning Chronicle*, is written throughout 'in a tone of high moral feeling, and with great eloquence, and must leave a deep and lasting impression on the mind of every reader.'[20] Hogarth is not referring to the indignation of the reformer but to the horror and the resulting pathos created more by the inhabitants and the actions that have brought them there than by conditions in the prison itself. Dickens may have read Hugo's *Le Dernier Jour d'un condamné* (Paris, 1829), for he had probably studied French at Wellington House Academy (the work was not translated into English until 1840). But if he had not read it, possibly because his knowledge of French was too limited, Hogarth surely had and must at least have described and perhaps even translated parts of the work for Dickens, or directed him to reviews that contained summaries or partial translations of the work.[21] In any case, as Hogarth was aware, the similarity of purpose in the two essays is evident. Hugo himself, in a Preface written for a later

---

[19] *Pilgrim Letters*, I, 103. Dickens did, however, contemplate doing a magazine paper on the prison, which he planned to offer to the *Metropolitan Magazine*, and accordingly made a second trip to Coldbath Fields with his father on 23 December. But nothing came of it – see *Pilgrim Letters*, I, 701, to George Cruikshank, [21 December 1835], and I, 111, to Catherine Hogarth, [23 December 1835].

[20] Quoted in D[exter], 'The Reception of Dickens's First Book,' p. 44.

[21] Hugo's 'slender tale,' states Kenneth W. Hooker, in *The Fortunes of Victor Hugo in England* (New York: Columbia University Press, 1938), p. 25, 'was little read [in England], for no translation of it appeared until 1840, but its thesis became familiar to English readers through the efforts of reviewers.' Hugo's work is a series of forty-six short 'papers' from prison, supposedly written by a man condemned to die and dealing solely with his thoughts, movements, and observations in the cell block of condemned prisoners. It could only have directly influenced Dickens, then, in the concluding section of 'A Visit to Newgate,' which, generally speaking, might be seen as a compact condensation of what Hugo's prisoner undergoes over several days and a great many more pages. For the question of Dickens's ability to read French, see William J. Carlton, 'Dickens Studies French,' *Dickensian*, 59 (1963), 21–27, whose conclusions I have accepted. For reviews of Hugo's work, see Hooker, pp. 22–25.

edition of his work, wrote that he did not wish to give full publicity to his thoughts until the work proved to be fully understood by its audience. 'I may now, therefore,' he continued, 'unmask the political and social ideas, which I wished to render popular under this harmless literary guise. I avow openly, that "The last day of a Condemned" is only a pleading, direct or indirect, for *the abolition of punishment by death*.'[22] Dickens's purpose, though obviously not centered on the abolition of the death penalty, may have been along somewhat similar lines. A footnote that Dickens inserted in the essay in the 1837–39 edition of the *Sketches* indicates his somewhat later intense interest in prison reform, but it is possible that it has some bearing on his underlying intentions in 1835: 'The regulations of the prison relative to the confinement of prisoners during the day, their sleeping at night, their taking their meals, and other matters of gaol economy have been all altered – greatly for the better – since this sketch was written three years ago.'[23] Yet, at the same time, some of the very details that Dickens suppressed when he first wrote the piece (and probably not for the reasons offered by Hugo) would have emphasized the kind of moral indignation implicit in this footnote. His comments about a girl with 'pinched-up half-starved features,' who is visiting her mother in jail, illustrates, I believe, his much more general moral purpose:

> This girl belonged to a class – unhappily but too extensive – the very existence of which should make men's hearts bleed. Barely past her childhood, it required but a glance to discover that she was one of those children born and bred in poverty and vice, who have never known what childhood is; who have never been taught to love and court a parent's smile, or to dread a parent's frown. The thousand nameless endearments of childhood, its gaiety and its innocence, are alike unknown to them. They have entered at once upon the stern realities and miseries of life, and to their better nature it is hopeless to appeal in after times, by any of the references which will awaken, if it be only for a moment, some good feeling in ordinary bosoms, however corrupt they may have become. Talk to them of parental solicitude, the happy days of childhood, and the merry games of infancy! Tell them of hunger and the streets, beggary and stripes, the gin-shop, the station-house, and the pawnbroker's, and they will understand you.
>
> (First Series, I, 115–16)

We do find, it is true, a criticism somewhat less general in nature concluding Dickens's description of the prison chapel, but this is virtually unique:

---

[22] Victor Hugo, *The Last Days of a Condemned*, trans. Sir P. Hesketh Fleetwood (London: Smith, Elder, 1840), p. 158. Originally published as *Le Dernier Jour d'un condamné* (Paris: Gosselin, 1829).

[23] See p. 219. In the Cheap Edition, Dickens changed the last clause to 'since this sketch was first published' (p. 125), and in the Charles Dickens Edition added this sentence: 'Even the construction of the prison itself has been changed' (p. 117).

At one time – and at no distant period either – the coffins of the men about to be executed, were placed in that pew [for condemned prisoners], upon the seat by their side, during the whole service. It may seem incredible, but it is strictly true. Let us hope that the increased spirit of civilization and humanity which abolished this frightful and degrading custom, may extend itself to other usages equally barbarous; usages which have not even the pleas of utility in their defence, as every year's experience has shown them to be more and more inefficacious.

(First Series, I, 124–25)

No doubt Dickens felt properly indignant at the time, but the means he chose to communicate with his audience were subtler ones, dependent upon fictional rather than didactic expository techniques, and he was using them in the service of more general, consciously determined, literary ends. Moreover, the shifting tone of the essay, reflecting Dickens's changing attitudes toward the subjects of his description, is produced by considerable variety of scene and impression. While he sympathizes with such prisoners as the girl with 'pinched-up half-starved features' or the men awaiting the gallows (see First Series, I, 126–30), he describes others in a tone touched by a mixture of sarcasm and pity, as in his study of the boys in the schoolroom:

There were fourteen of them in all, some with shoes, some without; some in pinafores without jackets, others in jackets without pinafores, and one in scarce any thing at all. The whole number, without an exception we believe, had been committed for trial on charges of pocket-picking; and fourteen such villanous little faces we never beheld. – There was not one redeeming feature among them – not a glance of honesty – not a wink expressive of any thing but the gallows and the hulks, in the whole collection. As to any thing like shame or contrition, that was entirely out of the question. They were evidently quite gratified at being thought worth the trouble of looking at; their idea appeared to be that we had come to see Newgate as a grand affair, and that they were an indispensable part of the show: and every boy as he 'fell in' to the line, actually seemed as pleased and important as if he had done something excessively meritorious in getting there at all. We never looked upon a more disagreeable sight, because we never saw fourteen such hopeless and irreclaimable wretches before.[24]

If Dickens excluded certain scenes he had witnessed at Newgate because he felt they would offend the sensibilities of his readers, he did so partly, I suspect, because he knew that in such a mixture of realistic description with a tone at once critical and emotional, he had found a subtler way of making his point.

---

[24] First Series, I, 120. In the Cheap Edition, Dickens toned down the sarcasm somewhat by changing 'fourteen such villanous little faces' to 'fourteen such terrible little faces,' and 'fourteen such hopeless and irreclaimable wretches' to 'fourteen such hopeless creatures of neglect' (pp. 125–26).

In one or two other places in the essay, Dickens drops into the somewhat artificial, somewhat irritating jocularity that occasionally mars other essays:

> Following our conductor by a door opposite to that at which we had entered, we arrived at a small room, without any other furniture than a little desk, with a book for visitors' autographs: and a shelf on which were a few boxes for papers, and casts of the heads and faces of the two notorious murderers, Bishop and Williams – the former, in particular, exhibiting a style of head and set of features which would have afforded sufficient moral grounds for his instant execution at any time, even had there been no other evidence against him. Leaving this room also by an opposite door, we found ourselves in the lodge which opens on the Old Bailey, one side of which is plentifully garnished with a choice collection of heavy sets of irons, including those worn by the redoubtable Jack Sheppard – genuine; and those *said* to have been graced by the sturdy limbs of the no less celebrated Dick Turpin – doubtful.[25]

Most impressive in the essay is the scene with which Dickens concludes. Having described the row of condemned cells, he states: 'Conceive the situation of a man, spending his last night on earth in this cell' (First Series, I, 131). From this point on, putting himself in the position of such a man – as he no doubt actually did when he wrote the scene – Dickens utilizes the melodramatic techniques that he was shortly to become noted for in his novels. The most noteworthy of these is his early use of a mixture of description, unexpected sounds such as the ticking and chiming of a clock, elaborate rhetorical phrasing, hallucination, reminiscence, and other devices to produce an effect somewhat suggestive of stream of consciousness, of which the following passage is a small part:

> Seven hours left! and he paces the narrow limits of his cell with rapid strides, cold drops of terror starting on his forehead, and every muscle of his frame quivering with agony. Seven hours! He suffers himself to be led to his seat, mechanically takes the bible which is placed in his hand, and tries to read and listen. No: his thoughts still wander. The book is torn and soiled by use – how like the book he read his lesson in at school just forty years ago! He has never bestowed a thought upon it since he left it as a child; and yet the place, the time, the room – nay, the very boys he played with, crowd as vividly before him as if they were scenes of yesterday; and some forgotten phrase, some childish work of kindness, rings in his ears like the echo of one uttered but a minute

---

[25] First Series, I, 110–11. Dickens added the following footnote at this point in the second edition (August 1836): 'The author of *Rookwood*, assures us, in his last elegant edition of that popular work, that these fetters are apocryphal. We have not the least doubt of the fact, when it is stated by such an authority. Mr. Ainsworth has made Turpin his own. After the ride he has given us in company with that renowned hero, we will implicitly believe anything he may please to write about him – and be very grateful for it, into the bargain' (I, 111). The footnote is not in the 1837–39 edition in parts or in subsequent editions.

since. The deep voice of the clergyman recals him to himself. He is reading from the sacred book its solemn promises of pardon for repentance, and its awful denunciation of obdurate men. He falls upon his knees and clasps his hands to pray. Hush! what sound was that? He starts upon his feet. It cannot be two yet. Hark! Two quarters have struck – the third – the fourth. It is! Six hours left. Tell him not of repentance or comfort. Six hours' repentance for eight times six years of guilt and sin! He buries his face in his hands, and throws himself on the bench.

(First Series, I, 132–33)

In 'A Visit to Newgate,' then, in addition to such specialized techniques as those used in the preceding passage, we see Dickens working on that subtle combination of pathos, sentimentality, irony, realistic objectivity, satire, and even waggery that will characterize his future writing. Here, in this early work, the combination is still somewhat crudely put together, it is true; on the other hand, the essay is structured in terms of the contrasting responses of the narrator to the objects of his view and builds, as does Hugo's much longer work, to a dramatic climax to which only the dullest reader would not respond emotionally.[26] He had used such structuring in earlier essays, but here the variety of scenes and characters is greater. Moreover, since all are part of one setting – Newgate Prison – they provide a relatively detailed picture of a place with its attendant complex, varied atmosphere. The container for action is here – a place, a variegated human background, potential themes, a range of tones, points of view, matters of psychological and sociological import. The essay needs only a group of more fully developed characters and something of a plot to evolve into a highly effective tale of terror or a melodramatic chapter in a novel, not unrelated, say, to one of several interpolated tales in *Pickwick Papers*; to certain scenes witnessed by Mr. Pickwick during his incarceration in the Fleet; to Fagin's last night in the condemned cell of Newgate (Chapter lii in modern editions – surely a refined version of the last section of 'A Visit to New-gate'); to the opening scene, the Marshalsea chapters, and the chapter describing Mr. Dorrit's death in *Little Dorrit* (Bk. II, Ch. xix); or, with different setting, to Jonas Chuzzlewit's murder of Tigg, with the murderer's later twinges of conscience evoked and paralleled by the setting itself (see Ch. xlvii). In *The Narrative Art of Charles Dickens*, Harvey P. Sucksmith states that Henry Thomson's 'Le Revenant,' one of numerous tales of terror published in *Blackwood's Edinburgh Magazine*, 'almost

---

[26] A full-length study of Dickens's rhetorical art (though dealing largely with works later than the *Sketches*) is Harvey P. Sucksmith, *The Narrative Art of Charles Dickens: The Rhetoric of Sympathy and Irony in His Novels* (Oxford: Clarendon Press, 1970). Sucksmith sees Dickens as the artist consciously working to create simple effects of antipathy, sympathy, and irony by 'piling up concrete details' and by 'appealing to the reader's senses' (p. 77) and complex effects, requiring a rhetoric of sympathy *and* irony, that 'intimately' involve the reader in the 'experience' of the novel and yet enable him to remain 'detached and able to make an objective and critical assessment of the experience he is living through' (p. 173).

certainly provided the source for Dickens's "Criminal Courts" [originally entitled "The Old Bailey," in the *Morning Chronicle*, 23 October 1834], the episode which concludes "A Visit to Newgate," and the penultimate chapter of *Oliver Twist*.'[27] 'A Visit to Newgate' is an excellent essay in itself, the culminating achievement of the essays that Dickens wrote between 1834 and 1836; but it also reveals, once again, the strong fictional elements in Dickens's newspaper and magazine pieces and the great contribution of these essays to the young author's preparation as a writer of fiction.

★

Perhaps the most intriguing of the three tales that Dickens wrote in late 1835 and early 1836 is 'The Black Veil,' a melodramatic story, portions of which are strongly reminiscent, Sucksmith points out, of chapters in Samuel Warren's *Passages from the Diary of a Late Physician* (2 vols., London, 1832; vol. 3, 1837) that had originally appeared serially in *Blackwood's* (1830–1837): 'The realistic picture of the physician's circumstances in "The Black Veil" recalls Warren's "Early Struggles," while Dickens' grisly but realistic preoccupation with the corpse of a hanged man and with the subject of "resurrection" is also found in Warren's "Grave Doings" and a note to "The Thunder-Struck. – The Boxer."'[28] Other elements in the tale may very likely have been suggested to Dickens by his visit to Newgate, and may have been a product of the thought processes from which he created 'A Visit to Newgate' and 'The Prisoners' Van,' both written immediately before 'The Black Veil.' He must certainly have been influenced here, too, by 'Le Revenant,' for it is the tale of a man who survives hanging – though a surgeon plays no part in the story. No matter how repulsive we find the rank melodrama, exaggerated sentiment, and gross unreality of this tale today,[29] I think we must concede that Dickens makes some advance in his handling of plot but a more significant development in his concept and effectuation of structure, in which plot, the balancing of narrative and

---

[27] See p. 79. Sucksmith emphasizes this point in greater detail in 'The Secret of Immediacy: Dickens' Debt to the Tale of Terror in *Blackwood's*,' *Nineteenth-Century Fiction*, 26 (1971/72), 145–57, where he also comments upon the possible influence of Hugo's *Le Dernier Jour d'un condamné* on Dickens (pp. 150–52). 'Le Revenant' is in *Blackwood's Edinburgh Magazine*, 21 (1827), 409–16.

[28] Sucksmith, 'The Secret of Immediacy,' pp. 149–50.

[29] In an introductory statement in the first edition of the First Series, appearing within brackets between the title and the opening paragraph of the tale, Dickens writes: 'We think it right to state that the circumstances upon which the following tale is founded, have often been related in our presence by an intimate friend of our own, whose veracity was never, to our knowledge, in the slightest degree impugned; and that frequently as we have heard the incident related by himself with great energy and emotion, it has invariably been without the slightest deviation from the manner in which he originally told it' (II, 77). Not only is this insistence upon the reality of the incident a conventional device in this type of tale, but Dickens must surely have intended the statement to heighten the effect of what was to follow. He had removed the statement by the third edition (1837), very likely in the second edition, vol. II of which I have not seen, but in which he made other revisions of this nature.

descriptive passages, characterization, point of view, setting, and tone combine to produce at least the effect initially desired by the author. The combination clanks a bit too much for a modern reader, of course, but it is aesthetically sound within the framework of the tale.

The plot itself is simple – almost too simple – and not as suspenseful, perhaps, as it might be. Within these limitations, however, it is fully developed, a characteristic seldom evident in the *Monthly Magazine* tales. A distraught woman, her face hidden by a black veil, appears in the office of a surgeon, requesting his services in a matter of life or death – not immediately, but at nine o'clock the following morning. Mystified by the apparent lack of urgency to such an urgent request and curious about the veiled woman's refusal to explain the situation further, the surgeon agrees to attend upon the unknown prospective patient at Walworth in the morning. There, after a mysterious delay during which the patient is apparently brought into the house to which the surgeon had been directed, the surgeon is taken to his bedside. Here he discovers not only that his patient is dead but also that the dead man, who had been hanged for a criminal offense that morning, is the woman's son. Having deluded herself into believing that, through some miracle or at least through some oversight or haste on the executioner's part, a spark of life might have remained that a skillful surgeon could have saved, the woman in the black veil goes mad when the surgeon must tell her that there is no hope of resuscitation.

The plot, then, is simply that of a mystery finally revealed. What conflict there is resides in the surgeon's (and the reader's) ignorance of why the woman requires his aid. Yet the story is more suspenseful and of more interest to students of Dickens's development as a writer than this brief summary reveals, for the plot is successfully reinforced and given life and dimension by other aspects of Dickens's growing craftsmanship. One evening in November 1835, Dickens wrote Catherine Hogarth that 'an extraordinary idea for a story of a very singular kind' had occurred to him that morning and he was 'anxious to commit it to paper' before the impression it had made upon him was lost.[30] Whatever the nature of this 'extraordinary' idea, it clearly involved more than the plot itself. The whole artist – the conscious craftsman – became involved at this point. And there is sufficient evidence in the tale itself that Dickens conceived it as a structured totality.

To begin with, the characters – the surgeon, the woman in the black veil, and even the man who answers the door of the house in Walworth – are created to reinforce the effect Dickens hoped to achieve in the story. The black veil hides the woman's secret from the reader as well as from the surgeon and early suggests death or some unknown horror connected

---

[30] *Pilgrim Letters*, I, 98, to Catherine Hogarth, [?27 November 1835]. I am accepting the suggestion by Butt and Tillotson (p. 42) and the editors of the *Pilgrim Letters* that the tale referred to is 'The Black Veil.'

with the grave, as 'mourning,' 'muffled,' 'concealment,' and 'shrouded' indicate:

> It was a singularly tall female, dressed in deep mourning, and standing so close to the door that her face almost touched the glass. The upper part of her person was carefully muffled in a black shawl, as if for the purpose of concealment, and her face was shrouded by a thick black veil. She stood perfectly erect; her figure was drawn up to its full height, and though the surgeon *felt* that the eyes beneath the veil were fixed on him, she stood perfectly motionless, and evinced, by no gesture whatever, the slightest consciousness of his having turned towards her.
>
> (First Series, II, 79–80)

Since Dickens does not use her in the story to achieve an impression of reality but to create suspense, mystery, and terror, the woman is an exceptionally 'flat' character. Her speech is in the melodramatic tradition, as are her actions:

> 'I am . . . very ill: not bodily, but mentally. It is not for myself, or on my own behalf . . . that I come to you. If I laboured under bodily disease, I should not be out alone at such an hour, or on such a night as this; and if I were afflicted with it twenty-four hours hence, God knows how gladly I would lie down and pray to die. It is for another that I beseech your aid, sir. I may be mad to ask it for him – I think I am: but, night after night, through the long dreary hours of watching and weeping, the thought has been ever present to my mind; and though even I see the hopelessness of human assistance availing him, the bare thought of laying him in his grave without it, makes my blood run cold!' And a shudder, such as the surgeon well knew art could not produce, trembled through the speaker's frame.
>
> (First Series, II, 81–82)

There is a 'desperate earnestness' in her actions; she 'passionately' clasps her hands, bursts into tears, weeps 'bitterly,' and in the last scene sobs hysterically, conveys a 'convulsive attitude of grief,' rushes 'frantically' to the bedside of her dead son and flings herself on her knees, then starts to her feet, beats her hands together, responds 'with a burst of passion amounting almost to frenzy,' chafes the forehead and breast and 'wildly' beats the cold hands of 'the senseless form before her,' throws herself before the surgeon to prevent him from letting light into the room, dashes off her bonnet and veil to exhibit a 'deadly pale' face, 'a nervous contortion of the lip, and unnatural fire in her eye,' and finally falls senseless at the feet of the surgeon, incurably insane (First Series, II, 82–86, 94–98).

The surgeon, on the other hand, is essentially a straight-forward, non-sensationalized creation. His characteristics do not seem to be exaggerated, he is a 'serious' as opposed to a 'comic' character, he speaks the language of educated people (as does the woman), he is poor but respectable, and he is an intelligent and sympathetic gentleman at all times. Although he does not tell his own story, like David Copperfield he is more an observer of the action than a participant in it. This is the first such character of this type in Dickens's writings, though he does derive most of his characteristics, except for the absence of wit and verbal cleverness, from the narrator of the earlier tales and essays, most noticeably, I think, from the narrator of the 'Our Parish' sketches and of the earlier essays that are more serious in tone, such as 'Gin-Shops' and 'The Streets – Morning.' The surgeon also serves as a focal point for the narrative point of view: it is through his eyes and mind that the reader sees and attempts to comprehend the action, a technique that Dickens uses to increase the suspense of the story, for we are allowed to know no more about the situation than the surgeon himself does. Following the opening scene in which he accedes to the woman's entreaty for his help the next day, the surgeon speculates upon what her request might signify, thus heightening the sense of mystery already aroused in us:

> The woman . . . spoke of another person – a man – and it was impossible to suppose that a mere dream or delusion of fancy would induce her to speak of his approaching dissolution with such terrible certainty as she had done. It could not be that the man was to be murdered in the morning, and that the woman originally a consenting party and bound to secrecy by an oath had relented, and though unable to prevent the commission of some outrage on the victim, determined to prevent his death if possible by the timely interposition of medical aid. The idea of such things happening within two miles of the metropolis appeared too wild and preposterous to be entertained beyond the instant.
>
> (First Series, II, 87)

Although we are being decoyed away from the truth of the situation, our minds are being directed to the right general area: there will be no pleasant or comic explanation for the woman's behavior. The tone, created largely by the nature of the narrator's thoughts, tells us this. Later, while the surgeon is waiting in the house at Walworth, the arrival of the son's body is likewise given a more vivid effect by being described from only the surgeon's point of view. He hears a vehicle approaching the house, the door opened, low talking, a 'shuffling noise of footsteps along the passage, and on the stairs, as if two or three men were engaged in carrying some heavy body to the room above,' and a later creaking of the stairs and closing of the door again as the men leave the house (First Series, II, 93–94). Thus, we are properly surprised and horrified by the climax of the tale.

The transitions from pure description to pictorial scene to dramatic scene are not only smoother in 'The Black Veil' than in the tales Dickens had written for the *Monthly Magazine* and even for *Bell's Life in London*, but each type of description or narration is appropriate for the purpose it serves. The two dramatic scenes contain the most important moments in the plot, that in which the woman first approaches the surgeon, where the action to follow is carefully prepared for, and that in which the surgeon is first shown the son's body, the climactic moment of the story. The pictorial scenes and description are used to get the surgeon from one day to the next, to move him from one area of London to another, to paint the various settings in which the action takes place, and to increase the tension by lengthening the space between the key dramatic scenes.

Finally, the setting itself contributes greatly to the structural unity of 'The Black Veil.' Dickens had earlier used setting, in an incidental way, to establish the mood of a particular scene, but in this story each setting – the surgeon's office, Walworth, the drawing room of the house, and the bedroom upstairs – contributes to the overall mood. In emphasizing the dismal weather outside, the opening paragraph in the tale has a subduing effect on the relative cheerfulness of the parlor within, preparing us for the disturbing effect of the mysterious woman:

> One winter's evening, toward the close of the year 1800, or within a year or two of that time, a young medical practitioner, recently established in business, was seated by a cheerful fire in his little parlour, listening to the wind, which was beating the rain in pattering drops against the window, and rumbling dismally in the chimney. The night was wet and cold: he had been walking through mud and water the whole day, and was now comfortably reposing in his dressing-gown and slippers, more than half asleep and less than half awake, revolving a thousand matters in his wandering imagination. First he thought how hard the wind was blowing, and how the cold, sharp rain would be at that moment beating in his face if he were not comfortably housed at home. Then his mind reverted to his annual Christmas visit to his native place and dearest friends; he thought how glad they would all be to see him, and how happy it would make Rose if he could only tell her that he had got a patient at last, and hoped to have more, and to come down again in a few months' time, and marry her, and take her home to gladden his lonely fireside. . . .
>
> (First Series, II, 77–78)

The surgeon's reflections about friends and sweetheart serve as a contrast, certainly, to the situation of the woman in the black veil, but even the cheerful fireside at which he is doing his dreaming becomes, in the course of the paragraph, a 'lonely' one. Because the woman herself, her actions, and her story, as well as the surgeon's speculations upon her visit, maintain the mood of disturbing mystery, of some nameless, foreboding terror, to the end of the scene, Dickens need not elaborate the setting further; the dramatic scene itself conveys all the suspense needed.

The second scene is pictorial, beginning with a description of 'the back part of Walworth' on the following day:

> The appearance of the place through which he walked was not calculated to raise the spirits of the young surgeon, or to dispel any feeling of anxiety or

depression that the singular kind of visit he was about to make might have awakened. Striking off from the high road, his way lay across a marshy common, through irregular lanes, with here and there a ruinous and dismantled cottage, fast falling to pieces with decay and neglect. A stunted tree, or pool of stagnant water, roused into a creeping, sluggish action, by the heavy rain of the preceding night, skirted the path occasionally, and now and then a miserable patch of garden-ground, with a few old boards knocked together for a summer-house, and old palings imperfectly mended with stakes pilfered from the neighbouring hedges, bore testimony at once to the poverty of the inhabitants, and the little scruple they entertained in appropriating the property of other people to their own use. Occasionally a filthy-looking woman would make her appearance from the door of a dirty house, to empty the contents of some cooking utensil into the gutter in front, or to scream after a little slipshod girl who had contrived to stagger a few yards from the door under the weight of a sallow infant almost as big as herself; but scarcely any thing was stirring around, and so much of the prospect as could be faintly traced through the cold damp mist which hung heavily over it, presented a lonely and dreary appearance, perfectly in keeping with the objects we have described.

(First Series, II, 88–90)

As we can tell from the generalizations Dickens makes about this setting in his first and last sentences, the details have been carefully and consciously selected to create a 'lonely and dreary appearance,' one 'not calculated to raise the spirits' or 'to dispel any feeling of anxiety or depression.' The objects noted and the adjectives used to characterize them – a combination of irregular lanes, ruined cottages, stunted trees, pools of stagnant water, coldness, damp mist, poverty manifested in run-down buildings, miserable patches of land, and screaming, filthy-looking women – contribute to the total effect. We get an impression of the people from the setting, and of the environment from both. In addition, the setting also reflects the puzzled, depressed mood of the surgeon and, operating as crude image or symbol, reinforces the all-enveloping tone of the entire story.

The exterior of the house is 'desolate and unpromising.' The house itself is low, standing 'at an angle of a narrow lane,' appearing closed up and withdrawn, too, from the other buildings in the vicinity, there being 'no other habitation in sight' (First Series, II, 90). The man who lets the surgeon in is 'a tall, ill-favoured man, with black hair, and a face as our friend [the surgeon] often declared afterwards, as pale and haggard, as the countenance of any dead man he ever saw' (First Series, II, 92). The description of the back parlor in which the young man is directed to wait also reinforces the cold, desolate, lonely, frightening atmosphere found in the earlier scenes. It is a sparsely furnished room. A 'handful of fire' is burning in the grate, but this only brings out the damp, for 'unwholesome moisture' is 'stealing down the walls in long, slug-like tracks.' The broken, patched window overlooks a bit of ground 'almost covered with water.' And an eerie silence dominates the scene (First Series, II, 93). The bedroom receives only the most cursory description. Like the room downstairs, it is poorly furnished. In addition, the dim light from the curtained window makes the objects and people in the room indistinct and uniform of hue (First Series, II, 95). But further description of the room to maintain the tale's overall mood is unnecessary, for the woman's hysteria, swooning, and madness achieve the same end much more dramatically.

In his descriptions, Dickens places great emphasis on water: on rain and mud in the first scene, on mist and pools of stagnant rain in the second, and on the dampness in the parlor and the water in the yard in the third. His use of 'unwholesome' to describe the moisture on the parlor walls reveals the effect he wanted to achieve with this description. Also noticeable, though not in every scene, is Dickens's reliance on loneliness, bareness, dirtiness, crookedness, and silence to reinforce the mood. Certainly one finds in this early work a rudimentary and surely a conscious use of weather, topography, and other physical manifestations to create an atmosphere. In the later novels such descriptions will form images that not only convey mood and reveal character and environment but also comment upon institutions and social systems, upon the nature of man, and upon man's relationship to greater, more spiritual and, in some instances, more virulent forces loose in the universe. The young author of 'The Black Veil' had no interest in, perhaps no awareness of, such profundities at this stage in his career. Dickens meant the tale to be a striking piece of mystery, suspense, and horror, but really nothing more, an imitation of similar tales he had surely been reading in *Blackwood's Edinburgh Magazine*, and perhaps an improvement upon them. Nevertheless, we can observe him already making conscious and – given the limitations of this type of tale – effective use of techniques that will later, particularly from the Christmas novels on, artistically reinforce deeper themes in his novels.

*

'The Great Winglebury Duel' and 'The Tuggs's at Ramsgate,' the two remaining tales that Dickens wrote during this period, the first in October 1835, the other in February 1836, return him, in a way, to the start of his career as a professional author. Farcical like the *Monthly Magazine* tales and about the same length as 'The Bloomsbury Christening' and 'The Steam Excursion,' they are developed mainly by dramatic scenes rather than the pictorial ones that predominate in the tales for *Bell's Life in London*. They, too, bear strong marks of the popular theatrical farces and magazine stories of the day, and the author's purpose is still to present a picture of human foibles. But at times they are also vaguely reminiscent of the eighteenth-century novels of Fielding and Smollett and, in several respects, improvements over the first tales that Dickens wrote. For one thing, they are better plotted and better structured overall than are the earlier tales. Later, it is true, the more mature, more technically experienced author will formulate his plots with greater finesse and surer skill, and will follow with fuller understanding and with striking variations and elaborations the patterns laid down by his important predecessors in the novel. In the meantime, these two tales exhibit, I believe, Dickens's growing concern with literary form.

Even though we may now look somewhat askance at the mechanical plot of 'The Great Winglebury Duel,' involving a familiar if extravagant case of mistaken identity, the emphasis that Dickens gives to the plot of this tale shows, I suspect, this new interest in plot and structure. Following a picturesque and somewhat lengthy description of the town of Great Winglebury and the Winglebury Arms, the narration takes us into the inn, where Mr. Alexander Trott is delivered a written challenge to a duel from Horace Hunter, his rival for the affections of Miss Emily Brown, whom Trott has arranged to meet at the inn for the purpose of eloping to Gretna Green. This challenge initiates the action that follows and creates the suspense that will continue throughout the story as we wait to discover exactly how Trott – not the bravest of men – will manage to avoid the duel promised in the story's title and meet and steal away with his beloved. The co-ordinate plot (the first such in Dickens), of which the widowed Julia Manners is the protagonist, also moves forward at the same time. Her arrival at the inn by coach precedes the delivery of Hunter's letter to Trott, and Dickens continues her story immediately following the scene in which Trott, in hopes of being restrained from even attending upon Hunter, writes an anonymous letter to the mayor of the town to warn him of a young gentleman at the inn (meaning himself, of course) who is 'bent on committing a rash act to-morrow morning at an early hour' (First Series, II, 226). The widow's plan, to meet and elope with a Lord Peter, also involves the mayor of Great Winglebury, whom she knows from her earlier marriage to an elderly gentleman of his acquaintance. To one familiar with such intricately plotted tales, a clever and surprising working-out of these schemes ought to follow – and it does. The promised duel does not come off, and the mix-up occasioned by the mayor's mistaking Trott for Lord Peter is not straightened out in time for the original marital plans of Trott and Miss Manners to be fulfilled. Instead, finding themselves, as a result of the mayor's mistake, in the coach, on the way to Gretna Green, and discovering that the other is not the intended fellow eloper, they scrutinize each other, Mr. Trott 'gently squeezing Miss Julia's waist,' and proffer explanations for a day and night of mistakes. The narrative cleverly summarizes what follows:

> Mr. Trott was a young man, had highly promising whiskers, an undeniable tailor, and an insinuating address – he wanted nothing but valour; and who wants that with three thousand a-year? The lady had this, and more; she wanted a young husband, and the only course open to Mr. Trott to retrieve his disgrace was a rich wife. So they came to the conclusion that it would be a pity to have all this trouble and expense for nothing, and that as they were so far on the road already, they had better go to Gretna Green, and marry each other, and they did so.
>
> (First Series, II, 242)

127

Even as he manipulates the plot to comment upon how silly human beings are, Dickens cleverly brings the tale to at least an ostensibly happy ending for these two thwarted lovers – and for most of the other characters as well. Horace Hunter marries Emily Brown, both Mr. Hunter and Mr. Trott are pardoned by their families, and Lord Peter (the exception), who had been unconscionably delayed by champagne-drinking and riding a steeple-chase, went back to his host's, 'drank more champagne, and rode another steeple-chase, and was thrown and killed.' And all these circumstances, as Dickens concludes the story, 'were discovered in time, and carefully noted down: and if ever you stop a week at the Winglebury Arms, they'll give you just this account of The Great Winglebury Duel' (First Series, II, 243). The entire tale is unbelievable, of course, but within the artificial world that the author creates, the unexpectedness of the ending is nevertheless plausible, acceptable, and pleasingly witty. The 'happy' ending is far truer to the comic spirit than the breach of promise suits, separations, abandonments, and suicides with which several of the *Monthly Magazine* tales concluded, with an enrichment rather than a diminishing of satiric effect. It has the fulfilled structure that the earlier tales do not have and, accordingly, is closer in its design, if not always in its comic richness, to individual chapters in *Pickwick Papers*.

The plot of 'The Tuggs's at Ramsgate' lacks the suspense and complexity of that of 'The Great Winglebury Duel' and is, in its more episodic pattern, therefore, a closer cousin to the tales in both the *Monthly Magazine* and *Bell's Life in London*. Having inherited a large sum of money, Mr. Tuggs gives up his grocery business and takes his family on a vacation to Ramsgate as a first step in a move upward in society. What follows in loosely picaresque fashion depends for its comic effect upon the Tuggses' gullibility, their ignorance of the social graces, and their newly reinforced class snobbery. At the end of the tale, we discover that the costly flirtation of Simon Tuggs (or 'Cymon,' as he insists), the son of the family, with Mrs. Captain Waters had been initiated by the woman, her military husband, and one of his subordinate officers. But this discovery is not sufficiently exciting to compensate for the relatively episodic nature of the tale. It is too much like the anticlimactic plot of 'Horatio Sparkins' to be entirely satisfying. Nevertheless, the tale moves more inevitably toward its predestined end than do Dickens's earlier stories, more as does 'The Dancing Academy.' Given Simon Tuggs's romantic nature, his social pretentions, his father's inheritance of twenty thousand pounds, and his 'tendency to weakness in his interesting legs' (*Library of Fiction*, No. 1 [April 1836], p. 1), we suspect that not only is he due for a fall later in the story, but the fall will somehow result from his snobbery, sentimentality, and vanity, if not from the weakness of his legs. Because Dickens sends the Tuggses to Ramsgate, where they will be quite out of their social depth, and because they are from the beginning such silly, pretentious people, we know that he intends to dabble in farce and satire. When he introduces the Tuggses to Captain and Mrs.

Waters and causes 'Cymon' to fall immediately in love with the wife, any reader of eighteenth-century fiction and farce knows that the author is preparing for pledges of undying love, the unexpected but destined return of the husband, the innocent but compromising situation, the attempts to hide, and the ultimate, inevitable discovery. These will be followed by a duel if the story is remotely serious or by farcical disgrace and perhaps (as in Dickens's tale) by the revelation of a successful confidence game. But the last may not be the most effective conclusion an author could select, for it puts the concluding emphasis on the dupers rather than the duped, on antagonist rather than protagonist.

Yet the combination of techniques in which Dickens had shown considerable improvement in the tales and essays written between 1833 and 1836 to some extent rescues 'The Great Winglebury Duel' and 'The Tuggs's at Ramsgate' from their flaws. We are not surprised to find effective scenes, humorous and relatively well-developed characters, a fairly artistic handling of descriptive and narrative techniques, and a reasonably complex tone and atmosphere consistent with the author's intentions. Brighter dialogue serves to develop characters more fully in 'The Tuggs's at Ramsgate' and aids in forwarding the intricacies of the plot in 'The Great Winglebury Duel.' It is less stilted than it had been earlier, less cluttered with self-indulgent word-play, and more dependent upon Dickens's developing ear for speech patterns, dialects, and nuances of tone and meaning. We even notice some attempt to separate more clearly the speech of one character from that of another. In 'The Tuggs's at Ramsgate,' for example, the Waterses speak fluent, educated English while the Tuggses frequently relapse into colloquialisms and slang expressions that betray their origins. Captain Waters, though suave in his speech, is sometimes blustery; his wife, appropriately named Belinda, uses words with highly sentimental connotations almost every time she speaks.[31] Dickens's characterizations also rely more heavily in these later stories on action that is comic in itself, as well as on description that more carefully delineates appearance, mannerisms, and attitudes. Both are evident in what is, I think, the best scene in

---

[31] One clue that Dickens gives the reader to the character of Mrs. Captain Waters is surely a reference to the opportunistic Mrs. Waters of *Tom Jones*, whose husband is a captain in the army, but whose Christian name is Jenny. Another clue may possibly be provided by the heroine of 'Belinda Waters,' a poem of some 141 lines by George Crabbe, which was originally published in *Posthumous Tales*, Vol. VIII of *The Poetical Works of the Rev. George Crabbe: With His Letters and Journals, and His Life by His Son* (London: John Murray, 1834), and reprinted in George Crabbe, *Poems*, ed. Adolphus W. Ward, Vol. III (Cambridge: Cambridge University Press, 1907), pp. 311–14. Crabbe's Belinda Waters is a proud, self-indulgent young beauty much given to reading of 'strange and bold escapes,/Of plans and plottings, murders and mishaps,/Love in all hearts, and lovers in all shapes' (ll. 50–52). While she is bored by *Clarissa*, throwing the volume down 'ere Clarissa reach'd the wicked town' (l. 75), 'tales of terror are her dear delight' (l. 61). Poetic justice eventually catches up with Belinda Waters: she marries a surgeon's mate retired on half-pay and spends the rest of her life in sorrow, sadness, and 'anxious fretfulness,' which her incapacity for household matters only exacerbates.

'The Tuggs's at Ramsgate,' the comic donkey ride of Simon, his sister, and Mrs. Waters:

'Kum up!' shouted one of the two boys who followed behind to propel the donkeys, when Belinda Waters and Charlotta Tuggs had been hoisted, and pushed, and pulled into their respective saddles.

'Hi – hi – hi!' groaned the other boy behind Mr. Cymon Tuggs. Away went the donkey, with the stirrups jingling against the heels of Cymon's boots, and Cymon's boots nearly scraping the ground.

'Way – way! Wo-o-o-o—!' cried Mr. Cymon Tuggs as well as he could, in the midst of the jolting.

'Don't make it gallop!' screamed Mrs. Captain Waters, behind.

'My donkey *will* go into the public-house!' shrieked Miss Tuggs, in the rear. . . .

Everything has an end, however; and even the galloping of donkeys will cease in time. The animal which Mr. Cymon Tuggs bestrode, feeling sundry uncomfortable tugs at the bit, the object of which he could by no means understand, abruptly sidled against a brick wall, and expressed his uneasiness by grinding Mr. Cymon Tuggs's leg on the rough surface. Mrs. Captain Waters's donkey, apparently under the influence of some playfulness of spirit, rushed suddenly, head first, into a hedge, and declined to come out again: and the quadruped on which Miss Tuggs was mounted expressed his delight at this humourous proceeding by firmly planting his fore-feet against the ground, and kicking up his hind-legs in a very agile, but somewhat alarming manner.

This abrupt termination to the rapidity of the ride naturally occasioned some confusion. . . . The efforts of the boys, however, assisted by the ingenious expedient of twisting the tail of the most rebellious donkey, restored order in a much shorter time than could have reasonably been expected, and the little party jogged slowly on together.

'Now let 'em walk,' said Mr. Cymon Tuggs. 'It's cruel to over-drive 'em.'

(*Library of Fiction*, No. 1, pp. 11–12)

The picture of the long-legged Mr. Tuggs on the short-legged donkey, his obvious inexperience in riding such a beast, the suggested characterizations of the donkeys themselves as we momentarily enter the thoughts of one of them, the comic tableau of chaos and confusion that temporarily brings the ride to a standstill, and the implications of Tuggs's last remark not only characterize the young man's pretentiousness but also explode it. In addition, each of these details contributes to the unified, consistent comic conception of the story.

Merely one episode in a tale of many, this scene does little to forward the plot, and does not, for that matter, reveal anything particularly new about Simon Tuggs. Yet by contributing an additional layer of detail, character, incident, and comedy to an already substantial accumulation of such material, it plays its part in reinforcing the tonal setting of the tale. The concluding paragraph of this excerpt is particularly clever. It not only rings with irony and humor, it also caps Dickens's characterization of young Tuggs and, in giving sharper focus to the author's satiric intent, successfully unifies the scene. We see even more clearly that nothing at Ramsgate, obviously, is going to turn out well for our newly-rich family. This realization, with the laughter accompanying it, comes very close, I think, to being what the story is all about.

At times in the two tales, the richness of detail and comedy is considerably reinforced by the settings Dickens creates to contain the action. This is particularly evident in 'The Great Winglebury Duel.' Dickens's essays contain well-detailed descriptive passages, but the tales do not; even those in *Bell's Life in London* are relatively empty of fully described settings *per se*. But 'The Great Winglebury Duel' has a quality that G. K. Chesterton finds in a number of the tales, though he indiscriminately refers to 'Horatio Sparkins' as well as to 'The Tuggs's at Ramsgate': 'an indefinable flavour of emphasis and richness, a hint as of infinity of fun.'[32] It is just such a hint that Dickens conveys in his setting at the beginning of the tale:

> The day was hot and sunny, the town in the zenith of its dulness, and with the exception of these few idlers not a living creature was to be seen. Suddenly the loud notes of a key-bugle broke the monotonous stillness of the street; in came the coach, rattling over the uneven paving with a noise startling enough to stop even the large-faced clock itself. Down got the outsides, up went the windows in all directions; out came the waiters, up started the ostlers, and the loungers, and the post-boys, and the ragged boys, as if they were electrified – unstrapping, and unchaining, and unbuckling, and dragging willing horses out, and forcing reluctant horses in, and making a most exhilarating bustle.
>
> (First Series, II, 212–13)

The description of the Winglebury Arms, immediately preceding this passage, prepares the reader, by a kind of associative process, for a variety of picaresque complications and delights plucked from the pages of Fielding and Smollett:

> The house is a large one with a red brick and stone front; a pretty spacious hall, ornamented with ever-green plants, terminates in a perspective view of the bar, and a glass case, in which are displayed a choice variety of delicacies ready for dressing, to catch the eye of a new-comer, the moment he enters, and excite his appetite to the highest possible pitch. Opposite doors lead to the 'coffee' and 'commercial' rooms; and a great, wide, rambling staircase, – three stairs and a landing – four stairs and another landing – one step and another landing – half a dozen stairs and another landing – and so on – conducts to galleries of bedrooms, and labyrinths of sitting-rooms, denominated 'private,' where you may enjoy yourself as privately as you can in any place where some bewildered being or other walks into your room every five minutes by mistake, and then walks out again, to open all the doors along the gallery until he finds his own.
>
> (First Series, II, 211)

---

[32] Chesterton, *Appreciations and Criticisms of the Works of Charles Dickens*, p. 8.

The rest of the story does not continue the richness of action, characterization, and authorial comment that we find in *Tom Jones*, *Peregrine Pickle*, *Pickwick Papers*, or even, though necessarily in bits and pieces, some of Dickens's essays of 1835 and 1836. But I think in 'The Great Winglebury Duel' and 'The Tuggs's at Ramsgate' we can see Dickens in the process of making the alterations in his very way of telling stories that prepare him for writing those masterly scenes in *Pickwick Papers* that made him famous and that elevated the work above the comic sporting novels of Surtees and Egan, which were themselves superior to the models Seymour had originally proposed to imitate.

At the beginning of 1836 Dickens was still grappling somewhat awkwardly with the complex mixture of setting, characterization, comic incident, and structure that he would need for *Pickwick Papers*; and the problems imposed by monthly serialization of a long story, a story most chapters of which (not to mention monthly parts of two or three chapters) were far longer than any he had hitherto attempted, still lay ahead. But in 'The Great Winglebury Duel' and 'The Tuggs's at Ramsgate' he is at least beginning to move within the circle of influence of better models than he had previously imitated. He seems to be thinking of himself no longer as the journalist but as the man of letters, even the *novelist*. We can observe him in these two tales, as well as in 'The Black Veil,' more effectively, if at times still awkwardly, merging the elements of fiction into a unified, structured work of literature. In all three and in the non-fictional 'A Visit to Newgate' we also see him experimenting with a variety of what are for him new techniques of narration, description, characterization, and tone and mood. His intentions no longer seem to be at cross-purposes with themselves. He knows, for example, that he must, while laughing, shake his head in disbelief and perhaps in disappointment at the behavior of such people as Simon Tuggs and Alexander Trott, Julia Manners and Belinda Waters, the Boots at the Winglebury Arms (another predecessor of Sam Weller) and the donkey boys at Ramsgate. He knows that happy endings can be as satiric as unpleasant ones. He knows that dialogue helps to create a dramatic scene by characterizing its participants and moving the plot along, and not simply by filling space on a page. He knows that a carefully described setting not only helps the reader to picture the story but also serves to create a mood, establish a time and place for action, provide an environment and atmosphere that contribute to the tone of the entire story as well as to that of the individual scene within it. He is, in other words, achieving some success in putting together, still in relatively uncomplicated and sometimes even crude ways, the various aspects of fiction, and in putting them together far more successfully than he had in the *Monthly Magazine* tales and in more complex ways than in the tales in *Bell's Life in London*. At this point in his career he is surely ready to tackle the larger work of fiction. The opportunity to do so lies just ahead of him.

CHAPTER SIX

Perspectives and Conclusions

PUBLISHED in two volumes on 8 February 1836, the First Series of *Sketches by Boz* had been in preparation since late October of the preceding year. By 27 October, at least, Dickens was proposing 'Sketches by Boz and Cuts by Cruikshank' or 'Etchings by Boz and Wood Cuts by Cruikshank' as a title for the work and was preparing to round up copies of essays and tales that had already been printed. He was also prepared, he wrote Macrone, 'if the whole collection fall something short of the two volumes, which we shall ascertain I suppose by the printing,' to be ready with 'two or three new Sketches to make weight.' He added that he was planning to do a piece on Newgate Prison for the edition and had a list of other topics on hand should further essays need to be written.[1]

The First Series contained 'Sentiment!' from *Bell's Weekly Magazine* and all of the *Monthly Magazine* tales except 'A Dinner at Poplar Walk.'[2] Four of the five 'Street Sketches' from the *Morning Chronicle* were included; only 'The Old Bailey' (reprinted in the Second Series as 'Criminal Courts') was omitted, possibly because Dickens felt it to be superseded by 'A Visit to Newgate,' as Butt and Tillotson suggest (p. 43). Seventeen of the twenty 'Sketches of London' from the *Evening Chronicle* were also used, the omissions being 'The House' and 'Bellamy's,' which were combined and considerably revised under the title of 'A Parliamentary Sketch. With a Few Portraits' in the Second Series, and 'The Streets – Morning,' which was very likely saved as a companion piece for 'The Streets at Night' (*Bell's Life in London*, 17 January 1836) – the two sketches, followed appropriately by 'Making a Night of It,' open the Second Series, a clue that Dickens and Macrone were thinking of doing another series even as Dickens was

---

[1] *Pilgrim Letters*, I, 82–84, to John Macrone, [?27 October 1835].
[2] As illustrated in Chapter II of this study, 'A Dinner at Poplar Walk' was considerably revised before being published in the Second Series as 'Mr. Minns and His Cousin.'

putting the first one together.[3] In addition to 'A Visit to Newgate,' 'The Black Veil,' and 'The Great Winglebury Duel,' which were being published for the first time, Dickens also included four of the twelve 'Scenes and Characters' that he was then in the process of writing for *Bell's Life in London*, namely, 'Miss Evans and "The Eagle,"' 'The Dancing Academy,' 'The Prisoners' Van,' and 'Christmas Festivities' (published 4 October, 11 October, 29 November, and 27 December, respectively).[4] In preparing the sketches for republication, Dickens 'made extensive cuts, rewrote whole paragraphs, and made innumerable minute changes both of substance and style,' as Butt and Tillotson indicate (p. 39). In the chapters above, we have seen that Dickens frequently excised opening and closing paragraphs that were unnecessary in a collection of essays, changed various details to make his description more forceful and vivid, modified or removed topical allusions, softened some of his harsher comments, polished phrasing and tightened sentence structure, and in general made revisions that often strikingly illustrate his conscious concern for craftsmanship.[5] He continued to make revisions in the various editions of the *Sketches* published during his lifetime, and a number of prefaces exist to illustrate his changing opinion of his earliest writings.[6]

On 10 February, two days after the publication of *Sketches by Boz* and

[3] Another early clue to the possibility of a second series is in *Pilgrim Letters*, I, 103, to John Macrone, [9 December 1835], where Dickens states that he intends to go over the House of Correction again but 'would much rather not describe it for this series.' He probably had decided by then to save most of the 'Scenes and Characters' he was writing for *Bell's Life in London* for a second series.

[4] 'On the whole,' Butt and Tillotson state, 'it seems fair to regard work published by the beginning of November and omitted from the First Series of *Sketches by Boz* as deliberately rejected; though sketches published later might be left out simply for lack of space, since the new ones were by then already written' (p. 42). Dickens did, however, include 'The Prisoners' Van,' published 29 November, and even 'Christmas Festivities,' published 27 December, some few days after he had originally expected the First Series to appear in the bookshops. By 17 December, some six days before he wrote the Christmas sketch, he had resigned himself to publication 'in the first week of the new Year' – see *Pilgrim Letters*, I, 108, to John Macrone. Because of the delay caused by Cruikshank's work on the illustrations, Dickens had the opportunity to add two sketches that presumably he thought might help 'make' the series. These were inserted at the end of the first volume.

[5] For additional details about Dickens's revisions for the First Series, see Butt and Tillotson, pp. 43–50. For matters concerning publication of the work, see Butt and Tillotson, pp. 38–43; Johnson, I, 104–09; and *Pilgrim Letters*, I, 80–130, *passim*.

[6] For revisions in later editions of *Sketches by Boz*, see Butt and Tillotson, pp. 50–61. Dickens wrote prefaces for the first edition of the First Series (dated February 1836), for the second edition of the First Series (dated 1 August 1836), for the Second Series (dated 17 December 1836), for the 1837–39 edition (dated 15 May 1839); and for the Cheap Edition (dated October 1850). The Charles Dickens Edition contains the preface (undated) originally written for the Cheap Edition. The author's object, Dickens wrote in the earliest preface, 'has been to present little pictures of life and manners as they really are; and should they be approved of, he hopes to repeat his experiment with increased confidence, and on a more extensive scale' (p. v). In the Cheap Edition, he informs his readers that the sketches were 'sent into the world with all their imperfections (a good many) on their heads,' and that he is 'conscious of their often being extremely crude and ill-considered, and bearing obvious marks of haste and inexperience; particularly in that section of the present volume which is comprised under the general head of Tales' (p. vii).

even before he was allowed to savor the acclamation of the reviewers,[7] Dickens was approached by William Hall of the publishing house of Chapman and Hall, to write a 'monthly something [that] should be a vehicle for certain plates to be executed by Mr. Seymour,' according to Dickens's account in the Preface to the Cheap Edition (1847) of *Pickwick Papers*. There was also, he added, 'a notion, either on the part of that admirable humourous artist, or of my visitor (I forget which), that a "NIMROD Club," the members of which were to go out shooting, fishing, and so forth, and getting themselves into difficulties through their want of dexterity, would be the best means of introducing these.' But Dickens objected that this was not an amenable subject for him, and that the idea 'had been already much used.' He told Hall 'that it would be infinitely better for the plates to arise naturally out of the text; and that I should like to take my own way, with a freer range of English scenes and people, and was afraid I should ultimately do so in any case.'[8] Acquiescing to the modifications strongly urged by Dickens, Chapman and Hall described the proposed work in the letter that stated the terms for the undertaking as 'a book illustrative of manners and life in the Country.'[9] Considering how much of the life and spirit of London is in *Pickwick Papers*, it was a deceptive compromise. Dickens scarcely hesitated over the additional strain he knew such a task would put on his time. 'The work,' he wrote Catherine, 'will be no joke, but the emolument is too tempting to resist.'[10]

He began the first number of *Pickwick* on 18 February, having promised Chapman and Hall that it would be completed by the first week in March, the second number by the end of the third week, with copy thereafter in hand five weeks in advance of publication (the first number was scheduled for a 31 March publication date).[11] From this time on he was to find himself constantly under pressure to begin and to complete each month's installment, and soon fell behind the proposed schedule. He had no intention then, at least, of sacrificing any of the projects he was working on or contemplating for the near future; he even took on more work. He had written a play, *The Strange Gentleman*, based on 'The Great Winglebury Duel,' and had completed the book and lyrics for an operetta, *The Village Coquettes*, for which John Hullah, a young composer, wrote the

---

[7] For excerpts from a number of these reviews, see D[exter], 'The Reception of Dickens's First Book,' pp. 43–50. George Hogarth's review in the *Morning Chronicle* – 'Hogarth's beautiful notice,' Dickens called it (*Pilgrim Letters*, I, 129, to John Macrone, [11 February 1836]) – was apparently the only review that Dickens had seen at the time, but, as mentioned earlier, he had been assured of the literary value of his *Sketches* by several men whose views he respected. For his activities in getting copies to the reviewers and seeing to it that advertisements and notices of the book's publication appeared in the important journals and papers, see *Pilgrim Letters*, I, 116–17, 123–30, 137, 140.

[8] Reprinted in the Penguin edition of *Pickwick Papers*, ed. Patten, p. 44.

[9] Reprinted in *Pilgrim Letters* (Appendix C), I, 648. The letter of agreement is dated 12 February 1836.

[10] *Pilgrim Letters*, I, 129, to Catherine Hogarth, [10 February 1836].

[11] *Pilgrim Letters*, I, 131–32, to Messrs. Chapman and Hall, 16 February 1836.

music. [12] These two works underwent revisions during the spring and summer, and Dickens later became involved with rehearsals as well. In the spring he wrote a pamphlet (published June 1836) entitled *Sunday Under Three Heads: As It Is; As Sabbath Bills Would Make It; As It Might Be Made*, under the pseudonym of 'Timothy Sparks.' Also during the year he signed agreements with John Macrone, on 9 May, to write a three-volume novel to be called *Gabriel Vardon, the Locksmith of London* (an early title for the work that eventually became *Barnaby Rudge*); with Thomas Tegg, on 11 August, to write a children's book in time for the Christmas season with the title of *Solomon Bell the Raree Showman*; and with Richard Bentley, on 22 August, for the rights to his first *two* three-volume novels, one presumably to be *Gabriel Vardon*.[13] Dickens also continued as a reporter for the *Morning Chronicle* until 5 November, when the demands upon his time, the success of *Pickwick Papers*, and an agreement with Bentley to undertake the editorship of a new monthly magazine to be called *The Wits' Miscellany* (but ultimately published as *Bentley's Miscellany*) made it desirable for him to resign his position on the paper.[14]

As if he were not busy enough, Dickens also wrote nine more sketches during the year and greatly revised a number of others for the Second Series of *Sketches by Boz*. In addition, he made minor revisions and wrote a new preface for the second edition of the First Series (August 1836). One of the new pieces, 'A Little Talk about Spring, and the Sweeps' (republished in the Second Series as 'The First of May'), appeared in the June issue of the *Library of Fiction*. Two others, 'The Hospital Patient' and 'Hackney Cabs, and Their Drivers,' were published in the issues of 6 August and 17 September of the *Carlton Chronicle*, the only entries in a series that Dickens ambitiously began with the general heading of 'Leaves from an Unpublished Volume. By "Boz," (which will be torn out once a fortnight).'[15] Not only was the second essay published some six weeks after the first, but

---

[12] Dickens finished *The Village Coquettes* during the last week of January 1836, and it was promptly accepted by John Braham for the St. James's Theatre – see *Pilgrim Letters*, I, 122, to George Cruikshank, [?1 February 1836]; I, 118, n. 2; and I, 120, to Catherine Hogarth, [?23 January 1836]. But numerous revisions, including the addition of a low comedy part for J. P. Harley, were to be made by Dickens before the piece went into rehearsal – see *Pilgrim Letters*, I, 151–77, *passim*. Dickens sent an 'entirely rewritten' version to Braham on 30 July (I, 158) but was still making revisions in this version as late as 25 September (I, 177, to J. P. Hullah). The operetta opened at the St. James's Theatre on 6 December to mixed reviews – see Johnson, I, 153–54.

[13] See *Pilgrim Letters*, I, 150, 163, 648–49, respectively. Dickens never did the volume for Tegg; though Tegg published a work with approximately the same title in 1839, it was by another author – see *Pilgrim Letters*, I, 163, n. 2. For the problems and disputes connected with the publishing agreements concerning *Gabriel Vardon*, see *Pilgrim Letters*, I, 164–65, n. 1, and Johnson, I, 143, 150–51, 183–85, and 234–53.

[14] See *Pilgrim Letters*, I, 190–91, to John Easthope, 5 November [1836].

[15] 'Hackney Cabs, and Their Drivers' was considerably revised when it was combined with 'Some Account of an Omnibus Cad' (*Bell's Life in London*, 1 November 1835) to form the first half of 'The Last Cab Driver, and the First Omnibus Cad' in the Second Series of *Sketches by Boz*. See Appendix B, below, for further details and a reprinting of the original essay.

Dickens apparently abandoned the series to begin a new one in the *Morning Chronicle* under the title of 'Sketches by "Boz." New Series.' He published only four sketches here before his resignation from the paper: 'Meditations in Monmouth-Street' (24 September), 'Scotland-Yard' (4 October), 'Doctors' Commons' (11 October), and 'Vauxhall-Gardens by Day' (26 October).[16] The last two pieces that Dickens wrote in 1836, 'Our Next Door Neighbours' and 'The Drunkard's Death,' were first published in the Second Series of the *Sketches*.[17]

These nine pieces range from roughly 1200 words ('Hackney Cabs, and Their Drivers') to 4200 ('The Drunkard's Death') with most about 2000 to 2500 words in length. 'The Hospital Patient' and 'The Drunkard's Death' are alike in a number of respects, dealing, in the former, with a brutal man whose wife is dying in a hospital from blows inflicted by him, and, in the latter, with a drunkard whose behavior leads to the death of his wife and, after some passage of time, to his son's apprehension and execution for robbery and murder, to abandonment by his daughter, and ultimately to his own suicide. Both begin in the expository mode, end with a melodramatic death scene, and, while relying on realistic detail, play heavily on sentimentality. A number of these characteristics are evident in the concluding paragraphs of 'The Drunkard's Death,' perhaps the most effective and the most melodramatic passage in the two pieces:

The tide was in, and the water flowed at his feet. The rain had ceased, the wind was lulled, and all was, for the moment, still and quiet – so quiet that the slightest sound on the opposite bank, even the rippling of the water against the barges that were moored there, was distinctly audible to his ear. The stream

---

[16] Dickens had planned to publish a new series of sketches, apparently in the *Evening Chronicle*, at least as early as March 1836, and may even have written something for it, as the editors of the *Pilgrim Letters* suggest (I, 149, n. 3). 'I am perfectly aware,' Dickens wrote to John Easthope, one of the proprietors of the newspaper, 'that the heavy press of other matter at this season of the year, would have rendered the insertion of the new series I commenced, a task of great difficulty: but I merely wish to remind you, that I left the arrangement entirely to you. . . .' He adds that he has no intention of departing from the promise to continue his sketches that he made to the *Evening Chronicle* readers at the end of the last of the 'Sketches of London' in the 20 August 1835 issue – see *Pilgrim Letters*, I, 149, [?April 1836]. The four new sketches that he did for Easthope were first published in the *Morning Chronicle*, however, though they were reprinted in the *Evening Chronicle* almost immediately. Four days before he officially resigned from the *Chronicle* staff, he wrote Easthope to explain 'why No. 5 has not yet appeared.' A severe cold had rendered him 'wholly unable to set pen to paper for some days past.' But he reported that the cold had lessened and he would 'prepare another sketch immediately' – *Pilgrim Letters*, I, 188 [1 November 1836]. If he actually did so, this must have been 'Our Next Door Neighbours,' the only new piece in the Second Series whose time of conception has not been accounted for at all.

[17] Dickens did not finish 'The Drunkard's Death' until 7 December, on which date he wrote to T. C. Hansard, the printer of the Second Series, that the 'little tale I am on, is a very good one (I think). I have taken great pains with it, as I wished to finish the Volume with *eclat*. It will run to 28 slips, and I am on the 26th. but I must keep the whole to read, in order that I may give it the finishing touch here and there' – *Pilgrim Letters*, I, 208.

stole languidly and sluggishly on. Strange and fantastic forms rose to the surface, and beckoned him to approach; dark gleaming eyes peered from the water, and seemed to mock his hesitation, while hollow murmurs from behind, urged him onwards. He retreated a few paces, took a short run, a desperate leap, and plunged into the river.

Not five seconds had passed when he rose to the water's surface, but what a change had taken place in that short time, in all his thoughts and feelings. Life, life, in any form, poverty, misery, starvation, anything but death. He fought and struggled with the water that closed over his head, and screamed in agonies of terror. The curse of his own son rang in his ears. The shore, but one foot of dry ground – he could almost touch the step. One hand's breadth nearer, and he was saved – but the tide bore him onward, under the dark arches of the bridge, and he sank to the bottom.

Again he rose, and struggled for life. For one instant – for one brief instant – the buildings on the river's banks, the lights on the bridge through which the current had borne him, the black water, and the fast flying clouds, were distinctly visible – once more he sunk, and once again he rose. Bright flames of fire, shot up from earth to heaven, and reeled before his eyes, while the water thundered in his ears, and stunned him with its furious roar.

A week afterwards the body was washed ashore, some miles down the river, a swollen and disfigured mass. Un-recognised and un-pitied, it was borne to the grave; and there, it has, long since, mouldered away.

(Second Series, pp. 375–77)

The other seven pieces are clearly essays, most of which illustrate the variety in tone and content that characterize 'A Visit to Newgate' and a number of earlier essays. In these pieces we see Dickens at the height of his early expository and descriptive powers, pretty much in control of the techniques he had been using and experimenting with over the many months since his first tale had appeared in the *Monthly Magazine*. To pick just one as an example, 'Meditations in Monmouth-Street' (*Morning Chronicle*, 24 September 1836), the best of the group, is reminiscent of the earlier 'Brokers' and Marine-Store Shops' but clearly superior to it. There Dickens humanized the objects in a shop window. In 'Meditations in Monmouth-Street,' describing an area of old-clothes shops in London, 'Boz' gives shape and life to the articles of clothing hanging in the windows by filling them with people of his imagination. Conceiving of the street as the 'burial-place of the fashions,' he writes: 'We love to walk among these extensive groves of the illustrious dead, and to indulge in the speculations to which they give rise; now fitting a deceased coat, then a dead pair of trousers, and anon the mortal remains of a gaudy waistcoat upon some being of our own conjuring up, and endeavouring, from the shape and fashion of the garment itself, to bring its former owner before our mind's eye.' Two long examples follow, giving the reader, I think, some insight into the ways and methods of the creative writer. The first is in the solemn mood. Several suits of clothing hanging outside one of the windows appear to 'Boz's' mind to have belonged at different periods of time to the same individual, fantastic though he realizes the idea is. 'There was the man's whole life, written as legibly on those clothes as if we had his autobiography engrossed on parchment before us,' he states. The narrator traces through the several suits the career of their former owner, from a small boy in tight-fitting outfit through several ages of boy and man – office messenger-lad, idler among blackguards, irresponsible husband and father, drunkard, criminal, transported prisoner – as if he were describing a series of plates by Hogarth; indeed, Dickens may have had some such series in mind. The descriptions of the stages in the life of this man reveal a great deal about Dickens's conception of character, indicating that even this early in his career, though his characters are described largely in terms of external details, he is quite aware that such details reveal much about the inner man. For example, in the description of the young boy's suit, he shows how conscious he is of the significance of detail, selecting each with great economy to suggest a character of some fullness:

The first was a patched and much-soiled little skeleton suit – one of those straight blue cloth cases in which small boys used to be confined before belts and tunics had come in, and old notions had gone out; an ingenious contrivance for displaying the full symmetry of a boy's figure, by fastening him into a very tight jacket, with an ornamental row of buttons over each shoulder, and then buttoning his trousers over it, so as to give his legs the appearance of being hooked on just under the arm-pits. This was the boy's dress. It had belonged to a town boy, we could see; there was a shortness about the legs and arms of the suit, and a bagging at the knees, peculiar to the rising youth of London streets. A small day-school he had been at, evidently. If it had been a regular boys' school they wouldn't have let him play on the floor so much, and rub his knees so white. He had had an indulgent mother too, and plenty of half-pence, as the numerous smears of some sticky substance about the pockets, and just below the chin, which even the salesman's skill could not succeed in disguising, sufficiently betokened. They were decent people, but not over-burdened with riches, or he would not have so far outgrown the suit when he passed into those corduroys with the round jacket; in which he went to a boys' school, however, and learnt to write – and in ink of pretty tolerable blackness too, if the place where he used to wipe his pen might be taken as evidence.

But Dickens deliberately shifts in his second example from the serious to a more cheerful tone, as he begins putting feet and legs into 'a cellar-board full of boots and shoes' – and then the people themselves. A pair of boots, 'a jolly, good-tempered, hearty-looking pair of tops,' is filled in his imagination by a 'fine red-faced jovial fellow of a market-gardener,' his 'huge fat legs bulging over the tops, and fitting them too tight to admit of his tucking in the loops he had pulled them on by, and his knee-cords with an interval of stocking, and his blue apron tucked up round his waist, and his red neckerchief and blue coat, and a white hat stuck on one side of his head; and there he stood with a broad grin on his great red face, whistling away as if any other idea but that of being happy and comfortable had never entered his brain.' In a neighboring pair of Denmark satin shoes the meditator in Monmouth-street places 'a coquettish servant-maid.' A 'very smart female, in a showy bonnet,' steps into 'a pair of grey cloth boots with black fringe and binding'; a very old, very gallant gentleman with a silver-headed cane totters into large list shoes; a laughing young man is put into 'a pair of long-quartered pumps'; and finally a whole group ready for dancing appears in a 'numerous *corps de ballet* of boots and shoes in the background.' But called back from his revery by a female shopkeeper who thinks he is staring impudently at her, 'Boz' takes flight out of the street. 'Here, and in other passages like this,' Edgar Johnson asserts, 'the volume reaches its climactic achievement, and foreshadows the incredible fecundity that was to be.'[18]

*

At this point, this study of Dickens's apprentice years has reached its end. By 24 September, when 'Meditations in Monmouth-Street' was published, Dickens had just finished writing the seventh number (October 1836) of *Pickwick Papers* – Mr. Pickwick had set off for Rochester with his fellow Pickwickians, encountered Alfred Jingle, been invited to Dingley Dell, pursued Jingle and Rachael Wardle to London, encountered Sam Weller and taken him on as his manservant, been discovered with Mrs. Bardell in his arms, survived the Eatanswill elections and Mrs. Leo Hunter's masquerade breakfast, re-encountered Jingle, been duped into the back garden of the Westgate House Establishment for Young Ladies, received notice of Mrs. Bardell's breach of promise suit, made his first visit to the offices of Dodson and Fogg, been introduced to Tony Weller – and is about to hear Jack Bamber's tale of the Queer Client, the fifth interpolated tale, with which the November number will begin. The novel is well underway. The plots and themes, the various loosely-related lines of development that will eventually unite this picaresque collection of characters and incidents, have been laid down. The time for exercises in the craft of fiction has ended; the apprentice must give way to the journeyman, beyond whom we already have glimpses of the master craftsman.

The transition from writing tales, descriptive essays, and character studies to writing *Pickwick Papers* was easier for Dickens than a person not familiar with his accomplishments in the *Sketches* might expect. For one thing, *Pickwick* began more as a series of sketches of people and places than it did as a novel. The advertisement for the first number of the work in the 26 March 1836 issue of *The Athenaeum*, probably written by Dickens himself, provides some evidence of this. Of Pickwick it states:

> This remarkable man would appear to have infused a considerable portion of his restless and inquiring spirit into the breasts of other members of the Club, and to have awakened in their minds the same insatiable thirst for Travel which so eminently characterized his own. The whole surface of Middlesex,

---

[18] Johnson, I, 114.

a part of Surrey, a portion of Essex, and several square miles of Kent, were in their turns examined, and reported on. In a rapid steamer, they smoothly navigated the placid Thames; and in an open boat they fearlessly crossed the turbid Medway. High-roads and by-roads, towns and villages, public conveyances and their passengers, first-rate inns and road-side public houses, races, fairs, regattas, elections, meetings, market days – all the scenes that can possibly occur to enliven a country place, and at which different traits of character may be observed and recognized, were alike visited and beheld, by the ardent Pickwick and his enthusiastic followers.

The Pickwick Travels, the Pickwick Diary, the Pickwick Correspondence – in short, the whole of the Pickwick Papers, were carefully preserved, and duly registered by the secretary, from time to time, in the voluminous Transactions of the Pickwick Club. These transactions have been purchased from the patriotic secretary, at an immense expense, and placed in the hands of 'Boz,' the author of 'Sketches Illustrative of Every Day Life, and Every Day People' – a gentleman whom the publishers consider highly qualified for the task of arranging these important documents, and placing them before the public in an attractive form. He is at present deeply immersed in his arduous labours, the first fruits of which will appear on the 31st March.[19]

Obviously, much of what is promised in this advertisement does not appear in the finished work; somewhere along the way, the miscellany of fictional episodes gives way to a somewhat more tightly structured plot with the beginning of the Bardell affair and its continuation, with the reappearance of Jingle, first at Dingley Dell and then in disguise at Mrs. Hunter's breakfast, and with the introduction and subsequent development of Sam Weller.[20] But, as Butt and Tillotson illustrate (pp. 67–70), the first few installments of *Pickwick Papers* were certainly in keeping with the original plan, for they were little more than collections of material similar in subject matter and form to that Dickens had already used in the essays and tales he had been writing. For example, No. IV (July 1836, Chs. ix–xi), they point out, 'makes no marked departure from the pattern' (p. 69). It begins with the elopement of Jingle and Miss Wardle, which ends with the settlement at the White Hart Inn. This farcical episode is followed by Pickwick's antiquarian discovery of the stone inscribed, as it turns out, with 'Bill Stumps His Mark.' And this is followed immediately by 'The Madman's Manuscript,' one of the several interpolated tales in the work. The author's object, Dickens himself stated in the first preface to the work

---

[19] Quoted from a photographic facsimile of the advertisement in Arthur Waugh, *A Hundred Years of Publishing, Being the Story of Chapman & Hall, Ltd.* (London: Chapman & Hall, 1930), facing p. 26. A photographic facsimile is also in Hatton and Cleaver, *A Bibliography of the Periodical Works of Charles Dickens*, following the Introductory Chapter; the advertisement is also reprinted in the Penguin edition of *Pickwick Papers*, ed. Patten, pp. 899–900.

[20] Sam's development from No. V on, state Butt and Tillotson (p. 70), 'gives a new depth and a new motive force to *Pickwick*; henceforward it is built, not simply upon events, but upon the deepening relation between him and his master.'

(written in 1837), 'was to place before the reader a constant succession of characters and incidents; to paint them in as vivid colours as he could command; and to render them, at the same time, life-like and amusing.'[21] Dickens might have been writing about *Sketches by Boz*. What continuity there is in the early numbers of *Pickwick* is only a shade more elaborate than that which worked its way into the 'Our Parish' sketches that he wrote for the *Evening Chronicle* in 1835, or that he alludes to but does not use in the concluding paragraph of Chapter Two of 'Passage in the Life of Mr. Watkins Tottle,' where he proposes publishing, at some time in the future, the posthumous papers of Watkins Tottle containing 'the materials collected in his wanderings among different classes of society,' which, supplied by Tottle's landlady, 'will be carefully arranged, and presented to the public from time to time, with all due humility, by BOZ.'[22]

Nor did the creation of the characters in the first few installments of *Pickwick Papers* exert any greater demands upon Dickens's creative imagination than had some of those in the better tales and sketches. Pickwick, Tupman, Snodgrass, and Winkle certainly begin as stock figures. Dickens characterizes the last two simply as 'the poetic Snodgrass, and . . . the sporting Winkle, the former poetically enveloped in a mysterious blue cloak with a canine-skin collar, and the latter communicating additional lustre to a new green shooting coat, plaid neckerchief, and closely fitted drabs' (Ch. i, p. 3). He does little more with Tupman or even with Pickwick himself in the opening chapters. He will develop these characters at greater length, obviously, in succeeding chapters, but he will do so largely along the lines set down from the beginning. Admittedly these satirical figures are given some roundness by the tone of amiability with which the narrator views their actions – but then, as we have seen, such characters had long dominated the scene in the sketches. In other aspects of characterization in *Pickwick*, Dickens was certainly limited at first by the brevity of the 'exercises' in characterization that the sketches afforded him. There, space restrictions and the expositional requirements of the essays had not given him the opportunity to create fully realized characters, and the farcical and melodramatic tales he had written required no more than the simplest sort of stock figures. Even the better major figures in the stories – Watkins Tottle, Potter and Smithers (in 'Making a Night of It'), and Simon Tuggs, for example – were significant predecessors only of such characters in *Pickwick Papers* as Tracy Tupman, Benjamin Allen and Bob Sawyer, and Winkle, to suggest respective parallels, but even these are inevitably much more fully developed characters than the earlier ones. It was natural for Dickens

---

[21] See p. vii (originally in the prefatory matter at the end of No. XIX/XX [November 1837]). Dickens's comments in later prefaces attempt to impose greater structure on the work, but the statement from the earliest preface undoubtedly comes closest to describing his original plans. See the Penguin edition of *Pickwick Papers*, ed. Patten, pp. 41–53, for reprintings of all the prefaces.

[22] *The Monthly Magazine*, N.S. 19 (February 1835), 137.

to begin *Pickwick* with stock figures; he surely felt most secure with them. Even Alfred Jingle, whom Dickens singled out in a letter to Catherine as 'a very different character from any I have yet described, who I flatter myself will make a decided hit,'[23] was a stock character based, as scholars have noted, upon characters from earlier novels and plays.[24]

There is also a strong continuity from the *Sketches* to *Pickwick* where other elements of the craft of fiction are concerned. The editor-narrator whom Dickens uses in the novel had already appeared in a good many sketches as 'Boz' or 'Tibbs.' Dickens did more with the setting in 'The Black Veil' and even in 'The Great Winglebury Duel' and certainly in a number of fine descriptive essays than he does in most chapters in *Pickwick*. His adequate technical ability with narrative and pictorial scene and his developing facility with dialogue and dramatic scene continued to advance as his first long work progressed to its conclusion. But again, the early numbers are not striking improvements in these respects over the essays and tales that Dickens wrote in late 1835 and early 1836.

The transition, then, from essay and tale to novel was accomplished smoothly. Dickens fell easily into the writing of *Pickwick Papers* because it was in many respects very little different from the writing he had been doing for the past two and a half years. His main problem was merely the greatly increased length of his monthly writing assignment. 'Pickwick is not yet completed,' he wrote Catherine in March. 'The sheets are a weary length – I had no idea there was so much in them.'[25] Of course it was this 'problem' that was to prove a blessing, for the additional space the Pickwick number forced Dickens to fill also required him to develop scenes more fully, to describe setting and action in a more leisurely fashion, and to create characters in richer detail and developed with somewhat greater roundness than hitherto. And these and other such accomplishments would prove the making of him as a novelist – granting him, obviously, the creative imagination and the technical ability that were already fairly well developed by 1836.

Thus, as *Pickwick* progressed, Dickens naturally continued to develop as a craftsman not only of the individual story within a chapter or covering

[23] *Pilgrim Letters*, I, 133, to Catherine Hogarth, [21 February 1836].
[24] See, for example, W. H. D. Rouse, 'Dickens and Jorrocks,' *Times Literary Supplement*, 19 April 1934, p. 282, with replies by R. H. Case (26 April, p. 303), Lascelles Abercrombie (3 May, p. 322), and W. S. Mackie (14 June, p. 424). Respectively, they advocate 'a gentleman in green' whom Jorrocks encounters in R. S. Surtees's *Jorrocks' Jaunts and Jollities* (1838, but serialized in the *New Sporting Magazine*, 1831–34); Major Overall in Theodore Hook's *Maxwell* (1830); Goldfinch in Thomas Holcroft's drama, *The Road to Ruin* (1792); and Latitat, a lawyer, in Frederick Reynolds's comedy, *How to Grow Rich* (1793). Elsewhere, other sources have occasionally been suggested, including one or more of Charles Mathews's characterizations, with which Dickens would also certainly have been familiar.
[25] *Pilgrim Letters*, I, 137, to Catherine Hogarth, [?4 March 1836]. The first two numbers were roughly 12,000 words each in length, nearly one-half again as long as the four essays combined that Dickens wrote for the *Evening Chronicle* in April 1835, probably his most productive month previously.

two or three chapters (not necessarily consecutive ones) but also of the novel. He seems gradually to have realized what *Pickwick Papers* was capable of being, what he had perhaps only partly unconsciously worked into it by way of structure, and to have made the requisite changes in direction and emphasis. Pickwick never makes it to that open boat on the Medway, or to the fairs, regattas, and market-days that were some of his original destinations. Instead, he keeps returning to London and Dingley Dell, where unfinished business awaits him. He remains in the Fleet Prison for two and a half installments of the novel, not only because the story is now more concerned with his principles for living a decent life and his more overtly expressed sympathy for down-trodden humanity than with his perambulations and sporting transactions, but also because conditions in a London prison were of greater interest, concern, and personal nearness to Dickens than were 'all the scenes that can possibly occur to enliven a country place.' Strong elements of the picaresque remain, but in the modifications of the form made nearly a century earlier by Fielding in *Tom Jones* and *Joseph Andrews*. Indeed, Dickens's growing awareness and more conscious manipulation of the structure of the work is indicated in his comments in the 1837 preface. Pointing out that he gradually abandoned the machinery of the Pickwick Club because it proved unworkable, he further reminds his reader that monthly publication 'rendered it an object of paramount importance that, while the different incidents were linked together by a chain of interest strong enough to prevent their appearing unconnected or impossible, the general design should be so simple as to sustain no injury from this detached and desultory form of publication'; thus it was necessary that every number be 'to a certain extent, complete in itself,' yet join together with the other nineteen parts to 'form one tolerably harmonious whole, each leading to the other by a gentle and not unnatural progress of adventure.' Accordingly, the reader should expect 'no artfully interwoven or ingeniously complicated plot.' Even more than this, Dickens concludes, 'if it be objected to the Pickwick Papers, that they are a mere series of adventures, in which the scenes are ever changing, and the characters come and go like the men and women we encounter in the real world, he [the author] can only content himself with the reflection, that they claim to be nothing else, and that the same objection has been made to the works of some of the greatest novelists in the English language.'[26]

Dickens's conception of characterization matures also. Sam Weller, to select what I think is the finest example, is introduced in Chapter x as the stock figure of a 'Boots' at the White Hart Inn, a type whom Dickens had depicted in 'The Great Winglebury Duel,' and with different occupations even earlier.[27] However, as his relationship with Pickwick develops, so,

[26] *Pickwick Papers* (1837), pp. vii-viii.
[27] Butt and Tillotson also see his predecessors in such figures as the omnibus cad in 'Some Account of an Omnibus Cad' (*Bell's Life in London*, 1 November 1835) and the 'stock comic servant of the eighteenth-century tradition' (p. 70).

accordingly, does the significance of Sam's character deepen. We get to know him as well as Dickens does – through what we find out about his earlier life; through his relationship with Mary, his father, step-mother, and the Reverend Mr. Stiggins; through his involvement with Jingle and particularly Job Trotter; through his reactions to Tupman, Winkle, and Snodgrass; and most importantly through his relationship with Pickwick. Even before the Bardell *vs.* Pickwick trial, he has become much more than Pickwick's servant. We have come to know him as the practical and honest man of experience who stands, not always successfully, as a bulwark between the innocence of Pickwick and the inhumanity of men and the indifference of institutions, so opposed to kindness and benevolence. Yet what is most intriguing and original about Sam is his forthright, outspoken, good-hearted, roguish, Cockney-tongued personality. Despite the profounder aspects of his character, he is still basically a strong comic creation.

Dickens develops in other areas also, particularly in his handling of the dramatic scene. The Bardell *vs.* Pickwick trial is the apex of Dickens's comic inventiveness in the work, but there are many other fine dramatic scenes as well. The brilliance of the dialogue in such scenes contributes greatly to their effectiveness, for the dialogue not only moves the plot along, it also characterizes the speakers, has an air of naturalness missing from Dickens's earlier writing, and makes for excellent humor. But the quality here is more a product of *Pickwick Papers* than of the *Sketches*, I suspect. Even in such tales as 'The Great Winglebury Duel' and 'The Tuggs's at Ramsgate' the dialogue is still too often stilted – though by no means as ineffective and crude as that of the earliest tales. The need to fill a goodly amount of space each month may first have led Dickens to write fuller dialogue, and practice in doing so may very well have produced better scenes.

Dickens's first novel has its virtues without a doubt. It is more purely comic, more optimistic in outlook, occasionally even more inventive in individual scenes than Dickens's later novels. It is the best comic work of its decade, and, at least in terms of pure comic fun, possibly the best of the century. As a novel, however, it lacks much, as a study of Dickens's development as a novelist from *Pickwick* to *Drood* would show. Certain important realizations about multi-plot structure and structural unity, about the relationships between theme, form, and recurrent imagery, and about the subtleties of technique and tone will not even come to Dickens until at least the 1840's. Even then, his new insights into the construction and content of novels will come slowly and will take time to work their way effectively into the novels. But certainly by the writing of *Bleak House* we find Dickens consciously weaving the threads of a multi-sided plot and a dual point of view through nineteen (as twenty) monthly numbers with skill and artistry. We also find there that his view of life and his concepts of man and of the social structure have deepened and pervade that magnificent work at every level.

But we are still at the beginning of *Pickwick Papers*. Whatever Dickens may have accomplished in the future as craftsman and artist is at this point in his career to be seen only as the undoubted promise he shows in *Sketches by Boz*. These pieces quite clearly formed the base for Dickens's later achievements; they served as the early proving ground. He simply could not have written a work like *Pickwick Papers* without first having written the essays and tales of 1833–36. He needed the exercises in writing, the practice in the craft of fiction, that these sixty pieces afforded him. The development of Dickens's imagination during childhood and his movement from one occupation to another were necessary stages in his development into a writer. More importantly, as I trust this study has shown, this early unconscious preparation for a career as a writer and his increasingly more conscious development as a professional author between 1833 and 1836 enabled him to meet the challenge of success. Looking back from the vantage point of 1836, we can make out clearly the stages in his early development as a conscious craftsman. Seen from the vantage point of the present, *Pickwick Papers* occupies a relatively late position in Dickens's progress from that imaginative, lonely boy writing to amuse himself to the successful author, but an early position, of course, in his progress from the young author beginning to work consciously with the elements of fiction to the accomplished artist of *Bleak House*.

Studying the essays and tales that Dickens wrote before *Pickwick Papers* in roughly chronological order, as we have, we have observed Dickens changing from a young man with a desire to write stories and sketches that will amuse others, but not knowing quite how to achieve his goal, into an author fairly well-practiced in the techniques of fiction writing, increasingly conscious of the effects he can attain with these techniques, and rather proficient in combining them to produce a reasonably unified, often effective comic or serious story. This is the Dickens of 1836, the ambitious, eager, competent young man beginning to be recognized by his colleagues and contemporaries, impatient, no doubt, to write his first three-volume novel; the developing craftsman in the art of fiction; a man somehow fated, from his earliest years, for the glorious future that lay before him. His apprentice years, when he wrote the pieces that comprise *Sketches by Boz*, played an important part in making that future possible.

APPENDIX A

The Publishing History of *Sketches by Boz*

I. PUBLICATION OF THE INDIVIDUAL SKETCHES

All of the sketches were subject to minor revisions of punctuation, spelling, and phrasing in editions published in Dickens's lifetime. Only substantial revisions are indicated below.[1]

1. 'A Dinner at Poplar Walk' [unsigned]. *Monthly Magazine*,[2] N.S. 16 (December 1833), 617–24.

   Reprinted in the *London Weekly Magazine* [formerly *The Thief*], 7 December 1833; in *The Albion* (New York), N.S. 2 (5 April 1834), 106–07; and in *Sketches by Boz*, Second Series, pp. 256–82,[3] as 'Mr. Minns and his Cousin,' with substantial revisions.

2. 'Mrs. Joseph Porter, "Over the Way"' [unsigned]. *Monthly Magazine*, N.S. 17 (January 1834), 11–18.

   Reprinted in *The Albion*, N. S. 2 (29 March 1834), 104; in *Waldie's Select Circulating Library* (Philadelphia), Part II, No. 9 (26 August 1834), 136–38 (not seen); and in First Series, II, 253–72, as 'Mrs. Joseph Porter.'

---

[1] I am considerably indebted in the compilation of this appendix to Hatton and Cleaver, *A Bibliography of the Periodical Works of Charles Dickens*, pp. 89–128; *Pilgrim Letters* (Appendix F), I, 692–94; Butt and Tillotson, pp. 35–61, *passim*; Herman L. Edgar and R. W. G. Vail, 'Early American Editions of the Works of Charles Dickens,' *Bulletin of the New York Public Library*, 33 (1929), 302–19; and William C. Bennett, 'America's Early Recognition of Dickens's Genius: Earliest Sketches Published Anonymously in a New York Weekly,' *Dickensian*, 35 (1938/39), 47–48. Except where indicated, I have checked my listings against the originals or photographic facsimiles.

[2] The full title, as of January 1833, was *The Monthly Magazine, or British Register of Politics, Literature, Art, Science, and the Belles-Lettres*.

[3] For fuller bibliographical descriptions of the First and Second Series of *Sketches by Boz*, see Part II, Nos. 1 and 3, below. Hereafter, I shall refer to these two publications as First Series and Second Series. I have not seen the *London Weekly Magazine*.

3. 'Horatio Sparkins' [unsigned]. *Monthly Magazine*, N.S. 17 (February 1834), 151–62.
Reprinted in First Series, II, 110–41.

4. 'The Bloomsbury Christening' [unsigned]. *Monthly Magazine*, N.S. 17 (April 1834), 375–86.
Reprinted in *The Albion*, N.S. 2 (10 May 1834), 147–48 (omissions), and First Series, I, 242–75.[4]

5. 'The Boarding-House' [unsigned]. *Monthly Magazine*, N.S. 17 (May 1834), 481–93.
Reprinted in *The Albion*, N.S. 2 (28 June 1834), 201–02 (omissions), and First Series, I, 147–80, as 'The Boarding-House. Chapter the First.'

6. 'Original Papers [Sentiment!]' [unsigned]. *Bell's Weekly Magazine*, 7 June 1834.[5]
Reprinted in First Series, II, 319–42, as 'Sentiment!'

7. 'The Boarding-House. – No. II' [signed 'Boz']. *Monthly Magazine*, N.S. 18 (August 1834), 177–92.
Reprinted in *The Albion*, N.S. 2 (11 October 1834), 323–24 [signed 'Boz'] (omissions), and First Series, I, 181–223, as 'The Boarding-House. Chapter the Second.'

8. 'Omnibuses,' Street Sketches – No. I [signed 'BOZ']. *Morning Chronicle*, 26 September 1834.
Reprinted in First Series, II, 244–52.

9. 'The Steam Excursion' [signed 'Boz']. *Monthly Magazine*, N.S. 18 (October 1834), 360–76.
Reprinted in *The Albion*, N.S. 2 (15 November 1834), 361–62 [signed 'Boz'] (omissions), and First Series, II, 273–318.

10. 'Shops, and Their Tenants,' Street Sketches. – No. II [signed 'BOZ']. *Morning Chronicle*, 10 October 1834.
Reprinted in First Series, I, 88–96.

11. 'The Old Bailey,' Street Sketches. – No. III [signed 'BOZ']. *Morning Chronicle*, 23 October 1835.
Reprinted in Second Series, pp. 49–62, as 'Criminal Courts.'

12. 'Shabby-Genteel People,' Street Sketches – No. IV [signed 'BOZ']. *Morning Chronicle*, 5 November 1834.
Reprinted in First Series, II, 101–09.

13. 'Brokers' and Marine Store Shops,' Street Sketches. – No. V [signed 'BOZ']. *Morning Chronicle*, 15 December 1834.
Reprinted in First Series, I, 233–41, with last paragraph omitted.

14. 'Passage in the Life of Mr. Watkins Tottle. Chapter the First' [signed 'BOZ']. *Monthly Magazine*, N.S. 19 (January 1835), 15–24.

---

[4] The omnibus scene was reprinted as 'The Omnibus' in *Seymour's Comic Album* (London: W. Kidd, [?November 1834]), pp. 83–89, with an illustration by Robert Seymour. See Kathleen Tillotson, 'Seymour Illustrating Dickens in 1834,' *Dickensian*, 54 (1958), 11–12.
[5] Not seen. Reported by Nielsen in 'Some Observations on *Sketches by Boz*,' pp. 243–45.

Reprinted in *The Albion*, N.S. 3 (7 February 1835), 43–44 [signed 'Boz'], and First Series, II, 1–29.

15. 'Hackney-Coach Stands,' Sketches of London. – No. I [signed 'BOZ']. *Evening Chronicle*, 31 January 1835.
   Reprinted in First Series, I, 224–32.

16. 'Passage in the Life of Mr. Watkins Tottle. Chapter the Second' [signed 'BOZ']. *Monthly Magazine*, N.S. 19 (February 1835), 121–37. Reprinted in *The Albion*, N.S. 3 (21 March 1835), 92–93 [signed 'BOZ'] (omissions),[6] and First Series, II, 30–76.

17. 'Gin Shops,' Sketches of London. – No. II [signed 'BOZ']. *Evening Chronicle*, 7 February 1835.
   Reprinted in First Series, I, 276–87.

18. 'Early Coaches,' Sketches of London. – No. III [signed 'BOZ']. *Evening Chronicle*, 19 February 1835.
   Reprinted in First Series, II, 171–81.

19. '"The Parish" [Chapter I. The Beadle – The Parish Engine – The Schoolmaster],'[7] Sketches of London. – No. IV [signed 'BOZ']. *Evening Chronicle*, 28 February 1835.
   Reprinted in First Series, I, 1–11, with last paragraph omitted.

20. '"The House,"' Sketches of London. – No. V [signed 'BOZ']. *Evening Chronicle*, 7 March 1835.
   Reprinted in Second Series, pp. 227–42, as the first half of 'A Parliamentary Sketch. With a Few Portraits,' pp. 225–55, with substantial revisions. See also No. 23, below.

21. 'London Recreations,' Sketches of London. – No. VI [signed 'BOZ']. *Evening Chronicle*, 17 March 1835.
   Reprinted in First Series, I, 136–46, with last paragraph omitted.[8]

22. 'Public Dinners,' Sketches of London. – No. VII [signed 'BOZ']. *Evening Chronicle*, 7 April 1835.
   Reprinted in First Series, I, 288–99.

23. 'Bellamy's,' Sketches of London. – No. VIII [signed 'BOZ']. *Evening Chronicle*, 11 April 1835.
   Reprinted in Second Series, pp. 242–55, as the second half of 'A Parliamentary Sketch. With a Few Portraits,' pp. 225–55, with substantial revisions. See also No. 20, above.

24. 'Greenwich Fair,' Sketches of London. – No. IX [signed 'BOZ']. *Evening Chronicle*, 16 April 1835.
   Reprinted in First Series, I, 314–30, with last paragraph omitted.

25. 'Thoughts about People,' Sketches of London. – No. X [signed 'BOZ']. *Evening Chronicle*, 23 April 1835.
   Reprinted in First Series, I, 97–106, with ending considerably revised.

---

[6] The reprinting of the two parts of this tale in *The Albion* has not been noted before.
[7] The bracketed titles for the 'Our Parish' essays are from the First Series.
[8] An excerpt [signed 'Boz'] from this essay was printed in *The Observer*, 20 April 1835 (not seen). See Walter Dexter, 'When Found,' *Dickensian*, 31 (1934/35), 158.

26. 'Astley's,' Sketches of London. – No. XI [signed 'BOZ']. *Evening Chronicle*, 9 May 1835.
Reprinted in First Series, I, 300–13, with last paragraph omitted.

27. 'Our Parish [Chapter II. The Curate – The Old Lady – The Captain],' Sketches of London. – No. XII [signed 'BOZ']. *Evening Chronicle*, 19 May 1835.
Reprinted in First Series, I, 12–23, with first and last paragraphs omitted.

28. 'The River,' Sketches of London. – No. XIII [signed 'BOZ']. *Evening Chronicle*, 6 June 1835.
Reprinted in First Series, II, 182–95 (last paragraph revised in 1837–39 edition – see Part II, No. 4, below).

29. 'Our Parish [Chapter III. The Four Sisters],' Sketches of London. – No. XIV [signed 'BOZ']. *Evening Chronicle*, 18 June 1835.
Reprinted in First Series, I, 24–33, with first paragraph considerably revised and last paragraph omitted.

30. 'The Pawnbroker's Shop,' Sketches of London. – No. XV [signed 'BOZ']. *Evening Chronicle*, 30 June 1835.
Reprinted in First Series, II, 142–57, with last paragraph omitted.

31. 'Our Parish [Chapter IV. The Election for Beadle],' Sketches of London. – No. XVI [signed 'BOZ']. *Evening Chronicle*, 14 July 1835.
Reprinted in First Series, I, 34–47.

32. 'The Streets – Morning,' Sketches of London. – No. XVII [signed 'BOZ']. *Evening Chronicle*, 21 July 1835.
Reprinted in Second Series, pp. 1–16, as 'The Streets by Morning.'

33. 'Our Parish [Chapter V. The Broker's Man],' Sketches of London. – No. XVIII [signed 'BOZ']. *Evening Chronicle*, 28 July 1835.
Reprinted in First Series, I, 48–66.

34. 'Private Theatres,' Sketches of London. – No. XIX [signed 'BOZ']. *Evening Chronicle*, 11 August 1835.
Reprinted in First Series, II, 196–208.

35. 'Our Parish [Chapter VI. The Ladies' Societies],' Sketches of London. – No. XX [signed 'BOZ']. *Evening Chronicle*, 20 August 1835.
Reprinted in First Series, I, 67–78.

36. 'Seven Dials,' Scenes and Characters. – No. I [signed 'TIBBS']. *Bell's Life in London*,[9] 27 September 1835.
Reprinted in Second Series, pp. 143–56.

37. 'Miss Evans and "The Eagle,"' Scenes and Characters – No. II [signed 'TIBBS']. *Bell's Life in London*, 4 October 1835.
Reprinted in First Series, I, 79–87, as 'Miss Evans and the Eagle.'

38. 'The Dancing Academy,' Scenes and Characters – No. III [signed 'TIBBS']. *Bell's Life in London*, 11 October 1835.
Reprinted in First Series, II, 158–70.

---

[9] The full title is *Bell's Life in London, and Sporting Chronicle.*

39. 'Making a Night of It,' Scenes and Characters – No IV [signed 'TIBBS']. *Bell's Life in London*, 18 October 1835.
Reprinted in Second Series, pp. 33–48.

40. 'Love and Oysters,' Scenes and Characters – No. V [signed 'TIBBS']. *Bell's Life in London*, 25 October 1835.
Reprinted in Second Series, pp. 298–308, as the second half of 'The Last Mr. John Dounce.'

41. 'Some Account of an Omnibus Cad,' Scenes and Characters – No. VI [signed 'TIBBS']. *Bell's Life in London*, 1 November 1835.
Reprinted in Second Series, pp. 298–308, as the second half of 'The Last Cab Driver, and the First Omnibus Cad,' pp. 283–308, with substantial revisions. See also No. 54, below, and Appendix B, below.

42. 'The Vocal Dress-Maker,' Scenes and Characters – No. VII [signed 'TIBBS']. *Bell's Life in London*, 22 November 1835.
Reprinted in Second Series, pp. 157–74, as 'The Mistaken Milliner. A Tale of Ambition.'

43. 'The Prisoners' Van,' Scenes and Characters – No. VIII [signed 'TIBBS']. *Bell's Life in London*, 29 November 1835.
Reprinted in First Series, I, 331–37, with a long opening paragraph omitted. See Appendix C, below.

44. 'The Parlour,' Scenes and Characters – No. IX [signed 'TIBBS']. *Bell's Life in London*, 13 December 1835.
Reprinted in *The Observer*, 14 December 1835, as 'The Parlour,' Scenes and Characters [signed 'TIBBS']; and in Second Series, pp. 309–23, as 'The Parlour Orator,' with first paragraph omitted and the last considerably revised. See Appendix C, below.

45. 'Christmas Festivities,' Scenes and Characters. – No. X [signed 'TIBBS']. *Bell's Life in London*, 27 December 1835.
Reprinted in *The Observer*, 28 December 1835 and 3 January 1836, as 'Christmas Festivities' [unsigned], with last paragraph omitted; and in First Series, I, 338–48, as 'A Christmas Dinner,' with last paragraph omitted.

46. 'The New Year,' Scenes and Characters. – No. XI [signed 'TIBBS']. *Bell's Life in London*, 3 January 1836.
Reprinted in *The Observer*, 4 January 1836, as 'The New Year' [unsigned]; and in Second Series, pp. 77–92 (last paragraph omitted in 1837–39 edition).

47. 'The Streets at Night,' Scenes and Characters. – No. XII [signed 'TIBBS']. *Bell's Life in London*, 17 January 1836.
Reprinted in Second Series, pp. 17–32, as 'The Streets by Night.'

48. 'A Visit to Newgate.' *Sketches by Boz*, First Series, I, 107–35.

49. 'The Black Veil.' *Sketches by Boz*, First Series, II, 77–100.

50. 'The Great Winglebury Duel,' *Sketches by Boz*, First Series, II, 209–43.

51. 'The Tugg's at Ramsgate' [signed 'BOZ']. *Library of Fiction*, Vol. I, Part 1 (April 1836), 1–18.[10]
Reprinted in *The Tuggs's at Ramsgate, by 'Boz.' Together with Other Tales, by Distinguished Writers* (Philadelphia: Carey, Lea & Blanchard, 1837), pp. 5–31; in *The Tuggs's at Ramsgate, and Other Sketches Illustrative of Every-Day Life and Every-Day People. By Boz . . . To Which Is Added The Pantomime of Life, by the Same Author* (Philadelphia: Carey, Lea & Blanchard, 1837); and in 1837–39 edition of *Sketches by Boz*, pp. 358–78. I have not seen the second work.
52. 'A Little Talk about Spring, and the Sweeps' [signed 'BOZ']. *Library of Fiction*, Vol. I, Part 3 (June 1836), 113–19.
Reprinted in Second Series, pp. 325–46, as 'The First of May' (last paragraph omitted in Cheap Edition [1850] – see Part II, No. 5, below).
53. 'The Hospital Patient,' Leaves from an Unpublished Volume. By 'Boz,' (which will be torn out once a fortnight). *Carlton Chronicle*, No. 9 (6 August 1836), 139.[11]
Reprinted in Second Series, pp. 132–42.
54. 'Hackney Cabs, and Their Drivers,' Leaves, from an Unpublished Volume. By 'Boz.' *Carlton Chronicle*, No. 11 (17 September 1836), 170.
Reprinted in Second Series, pp. 285–98, as the first half of 'The Last Cab Driver, and the First Omnibus Cad,' pp. 283–308, with substantial revisions. See also No. 41, above, and Appendix B, below.
55. 'Meditations in Monmouth-Street,' Sketches by 'Boz.' New Series, No. I [signed 'BOZ']. *Morning Chronicle*, 24 September 1836.
Reprinted in *Evening Chronicle*, 26 September 1836, as 'Meditations in Monmouth-Street,' Sketches by 'Boz.' – No. I [signed 'BOZ']; and in Second Series, pp. 93–112.
56. 'Scotland-Yard,' Sketches by 'Boz,' – No. II. (New Series) [signed 'BOZ']. *Morning Chronicle*, 4 October 1836.
Reprinted in *Evening Chronicle*, 5 October 1836, same title [signed 'BOZ']; in *Carlton Chronicle*, No. 14 (8 October 1836), pp. 222–23, as 'Scotland-Yard,' From Sketches by 'Boz.' New Series [signed 'BOZ'], with the first two paragraphs omitted; in *Bell's Life in London*, 9 October 1836, as 'Scotland Yard,' Sketches by 'Boz' [signed 'BOZ']; and in Second Series, pp. 63–76, with first two paragraphs omitted. See Appendix C, below.
57. 'Doctors' Commons,' Sketches by 'Boz.' – No. III. (New Series) [signed 'BOZ']. *Morning Chronicle*, 11 October 1836.
Reprinted in *Evening Chronicle*, 12 October 1836, same title [signed 'BOZ']; in *Carlton Chronicle*, No. 15 (15 October 1836), 238, as

---

[10] The full title is *The Library of Fiction, or Family Story-Teller; Consisting of Original Tales, Essays, and Sketches of Character*. The monthly parts were published in a collected edition at the end of the year as Volume I (London: Chapman and Hall, 1836) under this title.
[11] The full title is *The Carlton Chronicle and National Conservative Journal of Politics, Literature, Science and Art*. For further information, see Appendix B, below.

'Doctor's [*sic*] Commons,' From Sketches by 'Boz.' New Series [signed 'BOZ'], but comprising only the last one-third of the sketch; in *Bell's Life in London*, 16 October 1836, as 'Doctors' Commons,' Sketches by 'Boz' [signed 'BOZ' and crediting the sketch to the *Morning Chronicle*]; and in Second Series, pp. 175–90.

58. 'Vauxhall-Gardens by Day,' Sketches by 'Boz.' – No. IV. (New Series) [signed 'BOZ']. *Morning Chronicle*, 26 October 1836.

Reprinted in *Evening Chronicle*, 26 October 1836, same title [signed 'BOZ']; in *Bell's Life in London*, 30 October 1836, as 'Vauxhall-Gardens by Day,' Sketches by 'Boz' [signed 'BOZ']; and in Second Series, pp. 209–24.

59. 'Our Next Door Neighbours.' *Sketches by Boz*, Second Series, pp. 113–31.

60. 'The Drunkard's Death.' *Sketches by Boz*, Second Series, pp. 347–77.

II. Editions of *Sketches by Boz* Illustrating the Changing Arrangement of Contents

1. *Sketches by 'Boz,' Illustrative of Every-Day Life, and Every-Day People.* [The First Series.] Illustrations by George Cruikshank. 2 vols. London: John Macrone, [8 February] 1836.

Vol. I:

Preface (dated 'Furnival's Inn, February, 1836'), pp. iii–v.

The Parish

Chapter I. The Beadle – The Parish Engine – The Schoolmaster, pp. 1–11.[12]

Chapter II. The Curate – The Old Lady – The Captain, pp. 12–23.

Chapter III. The Four Sisters, pp. 24–33.

Chapter IV. The Election for Beadle, pp. 34–47.

Chapter V. The Broker's Man, pp. 48–66.

Chapter VI. The Ladies' Societies, pp. 67–78.

Miss Evans and the Eagle, pp. 79–87.

Shops, and Their Tenants, pp. 88–96.

Thoughts about People, pp. 97–106.

A Visit to Newgate, pp. 107–35.

London Recreations, pp. 136–46.

The Boarding-House.

Chapter the First, pp. 147–80.

Chapter the Second, pp. 181–223.

---

[12] Where there is any variation, the title is taken from the head of the sketch rather than from the table of contents. Fuller bibliographical descriptions of this and other editions will be found in John C. Eckel, *The First Editions of the Writings of Charles Dickens: Their Points and Values*, revised and enlarged edition (New York: Maurice Inman; London: Maggs Bros., 1932), pp. 1–16.

Hackney-Coach Stands, pp. 224–32.
Brokers' and Marine-Store Shops, pp. 233–41.
The Bloomsbury Christening, pp. 242–75.
Gin-Shops, pp. 276–87.
Public Dinners, pp. 288–99.
Astley's, pp. 300–13.
Greenwich Fair, pp. 314–30.
The Prisoners' Van, pp. 331–37.
A Christmas Dinner, pp. 338–48.

Vol. II:
Passage in the Life of Mr. Watkins Tottle.
    Chapter the First, pp. 1–29.
    Chapter the Second, pp. 30–76.
The Black Veil, pp. 77–100.
Shabby-Genteel People, pp. 101–09.
Horatio Sparkins, pp. 110–41.
The Pawnbroker's Shop, pp. 142–57.
The Dancing Academy, pp. 158–70.
Early Coaches, pp. 171–81.
The River, pp. 182–95.
Private Theatres, pp. 196–208.
The Great Winglebury Duel, pp. 209–43.
Omnibuses, pp. 244–52.
Mrs. Joseph Porter, pp. 253–72.
The Steam Excursion, pp. 273–318.
Sentiment!, pp. 319–42.

2. *Sketches by Boz: Illustrative of Every-Day Life, and Every-Day People.*
[The First Series.] The Second Edition. 2 vols. London: John Macrone,
[August] 1836.
The arrangement of the contents and the pagination are identical to those
of the First Edition, with the addition in Vol. I of a new Preface (dated
'Furnival's Inn, 1st. August, 1836'), pp. i–ii, followed by 'Preface to the
First Edition,' pp. iii–iv.[13]

3. *Sketches by Boz: Illustrative of Every-Day Life, and Every-Day People.*

---

[13] Macrone also published a Third Edition, 2 vols. (London: John Macrone, 1837), with
identical arrangement of contents but different pagination. I have seen only Vol. II. The
edition was apparently published by February 1837, according to 'Mr. Macrone's Select
List of New Works and New Editions, Preparing for Immediate Publication, or Recently
Published,' included at the end of the Second Edition of the Second Series of *Sketches by Boz*
(see next footnote). The 'Select List,' dated February 1837, lists the Third Edition of the
First Series and the Second Edition of the Second Series under Part II, 'New Works Just
Published.'

The Second Series. London: John Macrone, 1837 [actually 17 December 1836].[14]
Preface (dated 'Furnival's Inn. December 17, 1836'), pp. i–iii.

The Streets by Morning, pp. 1–16.
The Streets by Night, pp. 17–32.
Making a Night of it, pp. 33–48.
Criminal Courts, pp. 49–62.
Scotland-Yard, pp. 63–76.
The New Year, pp. 77–92.
Meditations in Monmouth Street, pp. 93–112.
Our Next Door Neighbours, pp. 113–31.
The Hospital Patient, pp. 132–42.
Seven Dials, pp. 143–56.
The Mistaken Milliner. A Tale of Ambition, pp. 157–74.
Doctors' Commons, pp. 175–90.
Misplaced Attachment of Mr. John Dounce, pp. 191–208.
Vauxhall Gardens by Day, pp. 209–24.
A Parliamentary Sketch. With a Few Portraits, pp. 225–55.
Mr. Minns and his Cousin, pp. 256–82.
The Last Cab Driver, and the First Omnibus Cad, pp. 283–308.
The Parlour Orator, pp. 309–23.
The First of May, pp. 325–46.
The Drunkard's Death, pp. 347–77.

4. *Sketches by Boz Illustrative of Every-Day Life and Every-Day People.*
With Forty Illustrations by George Cruikshank. New Edition,
Complete. London: Chapman and Hall, 1839. Originally published in
20 monthly parts, November 1837 to June 1839.[15]
Advertisement (a seven-line preface, dated 'London, May 15, 1839'), p. v.
Seven Sketches from Our Parish.
    Our Parish.

---

[14] A Second Edition of the Second Series (London: John Macrone, 1837), with identical arrangement of contents but slightly different pagination from p. 311 on (the volume ends on p. 375 rather than p. 377, as in the First Edition), was published by February 1837, as indicated in the preceding footnote.

[15] In addition to issue number and price, the monthly wrapper for all issues contains the following information: *Sketches by Boz.* Illustrated by George Cruikshank. London: Chapman & Hall, 1837. Pagination, which is identical for the parts issues and the one-volume edition, as the latter was gathered from the former, is as follows: No. I [November 1837], 1–24; No. II [December 1837], 25–48; No. III [January 1838], 49–72; No. IV [February 1838], 73–96; No. V [March 1838], 97–120; No. VI [April 1838], 121–44; No. VII [May 1838], 145–68; No. VIII [June 1838], 169–92; No. IX [July 1838], 193–216; No. X [August 1838], 217–40; No. XI [September 1838], 241–64; No. XII [October 1838], 265–88; No. XIII [November 1838], 289–312; No. XIV [December 1838], 313–36; No. XV [January 1839], 337–60; No. XVI [February 1839], 361–84; No. XVII [March 1839], 385–408; No. XVIII [April 1839], 409–32; No. XIX [May 1839], 433–88; No. XX [June 1839], 489–526, i–viii (prefatory material).

Chapter VII. Misplaced Attachment of Mr. John Dounce, pp. 260–66.
Chapter VIII. The Mistaken Milliner. A Tale of Ambition, pp. 267–73.
Chapter IX. The Dancing Academy, pp. 274–80.
Chapter X. Shabby-Genteel People, pp. 281–85.
Chapter XI. Making a Night of It, pp. 286–91.
Chapter XII. The Prisoners' Van, pp. 292–94.

Tales.
 Chapter I. The Boarding-House.
  Chapter the First, pp. 297–313.
  Chapter the Second, pp. 314–34.
 Chapter II. Mr. Minns and His Cousin, pp. 335–45.
 Chapter III. Sentiment, pp. 346–57.
 Chapter IV. The Tuggs's at Ramsgate, pp. 358–78.
 Chapter V. Horatio Sparkins, pp. 379–95.
 Chapter VI. The Black Veil, pp. 396–407.
 Chapter VII. The Steam Excursion, pp. 408–30.
 Chapter VIII. The Great Winglebury Duel, pp. 431–48.
 Chapter IX. Mrs. Joseph Porter, pp. 449–59.
 Chapter X. Passage in the Life of Mr. Watkins Tottle.
  Chapter the First, pp. 460–73.
  Chapter the Second, pp. 474–97.
 Chapter XI. The Bloomsbury Christening, pp. 498–514.
 Chapter XII. The Drunkard's Death, pp. 515–26.

5. *Sketches by Boz. Illustrative of Every-Day Life and Every-Day People.*
With a Frontispiece by George Cruikshank. [The Cheap Edition.]
London: Chapman and Hall, 1850.
The arrangement of contents is identical in this and succeeding editions
to that of the 1839 edition,[16] with the following substitution for the
'Advertisement':
Preface (dated 'London, October, 1850'), p. vii.

6. *Sketches by Boz. Illustrative of Every-Day Life and Every-Day People.*
With Eight Illustrations. [The Charles Dickens Edition.] London:
Chapman & Hall, 1868.
The arrangement of contents and the titles are identical to those in the
Cheap Edition. The Preface to the Cheap Edition is retained, but
undated. In this edition Dickens added running heads on right-hand
pages.

---

[16] The following titles in the Cheap Edition exhibit minor changes, the last made by
Dickens in his titles: 'Our Parish. Chapter I. The Beadle. The Parish Engine. The
Schoolmaster,' 'Our Parish. Chapter II. The Curate. The Old Lady. The Half-Pay Captain,'
'The Misplaced Attachment of Mr. John Dounce,' 'The Boarding-House. Chapter I,'
and 'A Passage in the Life of Mr. Watkins Tottle.'

APPENDIX B

'Hackney Cabs, and Their Drivers': A 'New' Sketch by 'Boz'

TECHNICALLY, I suppose, 'Hackney Cabs, and Their Drivers,' which appeared in *The Carlton Chronicle and National Conservative Journal of Politics, Literature, Science and Art*, 17 September 1836, is not a newly discovered sketch by Dickens, but the few details published concerning it are so scattered about that scholars are still pretty much accepting Hatton and Cleaver's inaccurate description of it (without reference to title) as a 'flagrant piracy' of a portion of 'Some Account of an Omnibus Cad,' which had appeared earlier in *Bell's Life in London, and Sporting Chronicle* (1 November 1835).[1] Walter Dexter referred to it by title, however, and was the first to note that, along with 'The Hospital Patient' (6 August 1836), it had been written especially for the *Carlton Chronicle*. But he is otherwise strangely unenlightening about it.[2]

The important facts, some of them new, are these. 'Hackney Cabs, and Their Drivers' is indeed a separate, distinct, 'new' sketch, raising to sixty the number of pieces that Dickens ultimately collected as fifty-six scenes, characters, and tales in all editions of *Sketches by Boz* from the parts issue of 1837–39 on. Sometime between mid-August, when he finished the piece, and early December, when he sent the last of the manuscript for the Second Series of the *Sketches* to the printer,[3] Dickens considerably revised 'Hackney Cabs, and Their Drivers' for this volume. It appeared, however, not as a

---

[1] Hatton and Cleaver, *A Bibliography of the Periodical Works of Charles Dickens*, p. 100.

[2] 'Dickens to His First Publisher: Some Hitherto Unpublished Letters,' *Dickensian*, 28 (1931/32), 38–39, and 'The Genesis of *Sketches by Boz*,' p. 111. Johnson (I, 152) notes Dexter's discovery but provides no additional information and does not mention the sketch by title.

[3] *Pilgrim Letters*, I, 160, to John Macrone, [3 August 1836], and 209, to Richard Bentley, [?10 December 1836]. The Second Series was published only eight days later on 17 December.

separate essay but as the first half of 'The Last Cab Driver, and the First Omnibus Cad.' Except for a passing reference by T. W. Hill, it is still assumed that Dickens simply expanded 'Some Account of an Omnibus Cad,' the second half of the combined piece, to twice its original length for the Second Series.[4]

The two essays for the *Carlton Chronicle* were products of Dickens's need to write enough sketches during 1836 to complete two volumes for the Second Series by Christmas, a goal wisely scaled down to one volume before publication.[5] As early as March 1836, Dickens had arranged with John Easthope, one of the proprietors of the *Morning Chronicle* and *Evening Chronicle*, to publish a new series of sketches, probably to run concurrently in both papers, and seems to have written at least one piece for this series, which had not yet appeared in print. Dickens wrote to Easthope in April to complain of the delay and to protest that, despite his employer's charge in a previous communication, he himself had no intention of abandoning the series. He had, after all, he pointed out, promised readers of No. XX of his 'Sketches of London' (*Evening Chronicle*, 20 August 1835) that the series would be continued.[6] But his time-consuming work on the monthly numbers of *Pickwick Papers*, his frequent stints as a Parliamentary reporter, the writing of *Sunday Under Three Heads* that spring, and revisions of *The Strange Gentleman* and particularly of *The Village Coquettes* apparently prevented him from continuing the series immediately. Moreover, he may not have been entirely satisfied with the arrangements proposed by Easthope. By mid-June he was making plans to visit Bedlam, '*for the New Series, specially* (fine subject),' but the projected essay may not have been intended for Easthope's papers.[7] Nothing came of this either; if anything, his summer activities were even more numerous, for he was also reading the proof sheets of the second edition of the First Series of the *Sketches* and gathering and probably already revising sketches for the Second Series.[8]

But an attractive offer from P. W. Banks, the new editor of the *Carlton Chronicle*, to write a 'series of short sketches' once a fortnight came along at the right moment. The pieces were to be about one-half the length of the 'Sketches of London,' and could easily be turned out in spare moments between his other activities. Besides, not only would the essays 'be very

---

[4] See Hatton and Cleaver, p. 100; Butt and Tillotson, p. 42; and *Pilgrim Letters*, I, 694, n. 2. In 'Notes on *Sketches by Boz*,' *Dickensian*, 47, p. 103, Hill mentions in a headnote for his comments on 'The Last Cab Driver, and the First Omnibus Cad' that the sketch was first printed as 'Some Account of an Omnibus Cad,' but that it 'also includes' 'Hackney Cabs, and Their Drivers.' He provides no additional information.

[5] See *Pilgrim Letters*, I, 181, 200.

[6] *Pilgrim Letters*, I, 149.

[7] *Pilgrim Letters*, I, 153, to John Macrone, [?17 June 1836]. Since he wrote this letter to Macrone, Dickens may have been planning to write this and possibly other essays specifically for first publication in the Second Series, as he had for the First Series.

[8] See *Pilgrim Letters*, I, 153, 157, 159.

short, and the terms long,' he wrote Macrone, 'the Carlton Club being as liberal as need be,' but in addition, the 'circulation I believe is a small one. So much the better – Fewer people will see the Sketches before they are collected. It is all among the nobs too – Better still. They'll buy the book.'[9] He was pleased, too, with the general heading he composed for the series:

LEAVES
FROM AN UNPUBLISHED VOLUME. BY 'BOZ,'
(which will be torn out once a fortnight).

'Hackney Cabs, and Their Drivers' was written for issue No. 11, which should have appeared on 20 August, the designated fortnight after the publication of 'The Hospital Patient.' But as Dexter points out, the issue was actually delayed for four weeks.[10] During this time, the editor wisely dropped the reference to fortnightly publication from the general heading. Although Dickens remained on good terms with Banks,[11] this was his last piece for the *Carlton Chronicle*. The remuneration may not have been all that Banks had promised, as Dexter and Butt and Tillotson suggest,[12] but it seems probable that Dickens had feared the journal was unlikely to resume publication and had found the time at last propitious for fulfilling his promise of a new series for the Easthope papers. His next four sketches appeared under the general heading of 'Sketches by "Boz." New Series' in the *Morning Chronicle* and *Evening Chronicle*, as concurrently as possible, during late September and early October. While two more sketches appeared in the *Carlton Chronicle*, these were unauthorized, abridged reprintings of 'Scotland-Yard' (8 October) and 'Doctors' Commons' (15 October), two of the sketches in the new series in Easthope's papers (see Appendix A, above).

In revising 'Hackney Cabs, and Their Drivers' for the Second Series, Dickens lengthened it by about six hundred words. In the process he turned a relatively pedestrian piece of writing into the first half of a striking essay. Some of the revisions are primarily stylistic.[13] For example, he replaces the 'I' of the original version with the more formal and occasionally more humorous 'we,' makes numerous changes in phrasing, particularly

---

[9] *Pilgrim Letters*, I, 160, to John Macrone, [3 August 1836].
[10] See 'Dickens to His First Publisher,' p. 38, and 'The Genesis of *Sketches by Boz*,' p. 111.
[11] See *Pilgrim Letters*, I, 178, 180, 195, 204, 207, 211–12.
[12] See Dexter, 'Dickens to His First Publisher,' pp. 38–39, and Butt and Tillotson, p. 50, n. 4.
[13] Except for two instances (in pars. 4 and 7) where I have silently corrected errors in the placement of quotation marks, 'Hackney Cabs, and Their Drivers' is reprinted below exactly as it appeared in the *Carlton Chronicle*. The reader who wishes to compare the original with its revisions may, short of consulting the first edition of the Second Series, feel fairly secure in using any modern edition of the *Sketches*. Although Dickens made a number of punctuation changes and minor stylistic revisions in editions after the first, the only alteration worth noting is that in the 1837–39 edition in parts, the 'loquacious little gentleman' who argues with the red-cab driver is given a *green* coat in exchange for the *brown* one he had acquired in the revision of par. 7.

in pars. 5 and 6, and omits several of the cabmen's direct quotations. The style in the revision is generally a bit more mannered, and the single cabman characterized in the revision seems more articulate somehow than his earlier compeers, who cared 'nuffin for no vun whatsomever' (par. 6), because he speaks largely through the paraphrases of 'Boz,' the narrative persona, who is witty and obviously well-educated. Dickens removes one topical allusion (all of par. 3) that helps to place the approximate time of composition of the essay some few days before Parliament recessed on 20 August, the very day on which the essay was scheduled for publication. Even by 17 September, when the piece *was* finally published, the allusion to the current legislative session was quite out of date. Elsewhere he adds an incidental bit of comic cynicism to the end of par. 2: 'In these days of derangement of the nervous system, and universal lassitude,' 'Boz' concludes, 'people are content to pay handsomely for excitement; and where can it be procured at a cheaper rate?'

But the most significant changes completely alter the emphasis of the piece in accordance with the new title, 'The Last Cab Driver, and the First Omnibus Cad.' The original sketch is about cab drivers in general; the revision focuses on one of them, namely the red-cab driver, the 'last' of his breed, just as, in smooth historical continuity, William Barker, the ex-waterman in 'Some Account of an Omnibus Cad,' becomes, with considerably less revision, the 'first' of the omnibus conductors. Using a single cabman throughout was undoubtedly suggested to Dickens by the cabman whom he incidentally depicted in the original version having an argument with a 'loquacious little gentleman' (see par. 7). He replaces the bland opening sentence of par. 1 of the original with a new, 250-word paragraph in which, following a few opening generalities, he describes first his new character, the red-cab driver, and then the vicissitudes and eccentricities of the cab itself. For the cab driver, he borrows the brown whiskers, white hat, coatless appearance, corduroy knee-smalls, and Wellington boots from that anonymous cabman of par. 7, but he also makes the red-cab driver more genuinely comic by suggesting that rather than meeting the knee-smalls, the boots only 'approach as near them as their dimensions would admit of.' He gives the red nose of the loquacious gentleman to the driver and the blue of the gentleman's legal case to the cabman's eyes. He adds a bright yellow handkerchief to the man's neck and informs us that he carries a flower in his mouth in summer and a straw in winter, 'slight, but to a contemplative mind, certain, indications of a love of nature, and a taste for botany.'

The cabriolet itself, 'Boz' adds, 'was gorgeously painted – a bright red; and wherever we went . . . there was the red cab, bumping up against the posts at the street corners, and turning in and out, among hackney coaches, and drays, and carts, and waggons, and omnibuses, and contriving by some strange means or other, to get out of places which no other vehicle but the red cab could ever by any possibility contrive to get into, at all. Our fondness for that red cab was unbounded.' It would, he concludes, 'have performed such evolutions' at Astley's circus as would have put the 'Indian chiefs, knights, Swiss peasants, and all' to shame.

The red cab and its driver become as ubiquitous in the revision as 'Boz' tells us they are in life. They continually turn up in incidents that were simply typical encounters with anonymous cab drivers in the original. Thus it is the red-cab driver who emerges 'so coolly' from a chemist's shop, where his injured passenger is being treated, and 'philosophically climbing into the little dickey,' starts off 'at full gallop,' away from the scene of the cab accident described in somewhat less detail in par. 4 of the original. Likewise, in the case being tried before the Lord Mayor in Mansion House, he reappears as the defendant who so amuses the court and onlookers with his 'native humour' that his fine is mitigated, and he goes away again 'full gallop, in the red cab, to impose on somebody else without loss of time.' Dickens expands the cabman's altercation with the loquacious gentleman by about one hundred words. We lose the gentleman's red nose and blue bag, as already mentioned, and also the cabman's crude threat to him to 'make that 'ere nose o' yours purple,' but the passenger is characterized a bit more fully by the 'angry pinch of snuff' he takes, which makes a 'visible impression on the mind of the red-cab-driver,' who, nevertheless, 'without more ado,' knocks the man down, but then calls the police himself 'with all the civility in the world.' He is a cooler customer indeed than his predecessor.

Dickens also provides the longer essay with a sequel to this last incident in the life of the red-cab driver. In the original sketch he had mentioned the House of Correction toward the end of par. 5; when he canceled this section in revision, he developed the sequel into an actual visit to the prison and gave a new comic twist to his original observation that the men working on the treadmill in one of the prison yards were predominantly cabmen. As if he had read the earlier version, 'Boz' specifically looks for the red-cab driver among the men working on the wheel, but does not find him there. He is not to be disappointed, however. Later, while crossing the kitchen-garden with the Governor of the prison, he hears a familiar voice 'pouring forth its soul in the plaintive air of "all round my hat," which,' he informs us, 'was then just beginning to form a recognised portion of our national music.' The Governor explains that the voice is that of a 'very sad' fellow who was placed in solitary confinement because he refused to join the others on the treadmill. 'He says he likes it very much though,' the official explains, 'and I am afraid he does, for he lies on his back on the floor, and sings comic songs all day!' – in what, surely, we are to recognize as the red-cab driver's modest paradise. 'Shall we add,' 'Boz' joyously concludes, 'that our heart had not deceived us; and that the comic singer was no other than our eagerly-sought friend, the red-cab driver?'

The final mention of 'Boz's' clever friend comes in the new conclusion that Dickens wrote for 'The Last Cab Driver, and the First Omnibus Cad.'

He replaced the original ending to 'Some Account of an Omnibus Cad,'[14] with a shorter conclusion applicable to the entire longer piece. The last half of the new conclusion refers to the red-cab driver:

> We have spoken of Mr. Barker and of the red-cab driver, in the past-tense, alas! Mr. Barker has again become an absentee [Dickens's comic euphemism for a person sentenced to imprisonment or transportation]; and the class of men to which they both belonged, are fast disappearing. Improvement has peered beneath the aprons of our cabs, and penetrated to the very innermost recesses of our omnibuses. Dirt and fustian will vanish before cleanliness and livery. Slang will be forgotten when civility becomes general; and that enlightened, eloquent, sage, and profound body, the Magistracy of London, will be deprived of half their amusement, and half their occupation.

'Boz's' complaint that improvements in modes of transportation in London are detrimental to all that is picturesque and pleasantly old is, of course, a comic lament, a satire on the romantic strain in the essays of Dickens's predecessors. It is, I think, a genuinely comic conclusion and, apart from the narrator's somewhat strained mode of expression, a beautifully appropriate device to unify the two earlier essays into one.

Much has been said of the slight revision that Dickens made in his early novels, of the spontaneous, exuberant flow of wit and humor, of character and incident from the confident young author's pen. But we see, too, that when Dickens turned his hand to rewriting, the improvement was often striking indeed.[15] In revision, 'The Last Cab Driver, and the First Omnibus Cad' becomes not merely a portrait of two comic denizens of the world of London transportation but a pseudo-sociological study of the changing times and a mock-melancholic longing for the far less comfortable past. Observer, satirist, and cynic merge in 'Boz,' who is as much a product of the young author's imagination as the red-cab driver. But in this essay it is particularly the latter – straw or daisy in mouth, a gap between knee-smalls and boots, in white hat and yellow neckerchief, sitting arrogantly in his cab, that *red* cab encountered with comically fatalistic frequency all over London in the worst possible but obviously typical situations – who is the brilliant product of revision. Without such rewriting, we should never have had this fascinating character and his equally vivacious vehicle. I should also like to think that without the discovery – or rediscovery – of 'Hackney Cabs, and Their Drivers,' we should never have been fully aware of what we might have missed had

---

[14] Most of the original ending to 'Some Account of an Omnibus Cad' has been reprinted in Butt and Tillotson, p. 54.

[15] Other studies of revisions that Dickens made in the pieces collected in *Sketches by Boz* will be found in Butt and Tillotson, pp. 35–61; Darton, *Dickens, Positively the First Appearance*, pp. 69–77; Carlton, 'Portraits in "A Parliamentary Sketch,"' pp. 100–09; Benignus, *Studien über die Anfänge von Dickens*, pp. 1–17; and my 'Two Glimpses of Dickens' Early Development as a Writer of Fiction' (see Preface, above).

Dickens been content, as he was with a number of his other sketches, to reprint it with only minor stylistic changes. Nor should we have had the opportunity to see the young craftsman in action, turning one barely adequate sketch into the first half of a longer, much more imaginative essay of definite literary merit. The original version of the essay follows.

LEAVES,

FROM AN UNPUBLISHED VOLUME BY 'BOZ,'
HACKNEY CABS, AND THEIR DRIVERS.

[Par. 1] Cabs I admire, and cab-drivers I positively doat upon. Some people object to the exertion of getting into cabs, and others object to the difficulty of getting out of them; but I think both these are objections which take their rise in perverse and ill-conditioned minds. I consider the getting into a cab a very pretty and graceful process. When it's well performed, it is essentially melo-dramatic. First, there's the expressive pantomime of every one of the eighteen cabmen on the stand, the moment you raise your eyes from the ground. Then there's your own pantomime in reply – quite a little ballet. Four cabs immediately leave the stand, for your especial accommodation; and the evolutions of the noble animals who draw them, are beautiful in the extreme, as they grate the wheels of the cabs against the curb-stones, and sport playfully in the kennel. You single out a particular cab, and dart swiftly towards it. One bound, and you are on the first step; turn your body lightly round to the right, and you are on the second; bend gracefully beneath the reins, working round to the left at the same time, and you are in the cab. There is no difficulty in finding a seat; the apron knocks you comfortably into it at once, and off you go.

[Par. 2] The getting out of a cab is perhaps rather more complicated in its theory, and a shade more difficult in its execution. I have studied the subject a good deal, and I think the best way is to throw yourself out, and trust to chance for your alighting on your feet. If you make the driver alight first, and then throw yourself upon him, you will find that he breaks your fall materially. In the event of your contemplating an offer of eightpence, on no account make the tender, or show the money, until you are safely on the pavement. It's very bad policy attempting to save the fourpence. You are very much in the power of a cabman, and he considers it a kind of fee not to do you any wilful damage. Any instruction, however, in the art of getting out of a cab, is wholly unnecessary if you are going any distance; because the probability is, that you will be shot lightly out, before you have completed the third mile. I believe there is no instance on record of a cab-horse having performed three consecutive miles without going down, once. What of that? It's all excitement.

[Par. 3] The legislature have a proposed enactment upon the subject of cabs, on their table at the present moment. Let them consider the whole question calmly, dispassionately, and maturely in the approaching recess. Cabs involve far higher considerations than the overturning of a few of his majesty's subjects. They are a portion of the national recreation – a part of the amusements of the people. Deprive them of the excitement and interest of cab accidents in the streets; and you set them brooding upon the closing of the public-houses at twelve o'clock at night, and other political grievances. Cabs, as at present constituted, form the great safety-valve of popular feeling.

[Par. 4] How stands the fact? Walk down Holborn, or Fleet Street, or any of the principal thoroughfares in which there is a great deal of traffic, and judge for yourselves. You have hardly turned into the street when you see a wheel or two lying on the ground, an uprooted post, a hat-box, a portmanteau, and a carpet-bag, strewed about in a very picturesque manner; a horse standing by, looking about him with great unconcern, and a crowd, shouting and screaming with delight, cooling their flushed faces against the glass windows of a chemist's shop. 'What's the matter here, can you tell me?' 'O'ny a cab, sir.' 'Anybody hurt, do you know?' 'O'ny the fare, sir. I see him a turnin' the corner, and I ses to another gen'lm'n, "that's a reg'lar little oss that, and he's a comin' along rayther sweet, an't he?" "He just is," ses the other gen'lm'n, ven bump they cums agin the post, and out flys the fare, like bricks.' 'Ah! is he hurt?' 'I b'lieve you, he is. He'll never have the toothache no more, he wont; but what pleases me is this here: it vos his own porkmanker as give him the whop on the head. So if there's any deodand at all, it must be on his own property. There's a game!'

[Par. 5] The ubiquity of these cabs, and the influence they exercise over the visible[16] muscles of the judicial character itself, is perfectly astonishing. Turn into the justice-room at the Mansion House; the whole court resounds with merriment. The Lord Mayor throws himself back in his chair in a state of unmitigated delight at his own joke; every vein in Mr. Hobler's countenance is swollen with laughter, partly at the Lord Mayor's facetiousness, and partly at his own; the constables and police-officers are in ecstacies of admiration, the spectators are convulsed, and the very paupers smile as even the beadle himself relaxes. What can it mean? 'Pray what *is* going forward here?' 'It's o'ny a cabman, as is sending the Lord Mayor's shuttlecock back as heavy as it came!' Go over the House of Correction for the county of Middlesex; ask what the majority of the men are, who are at work upon the wheel in the first yard you enter; and the reply will be, 'Oh, they're only cabmen.' Walk into the gallery at the Old Bailey, and twenty-to-one but the prisoner at the bar, who is being tried for manslaughter, is a cabman too. There's a stoppage in the street as you go home, and it's occasioned by a couple of cabmen in single combat.

[Par. 6] A regular thorough-bred cabman is but little influenced by the feelings or opinions of society; to speak in his own poetic language, he 'cares nuffin for no vun whatsomever.' A fare is to be regarded, inasmuch as he not only puts money in his pocket, but affords him an

---

[16] A typographical error; corrected to 'risible' in the Second Series of *Sketches by Boz*.

opportunity of running a heat against some smarter rival down a crowded street. Beyond this, he has no interest in him, unless, as we before hinted, he suspects him of an eightpenny intention, and then out he goes, offhand. They are a philosophical set of fellows, fond of the public-house, but caring not one jot for the House of Correction, so long as they can richly deserve the punishment to which they are consigned.

[Par. 7] I saw an instance of this the other evening. A brown-whiskered, white-hatted, no-coated cabman, with an old pair of Wellington boots, pulled up to meet his corderoy knee-smalls, was engaged in a loud altercation with the fare he had just set down – a loquacious little gentleman with a blue bag, and a red nose. The man had not received above a shilling more than his fare, and consequently laboured under a great deal of very natural indignation. The dispute had attained a pretty considerable height, when at last the loquacious little gentleman making a mental calculation of the distance, and finding that he had already paid more than he ought, avowed his unalterable determination to 'pull up' the cabman in the morning. 'No. Will you, by G—?' sneered the driver. 'I will,' said the little gentleman, in a tone of voice which sufficiently showed he was not jesting. 'Well,' said the driver, tucking up his shirt sleeves, very calmly. 'There'll be three veeks for that; that'll bring me up to the middle o' next month. Three veeks more'll bring me to my birth-day, and then I've got ten pound to draw. So I'll first make that 'ere nose o' yours purple, and get board, lodgen', and washen' till then out o' the county,' and the little gentleman's nose *was* rendered purple, in no time, and I have no doubt the board, lodging, and washing, were all provided in due course.

[Par. 8] I have strong reason to suspect that this man was a distant relation of a waterman of my acquaintance, who, on one occasion, when I was passing the coachstand over which he presides, after standing very quietly to see a tall man struggle into a cab, ran up very briskly, when it was all over, (as his brethren invariably do), and touching his hat, asked, as a matter of course, for 'a copper for the waterman.' Now the fare was by no means a handsome man; and waxing very indignant at the demand, he replied. 'Money! What for? Coming up and looking at me, I suppose.' 'Vell, sir,' rejoined the waterman, with a smile of immoveable complacency, '*That's* worth twopence, at least.'

(*The Carlton Chronicle*, No. 11, 17 September 1836, p. 170)

APPENDIX C

Three Canceled Introductory Sections

DICKENS revised or canceled a number of passages in previously published pieces when preparing them for inclusion in the two series of *Sketches by Boz*. Three of the longest canceled passages, all introductory sections, are reprinted below.

I. The opening paragraphs of 'The Prisoners' Van,' Scenes and Characters – No. VIII, *Bell's Life in London*, 29 November 1835.[1]

We have a most extraordinary partiality for lounging about the streets. Whenever we have an hour or two to spare, there is nothing we enjoy more than a little amateur vagrancy – walking up one street and down another, and staring into shop windows, and gazing about us as if, instead of being on intimate terms with every shop and house in Holborn, the Strand, Fleet-street, and Cheapside, the whole were an unknown region to our wondering mind. We revel in a crowd of any kind – a street 'row' is our delight – even a woman in a fit is by no means to be despised, especially in a fourth-rate street, where all the female inhabitants run out of their houses, and discharge large jugs of cold water over the patient, as if she were dying of spontaneous combustion, and wanted putting out. Then a drunken man – what can be more charming than a regular drunken man, who sits in a door-way for half an hour, holding a dialogue with the crowd, of which his portion is generally limited to repeated inquiries of 'I say – I'm all right, an't I?' and then suddenly gets up, without any ostensible cause or inducement, and runs down the street with tremendous swiftness for a hundred yards or so, when he falls into another door-way, where the first feeble words he imperfectly articulates to the policeman who lifts him up are 'Let's av – drop – somethin' to drink?' – we say again, can anything be more charming than this sort of thing? And what, we ask, can be expected but popular discontent, when Temperance Societies interfere with the amusements of the people?

---

[1] The first paragraph was earlier reprinted in Butt and Tillotson, p. 44.

There is one kind of street quarrel which is of very common occurrence, but infinitely amusing – we mean where a little crowd has collected round three or four angry disputants, and no one single person, not even among the parties principally concerned, appears to have a very distinct notion of what it's all about. The place is – Long-Acre, say, or Saint Martin's-lane – time, half-past eleven at night. Some twenty people have collected round a bow-legged, under-sized young gentleman, in a brown coat and bright buttons, who has upon his arm a small young woman in a straw bonnet, with one shawl on, and another folded up over her arm. Opposed to the under-sized pair is a tall young fellow, in a brownish white hat, and flash attire; and you arrive in time to hear some such dialogue as the following: – 'Who said anythin' to *you?*' (in a tone of great contempt, from the long gentleman, turning round with his hands in his pockets). 'Vy *you* did, Sir' (from the small individual, in a towering passion). 'Oh! do come away, George' (from the young lady, accompanied with a tug at the coat-tail, and a whimper). 'Never mind him, he an't worth your notice.' 'Ah! take him home' – sneers the tall gentleman as they turn away – 'and tell his mother to take care on him, and not let him out arter dark, fear he should catch a cold in his ed. Go on.' Here the small young man breaks from the small young woman, and stepping close up to the adverse party, valourously ejaculates in an under-tone, '*Now*, what have you got to say.' 'Niver mind,' replies the long gentleman with considerable brevity. 'What do you mean by insulting this 'ere young 'ooman, Sir?' enquires the short man. 'Who insulted the young 'ooman?' replies the long one. 'Vy you did, Sir,' responds the short one, waxing specially wroth – 'You shoved agin her, Sir.' 'You're a liar,' growls the long gentleman fiercely; and hereupon the short gentleman dashes his hat on the ground with a reckless disregard of expense, jerks off his coat, doubles his fists, works his arms about like a labourer warming himself; darts backwards and forwards on the pavement with the motion of an automaton, and exclaims between his set teeth – 'Come on, I an't afeard on you – come on,' – and the long gentleman might come on, and the fight might come off, only the young lady rushes upon the small man, forces his hat over his eyes, and the tails of his coat round his neck, and screams like a peacock, till a policeman arrives. After great squabbling, considerable persuasion, and some threatening, the short man consents to go one way, and the long man another; and the answer of all the by-standers who had seen the whole, to the urgent inquiry from a new comer up, 'Do you know what's the matter, Sir?' invariably is – 'No, Sir, I really can't make out.'

We were passing the corner of Bow-street. . . .

II. The opening paragraph of 'The Parlour,' Scenes and Characters – No. IX, *Bell's Life in London*, 13 December 1835.

A snug parlour in winter, with a sofa on one side the blazing fire, an easy chair on the other, and a table in the centre, bearing a liquor-stand, glasses, and cigars, the whole seen to the greatest advantage by the soft light of a French lamp, which falls delicately on the curtains you have carefully drawn to exclude the wind, and enables you to eye your damask with great complacency – a snug parlour under such circumstances is a temporary Elysium, and well deserves to be lauded by an abler pen than ours. A pair of parlours, 'genteelly furnished' for a single gentleman, with a French bedstead for one in the back parlour, and cane-bottomed chairs for six in the front – all for twelve shillings a week, and attendance included, have their charms also. A breakfast parlour's no bad thing, when you're spending a week with a pleasant family in the country; and an hour or two may be passed very agreeably in a dining parlour in town. But though each and every of the parlours we have just enumerated has its own peculiar merits and attractions, to no one among them are we about to make any further allusion. The question then very naturally arises, what kind of parlour *do* we mean? – and that question we will resolve at once.

We had been lounging, the other evening. . . .

III. The opening paragraphs of 'Scotland-Yard,' Sketches by 'Boz' – No. II. (New Series), *The Morning Chronicle*, 4 October 1836.[2]

If our recollection serves us, we have more than once hinted, confidentially, to our readers that we entertain a strong partiality for the queer little old streets which yet remain in some parts of London, and that we infinitely prefer them to the modern innovations, the wide streets with broad pavements, which are every day springing up around us. The old Exeter 'Change, for instance, and the narrow and dirty part of the Strand immediately adjoining, we were warmly attached to. The death of the elephant was a great shock to us; we knew him well; and, having enjoyed the honour of his intimate acquaintance for some years, felt grieved – deeply grieved – that in a paroxysm of insanity he should have so far forgotten all his estimable and companionable qualities as to exhibit a sanguinary desire to scrunch his faithful valet, and pulverize even Mrs. Cross herself, who for a long period had evinced towards him that pure and touching attachment which woman alone can feel. This was a sad blow to us. The constitution of the beef-eater at the door sunk beneath the loss of the elephant; this was another. They pulled down Exeter 'Change itself; this was a greater trial than either, but we got over it in time. And since that period the rage for improvement has exposed us to so many melancholy trials of a similar description, that we have grown callous to suffering, and the only effect of our persecutions is to render us more attached than ever to the few old spots that are yet left us.

Of these, there is no one which, having a peculiar character of its own, preserved it so tenaciously, or took an honest pride in it so long, as Scotland-yard. It is so thoroughly a little colony of itself, it is so utterly unlike any other part of London, that a slight account of its progress and history has always seemed to us to be imperatively called for. None has yet appeared, however, and we now take pen in hand, more with the view of throwing out a few slight hints for the guidance of future historians, than with any idea of developing with the ability which such a subject demands, the past and present state of this little empire.

Scotland-yard, then, is a small – a very small – tract of land. . . .

---

[2] The first two-thirds of the first paragraph was earlier reprinted in Butt and Tillotson, p. 55.

Dickens and Two Sketches by John Poole

A few years ago, Professor Kathleen Tillotson pointed out the possible influence of John Poole on Dickens when she examined some parallels between Dickens's early tale, 'The Steam Excursion' and Poole's 'Preparations for Pleasure; or, A Pic-Nic,'[1] both tales of a day excursion of dubious success on the Thames. While she found no direct imitation on Dickens's part ('Dickens,' she stated, 'as in so many of his early tales, decorates his farcical basis with a much more gay and subtle kind of humour'), she indicated that his knowledge of Poole's tale was 'beyond doubt.' Moreover, she suggested that Dickens's early tales in general 'are more like Poole's than any of his other predecessors,' a conclusion that anyone familiar with Poole's *Sketches and Recollections* would readily support. She found resemblances between 'Preparations for Pleasure' and 'The Steam Excursion' in the personnel of the two excursion parties (both include 'a young law student, a young lady who brings her guitar, a "funny man" given to practical jokes, and an uninvited child or children'), in the concert given aboard ship, and in the disruptive storm that mars the return voyage.[2]

There are also a great many differences in structure as well as in specific details, of course. Dickens's excursionists, numbering about fifty,

---

[1] 'Dickens and a Story by John Poole,' *Dickensian*, 52 (1955/56), 69–70. Poole's tale (signed P★) was originally published in the *New Monthly Magazine*, N.S. 26 (October 1829), 372–90, and reprinted in his *Sketches and Recollections*, 2 vols. (London: Henry Colburn, 1835), I, 259–314. Dickens's tale originally appeared in the *Monthly Magazine*, N.S. 18 (October 1834), 360–76.

[2] Tillotson, p. 70. The author also points out that the cousin of Mr. Minns in Dickens's 'A Dinner at Poplar Walk' (*Monthly Magazine*, December 1833) is named Octavius Bagshaw, surely 'an unconscious recollection' of Poole's Claudius Bagshaw, and that Augustus Snodgrass of *Pickwick Papers* owes his surname to Frederick Snodgrass, a minor character in Poole's tale. She believes that Dickens changed Bagshaw's name to Budden in the Second Series of *Sketches by Boz* because, 'presumably, when Poole republished his story in the collected *Sketches and Recollections* in 1835, Dickens noticed the reminiscence, and made the change to avoid any suspicion of plagiarism' (p. 70).

charter a steamboat to take them down the Thames as far as the Nore. Poole's, numbering about fourteen, rent a barge to take them (in the other direction) only as far as Twickenham. While a good portion of both tales is concerned with the preparations for the day trip, Dickens's people set up a committee and make elaborate plans from the start; except for the seasickness at the end, their excursion is relatively successful. In Poole's tale, the Bagshaws want to plan a small outing to celebrate their wedding anniversary, but it shortly turns into an elaborate picnic for fourteen, requiring, as they see it, three committees to ensure the success of the outing; the excursion comes close to being a total disaster. Dickens's tale is told from the point of view of Mr. Percy Noakes, the young bachelor lawyer and guiding light of the planning committee, while Poole's is told from that of Mr. Bagshaw. But despite these differences, the parallels are sufficiently numerous to indicate that Poole's tale, whether half-remembered or consciously used, must have served as something of a model for Dickens's. Two parallels, the latter not cited by Professor Tillotson, the former only mentioned, are worth noting.

1. Unwanted Children
From Poole's 'Preparations for Pleasure'

At length he [Mr. Bagshaw] was relieved by the return of Mrs. Snodgrass; but, to the horror and consternation of himself, and of all present, she introduced the aforesaid Master Charles, – an ugly, ill-tempered, blubbering little brat of seven years old, with a bloated red face, scrubby white hair, and red eyes; and with the interesting appendage of a thick slice of bread and butter in his hand. 'I'm sure you'll pardon this liberty,' said the affectionate Mama; 'but poor Charley has cut himself very much, and he would not be pacified till I consented to take him with us. He has promised to be very good. There, don't cry any more, darling!' and, accordingly, the urchin roared with tenfold vigour. There were no particular manifestations of joy at this arrival; and it is just possible, although nothing was uttered to that effect, that there did exist a general and cordial wish that young Master Snodgrass were sprawling at the bottom of the deepest well in England.

(*New Monthly Magazine*, N.S. 26, p. 382)

From Dickens's 'The Steam Excursion'

'Noakes,' exclaimed Hardy, who had been looking at every object, far and near, through the large telescope; 'it's the Fleetwoods and the Wakefields – and two children with them, by Jove.'

'What a shame to bring children!' said every body, 'how very inconsiderate!'

... The girl was about six years old; the boy about four; the former was dressed in a white frock with a pink sash, and a dog's-eared looking little spencer, a straw bonnet, and green veil, six inches by three and a half; the latter was attired for the occasion in a nankeen frock, between the bottom of which and the top of his plaid socks a considerable portion of two small mottled legs was discernible. He had a light blue cap with a gold band and tassel on his head, and a damp piece of gingerbread in his hand, with which he had slightly embossed his dear little countenance.

(*Monthly Magazine*, N.S. 18, pp. 368–69)

2. Boat for Hire

[The passage from Dickens's 'The Steam Excursion' is to be found in Chapter II, above, pp. 46–47; that from Poole's 'Preparations for Pleasure' follows.]

Mr. Bagshaw, who had been appointed to hire a boat, and make the most economical arrangement he could about the fare, went down to Westminster Bridge. He was instantly surrounded by a dozen of the gentlemen who habitually congregate at that place. 'Boat, your honour – all ready, your honour.' Mr. Bagshaw explained. He came 'to engage a boat, barge, or other aquatic vehicle, of sufficient capacity to convey a party of fourteen to Twickenham and back: – what would be the remuneration required?' A stout, impudent, half-drunken fellow, thrust himself forward, shouting, 'I'm your man for five guineas.' Mr. Bagshaw's only reply to this was, 'You are an extortionate scoundrel.' Hereupon, the 'jolly young waterman' struck Mr. Bagshaw a violent blow on the right eye. . . .

(*New Monthly Magazine*, N.S. 26, p. 380)

Another sketch by Dickens, 'Early Coaches,' bears even more striking similarities to a second piece by Poole, entitled 'Early Rising: – "I'll Pack My Portmanteau."' [3] The two essays begin differently. Poole rambles from his epigraph, attributed to the *Elegant Extracts*, that 'Promises, like pie-crusts, are made to be broken,' to the notion that it is impossible for someone not born to it ever to become accustomed to 'early rising.' He gives examples from his own experience and begins yet another one involving a visit to Bristol, from which it is important for him to return to London at the end of his holiday. This matter covers some 1100 words. In less than one-third of the space, Dickens comments on travel by post-chaise, particularly in early coaches, and then discusses the hurried arrangements connected with being suddenly summoned to undertake such a journey.

From this point on, until near the end, the two essays proceed in the same direction. Both first-person narrators find themselves entering a booking-office to inquire about an early morning coach, Dickens's deliberately, for he must leave early from London, and Poole's to assuage his astonishment and disbelief at seeing a coach advertised to leave Bristol for London so early as five in the morning. Both take an inside seat, horrified at the thought

---

[3] Poole's sketch (signed P★) was originally published in the *New Monthly Magazine*, N.S. 31 (January 1831), 25–32, and reprinted in *Sketches and Recollections*, I, 17–38. Dickens's appeared in the *Evening Chronicle*, 19 February 1835. Since Poole's *Sketches and Recollections* was not published until April 1835, Dickens must have seen Poole's sketch in the *New Monthly Magazine*.

of an outside one at that time of day and year (January in Poole's sketch and probably about that season in Dickens's, too); both are amazed by the clerk's nonchalant attitude toward the departure time, as if it were an everyday matter for him, which, of course, it is; both proceed home and with some trepidation ask to be awakened sufficiently early to catch their coaches. In the morning, both are forced from bed to face a cold, wet, foggy day and are required to make their ablutions under adverse conditions. At this point, the two essays diverge. Dickens's narrator goes off through the slush to catch his coach, giving us a vivid account of the unpleasant walk, his wait for the coach, and the departure. Poole's dawdles so long that it is past five o'clock before he finishes packing his portmanteau. Accordingly, he returns to bed, asking not to be called until 'This day three months at the earliest' (p. 32).

The two scenes in the booking-office have striking parallels. Dickens's is to be found in full in Chapter III, above, pp. 72–73; Poole's, which is much longer, follows.

From Poole's 'Early Rising: – "I'll Pack My Portmanteau"'

Having an appointment of some importance, for the eighth of January, in London, I had settled that my visit should terminate on Twelfth-night. On the morning of that festive occasion I had not yet resolved on any particular mode of conveyance to town; when, walking along Broad Street, my attention was brought to the subject by the various coach-advertisements which were posted on the walls. The 'Highflyer' announced its departure at three in the afternoon – a rational hour; the 'Magnet' at ten in the morning – somewhat of the earliest; whilst the 'Wonder' was advertised to start every morning at five precisely!!! – a glaring impossibility. . . . We often experience an irresistible impulse to interfere, in some matter, simply because it happens to be no business of our's; and the case in question being, clearly, no affair of mine, I resolved to inquire into it. I went into the coach-office, expecting to be told, in answer to my very first question, that the advertisement was altogether a *ruse de guerre*.

'So, Sir,' said I, to the book-keeper, 'you start a coach, to London, at five in the morning?'

'Yes, Sir,' replied he, – and with the most perfect *nonchalance!*

'You understand me? At *five? – –* in the MORNING?' rejoined I, with an emphasis sufficiently expressive of doubt.

'Yes, Sir; five to a minute – two minutes later you'll lose your place.'

This exceeded all my notions of human impudence. It was evident I had here an extraordinary mine to work, so I determined upon digging into it a few fathoms deeper.

'And would you, now, venture to *book* a place for me?'

'Let you know directly, Sir. (Hand down the Wonder Lunnun-book, there.) When for, Sir?'

I stood aghast at the fellow's coolness. – 'To-morrow.'

'Full outside, Sir; just one place vacant, *in.*'

The very word, 'outside,' bringing forcibly to my mind the idea of ten or a dozen shivering creatures being induced, by any possible means, to perch themselves on the top of a coach, on a dark, dull, dingy, drizzling morning in January, confirmed me in my belief that the whole affair was, what is vulgarly called, a 'take-in.'

'So you *will* venture then to *book* a place for me?'

'Yes, Sir, if you please.'

'And, perhaps, you will go so far as to receive half my fare?'

'If you please, Sir, – one-pound-two.'

'Well, you are an extraordinary person! Perhaps, now – pray be attentive – perhaps, now, you will carry on the thing so far as to receive the whole?'

'If you please, Sir – – two-pound-four.'

I paid him the money; observing, at the same time, and in a tone calculated to impress his imagination with a vivid picture of attorneys, counsel, judge, and jury, – 'You shall hear from me again.'

'If you please, Sir; to-morrow morning, at five *punctual* – start to a minute, Sir, – thank'ee, Sir – good morning, Sir.' And this he uttered without a blush.

'To what expedients,' thought I, as I left the office, 'will men resort, for the purpose of injuring their neighbours. Here is one who exposes himself to the consequences of an action at law, or, at least, to the expense of sending me to town, in a chaise and four, at a reasonable hour of the day; and all for so paltry an advantage as that of preventing my paying a trifling sum to a rival pro-prietor, – and on the preposterous pretence, too, of sending me off at five in the morning!

(*New Monthly Magazine*, N.S. 31, pp. 27–28)

Although Dickens's descriptions of the coaching office and the clerk are more detailed than Poole's, and although Poole's description of his narrator's response to the whole situation is much more fully explicated than Dickens's, there are, I think, a sufficient number of parallels to indicate that Dickens was at least generally influenced by Poole's piece. But isn't it also evident that the references of Dickens's narrator to the clerk's lack of sympathy for the inconveniences of early morning travel are not entirely clear except in the context of Poole's more diffusive scene?

The relatively close similarities between the two essays do not end here, however. Having returned to his hotel, Poole's narrator mournfully asks the Boots to call him at four o'clock in the morning. After deciding to wait until then to pack his portmanteau, he goes to bed:

My slumbers were fitful-disturbed. Horrible dreams assailed me. Series of watches, each pointing to the hour of FOUR, passed slowly before me – then, time-pieces – dials, of a larger size, – and, at last, enormous steeple-clocks, all pointing to FOUR, FOUR, FOUR. 'A change came o'er the spirit of my dream,' and endless processions of watchmen moved along, each mournfully dinning in my ears, 'Past four o'clock.' At length I was attacked by night-mare. Methought I was an hour-glass – old Father Time bestrode me – he pressed upon me with unendurable weight – fearfully and threateningly did he wave his scythe above my head – he grinned at me, struck three blows, audible blows, with the handle of his scythe, on my breast, stooped his huge head, and shrieked in my ear————

'Vore o'clock, zur; I zay it be vore o'clock.'[4]

'Well, I hear you.'

'But I doan't hear you. Vore o'clock, zur.'

'Very well, very well, that'll do.'

'Beggin' your pardon, but it woan't do, zur. 'Ee must get up – past vore, zur.'

'The devil take you, will you—'

'If you please, zur; but 'ee must get up. . . .' And here he thundered away at the door; nor did he cease knocking till I was fairly up, and had shown myself to him in order to satisfy him of the fact. 'That'll do, zur; 'ee toald I to carl 'ee, and I hope I ha' carld 'ee proper*ly*.'

I lit my taper at the rush-light. On opening a window-shutter, I was regaled with the sight of a fog, which London itself, on one of its most perfect November days, could scarcely have excelled. A dirty, drizzling rain was falling. My heart sank within me. It was now twenty minutes past four. I was master of no more than forty disposable minutes, and, in that brief space, what had I not to do! The duties of the toilet were indispensable – the portmanteau *must* be packed – and, run as fast as I might, I could not get to the coach-office in less than ten minutes. Hot water was a luxury not to be procured: at that villainous hour not a human being in the house (nor, do I firmly believe, in the universe entire,) had risen – my unfortunate self, and my companion in wretchedness, poor Boots, excepted. The water in the jug was frozen; but, by dint of hammering upon it with the handle of the poker, I succeeded in enticing out about as much as would have filled a tea-cup. Two towels, which had been left wet in the room, were standing on a chair bolt upright, as stiff as the poker itself, which you might almost as easily have bent. The tooth-brushes were riveted to the glass, of which (in my haste to disengage them from their strong hold,) they carried away a fragment; the soap was cemented to the dish; my shaving-brush was a mass of ice. In shape more appalling Discomfort had never appeared on earth. I approached the looking-glass. Even had all the materials for the operation been tolerably thawed, it was impossible to use a razor by such a light. – 'Who's there?'

'Now, if 'ee please, zur; no time to lose; only twenty-vive minutes to vive.'

I lost my self-possession – I have often wondered *that* morning did not unsettle my mind!

There was no time for the performance of any thing like a comfortable toilet. I resolved therefore to defer it altogether till the coach should stop to breakfast. 'I'll pack my portmanteau; that *must* be done.' *In* went whatever happened to come first to hand. In my haste, I had thrust in, amongst my own things, one of mine host's frozen towels. Every thing must come out again. – 'Who's there?'

'Now, zur; 'ee'll be too late, zur!'

'Coming!' – Every thing was now gathered together – the portmanteau would not lock. No matter, it must be content to travel to town in a *deshabille* of straps. Where were my boots? In my hurry, I had packed away both pair. It was impossible to travel to London, on such a day, in slippers. Again was

---

[4] This is the Boots speaking, in what Poole characterizes as 'a broad Somersetshire twang.' In *Sketches and Recollections*, Poole added the sentence, 'It was the awful voice of Boots,' and revised the narrator's response to read, ' "Well, I hear you," groaned I' (I, 35).

every thing to be undone. . . . [After a bit more of the same, the Boots finally comes to inform the narrator that the coach has left.]

(*New Monthly Magazine*, N.S. 31, pp. 30–31)

Dickens's account of the same period of time is somewhat more succinct, but, again, the parallels are close enough, it seems to me, to indicate a strong indebtedness to Poole's essay:

If there be one thing in existence more miserable than another, it most unquestionably is the being compelled to rise by candle-light. If you ever doubted the fact, you are painfully convinced of your error, on the morning of your departure. You left strict orders, over night, to be called at half-past four, and you have done nothing all night but doze for five minutes at a time, and start up suddenly from a terrific dream of a large church clock with the small-hand running round, with astonishing rapidity, to every figure on the dial-plate. At last, completely exhausted, you fall gradually into a refreshing sleep – your thoughts grow confused – the stage-coaches, which have been 'going off' before your eyes all night, become less and less distinct, until they go off altogether: one moment you are riding with all the skill and smartness of an experienced whip – the next you are exhibiting *à la* Ducrow, on the off-leader: anon you are closely muffled up, inside, and have just recognized in the person of the guard, an old school-fellow, whose funeral, even in your dream, you remember to have attended eighteen years ago. At last you fall into a state of complete oblivion, from which you are aroused, as if into a new state of existence by a singular illusion. You are apprenticed to a trunk-maker; how, or why, or when, or wherefore, you don't take the trouble to inquire; but there you are pasting the lining in the lid of a portmanteau. Confound that other apprentice in the back shop how he is hammering! – rap, rap, rap – what an industrious fellow he must be; you have heard him at work for half an hour past, and he has been hammering incessantly the whole time. Rap, rap, rap, again – he's talking now – what's that he said? Five o'clock! You make a violent exertion, and start up in bed as if you were rehearsing the tent scene in *Richard*. The vision is at once dispelled; the trunk-maker's shop is your own bedroom, and the other apprentice your shivering servant, who has been vainly endeavouring to wake you for the last quarter of an hour, at the imminent risk of breaking either his own knuckles, or the pannels of the door.

You proceed to dress yourself with all possible dispatch. The flaring flat candle with the long snuff, just gives light enough to show that the things you want are not where they ought to be, and you undergo a trifling delay in consequence of having carefully packed up one of your boots in your over anxiety of the preceding night. You soon complete your toilette, however, for you are not particular on such an occasion, and you shaved yesterday evening; so mounting your Petersham great coat, and green travelling shawl, and grasping your carpet bag in your right hand, you walk lightly down stairs lest you should awake any of the family; and after pausing in the sitting-room for one moment just to have a cup of coffee (the said sitting-room looking remarkably comfortable, with every thing out of its place, and strewed with the crumbs of last night's supper), you undo the chain and bolts of the street door, and find yourself fairly in the street.

176

A thaw, by all that's miserable! The frost is completely broken up. . . . The cold sleet is drizzling down with that gentle regularity which betokens a duration of four-and-twenty hours at least; the damp hangs upon the house-tops, and lamp-posts, and clings to you like an invisible cloak. . . . [For the rest of this descriptive paragraph, see Chapter III, above, p. 72.]

(*Evening Chronicle*, 19 February 1835)

The last example in particular illustrates the superior quality of Dickens's description, as well as the effectiveness of his use of the pictorial method for this particular scene. But the striking similarities, not only in general outline of the scene but to considerable extent in specific detail, strongly suggest that Dickens may very well have had Poole's essay before him when he wrote 'Early Coaches,' and that he had perhaps set himself the exercise not so much of paralleling or imitating Poole's piece as of improving upon it. Certainly Dickens's version is faster moving, more imaginative, and in vital ways less dependent upon overused conventions of stage farce than is Poole's. 'Perhaps,' Tillotson stated in her short essay on the two authors, 'Dickens's tender memories of an early admiration for Poole's stories played some part in the charitable and friendly assistance he gave the old man in his long and poverty-stricken decline' (p. 70). In the instance of Poole's 'Early Rising: – "I'll Pack My Portmanteau,"' at least, there may have been a greater indebtedness behind the admiration than Tillotson suspected.

Bibliography

Allen, M. L. 'The Black Veil: Three Versions of a Symbol.' *English Studies*, 47 (1966), 286–89.

Altick, Richard D. *The English Common Reader: A Social History of the Mass Reading Public 1800–1900*. Chicago: University of Chicago Press, 1957.

Amerongen, J. B. Van. *The Actor in Dickens: A Study of the Histrionic and Dramatic Elements in the Novelist's Life and Works*. London: Cecil Palmer, 1926.

Axton, William. *Circle of Fire: Dickens' Vision & Style & The Popular Victorian Theater*. Lexington: University of Kentucky Press, 1966.

Bagehot, Walter. 'Charles Dickens (1858).' *Literary Studies*. 2 vols. London: Longmans, Green, 1879, II, 184–220. Originally published in *National Review*, 7 (1858), 458–86.

Benignus, Siegfried. *Studien über die Anfänge von Dickens*. Doctoral Dissertation, University of Strasbourg, 1895; Esslingen: Langguth, 1895.

Bennett, William C. 'America's Early Recognition of Dickens's Genius: Earliest Sketches Published Anonymously in a New York Weekly.' *Dickensian*, 35 (1938/39), 47–48.

Block, Andrew. *The English Novel, 1740–1850: A Catalogue Including Prose Romances, Short Stories, and Translations of Foreign Fiction*. 2nd ed. London: Dawson of Pall Mall, 1961.

Boll, Ernest. 'Charles Dickens and Washington Irving.' *Modern Language Quarterly*, 5 (1944), 453–67.

— 'The Sketches by "Boz."' *Dickensian*, 36 (1939/40), 69–73.

Browning, Robert. '*Sketches by Boz.*' *Dickens and the Twentieth Century*. Ed. John Gross and Gabriel Pearson. Toronto: University of Toronto Press, 1962, pp. 19–34.

Buckstone, J. B. '*John Jones,*' and '*The Christening.*' (Dicks' Standard Plays, No. 816.) London: John Dicks, n.d.

Butt, John, and Kathleen Tillotson. *Dickens at Work*. London: Methuen, 1957.

Carlton, William J. 'Charles Dickens, Dramatic Critic.' *Dickensian*, 56 (1960), 11–27.
— *Charles Dickens, Shorthand Writer: The 'Prentice Days of a Master Craftsman*. London: Cecil Palmer, 1926.
— 'Dickens Studies French.' *Dickensian*, 59 (1963), 21–27.
— 'Fanny Dickens: Pianist and Vocalist.' *Dickensian*, 53 (1957), 133–43.
— 'John Dickens, Journalist.' *Dickensian*, 53 (1957), 5–11.
— ' "The Old Lady" in *Sketches by Boz*.' *Dickensian*, 49 (1952/53), 149–52.
— 'Portraits in "A Parliamentary Sketch." ' *Dickensian*, 50 (1953/54), 100–09.
— 'Postscripts to Forster.' *Dickensian*, 58 (1962), 87–92.
— ' "The Story without a Beginning": An Unrecorded Contribution by Boz to the *Morning Chronicle*.' *Dickensian*, 47 (1950/51), 67–70.
— 'The Strange Story of Thomas Mitton.' *Dickensian*, 56 (1960), 141–52.
— 'The Third Man at Newgate.' *Review of English Studies*, N.S. 8 (1957), 402–07.
Chesterton, G. K. *Appreciations and Criticisms of the Works of Charles Dickens*. London: Dent; New York: Dutton, 1911.
Collier, John Payne. *An Old Man's Diary, Forty Years Ago*. 4 parts. London: Printed by Thomas Richards for 'strictly private circulation,' 1871–72.
Collins, Philip. *Dickens and Crime*. (Cambridge Studies in Criminology. Ed. L. Radzinowicz. Vol. 17.) 2nd ed. London: Macmillan; New York: St. Martin's, 1965.
— 'Dickens on Chatham: An Uncollected Piece. With Introduction and Notes.' *Dickensian*, 59 (1963), 69–73.
— 'Dickens's Reading.' *Dickensian*, 60 (1964), 136–51.
Cox, C. B. 'Comic Viewpoints in *Sketches by Boz*.' *English: The Magazine of the English Association*, 12 (1958/59), 132–35.
Crabbe, George. *Poems*. Ed. Adolphus W. Ward. Vol. III. Cambridge: Cambridge University Press, 1907.
— *The Poetical Works of the Rev. George Crabbe: With His Letters and Journals, and His Life by His Son*. Vol. VIII: *Posthumous Tales*. London: John Murray, 1834.
Darton, F. J. Harvey. *Dickens, Positively the First Appearance: A Centenary Review. With a Bibliography of Sketches by Boz*. London: Argonaut Press, 1933.
— 'Dickens the Beginner: 1833–1836.' *Quarterly Review*, 262 (1934), 52–69.
Davis, Earle. *The Flint and the Flame: The Artistry of Charles Dickens*. Columbia: University of Missouri Press, 1963.
— 'Literary Influences upon the Early Art of Charles Dickens.' Doctoral Dissertation, Princeton University, 1935.
Dean, F. R. 'George Hogarth.' *Dickensian*, 43 (1946/47), 19–24.
DeVries, Duane. 'Two Glimpses of Dickens' Early Development as a

Writer of Fiction.' *Dickens Studies Annual.* Vol. I. Ed. Robert B. Partlow, Jr. Carbondale and Edwardsville: Southern Illinois University Press; London and Amsterdam: Feffer & Simons, 1970, pp. 55–64.

Dexter, Walter. 'Charles Dickens: Journalist.' *Nineteenth Century and After,* 115 (1934), 705–16.

— 'Contemporary Opinion of Dickens's Earliest Work.' *Dickensian,* 31 (1934/35), 105–08.

— 'Dickens to His First Publisher: Some Hitherto Unpublished Letters.' *Dickensian,* 28 (1931/32), 33–39.

— 'The Genesis of *Sketches by Boz.*' *Dickensian,* 30 (1933/34), 105–11.

— 'How Press and Public Received "The Pickwick Papers."' *Nineteenth Century and After,* 119 (1936), 318–29.

— 'Macrone and the Reissue of *Sketches by Boz.*' *Dickensian,* 33 (1936/37), 173–76.

— '"The Metropolitan Magazine" and Dickens's Early Work.' *Dickensian,* 33 (1936/37), 93–96.

— 'A New Contribution to "The Monthly Magazine" and an Early Dramatic Criticism in "The Morning Chronicle."' *Dickensian,* 30 (1933/34), 223–25.

— 'The Reception of Dickens's First Book.' *Dickensian,* 32 (1935/36), 43–50.

— 'When Found.' *Dickensian,* 31 (1934/35), 158.

— 'When Found: The Pirates.' *Dickensian,* 30 (1933/34), 239.

— ed. *The Letters of Charles Dickens.* 3 vols. (The Nonesuch Dickens.) Bloomsbury: Nonesuch Press, 1938.

— and J. W. T. Ley. *The Origin of Pickwick: New Facts Now First Published in the Year of the Centenary.* London: Chapman and Hall, 1936.

Dibelius, Wilhelm. *Charles Dickens.* 2nd ed. Leipzig and Berlin: B. G. Teubner, 1926.

Dickens, Charles. *Miscellaneous Papers.* Ed. B. W. Matz. 2 vols. (Gadshill Edition.) London: Chapman and Hall; New York: Charles Scribner's Sons, [1908].

— *The Nonesuch Dickens.* Ed. Arthur Waugh, Hugh Walpole, Walter Dexter, and Thomas Hatton. 23 vols. Bloomsbury: Nonesuch Press, 1937–38.

— *The Posthumous Papers of the Pickwick Club.* Ed. Robert L. Patten. Harmondsworth: Penguin Books, 1972.

'Dickens's First Contribution to "The Morning Chronicle"': Now Identified and Republished for the First Time.' *Dickensian,* 31 (1934/35), 5–10.

Eckel, John C. *The First Editions of the Writings of Charles Dickens: Their Points and Values.* Rev., enl. ed. New York: Maurice Inman; London: Maggs Bros., 1932.

Edgar, Herman L., and R. W. G. Vail. 'Early American Editions of the Works of Charles Dickens.' *Bulletin of the New York Public Library,* 33 (1929), 302–19.

Engel, Monroe. *The Maturity of Dickens*. Cambridge: Harvard University Press, 1959.

Fielding, Kenneth J., ed. *The Speeches of Charles Dickens*. Oxford: Clarendon Press, 1960.

Forster, E. M. *Aspects of the Novel*. London: E. Arnold; New York: Harcourt, Brace, 1927.

Forster, John. *The Life of Charles Dickens*. Ed. J. W. T. Ley. London: Cecil Palmer, 1928. Originally published in 3 vols., London: Chapman and Hall, 1872–74.

Frye, Northrop. *Anatomy of Criticism: Four Essays*. Princeton, New Jersey: Princeton University Press, 1957.

Ganz, Margaret. 'Humor's Alchemy: The Lesson of *Sketches by Boz*.' *Genre*, 1 (1968), 290–306.

Getzels, Jacob W., and Philip W. Jackson. *Creativity and Intelligence: Explorations with Gifted Students*. London and New York: John Wiley & Sons, 1962.

Gissing, George. *Charles Dickens: A Critical Study*. London: Blackie & Son, 1898.

Graham, Walter. *English Literary Periodicals*. New York: Thomas Nelson & Sons, 1930.

Grant, James. *The Great Metropolis*. 2 vols. New York: Saunders and Otley, 1837.

— *The Newspaper Press: Its Origin – Progress – and Present Position*. 2 vols. London: Tinsley Brothers, 1871.

Grubb, Gerald G. 'Dickens's First Experience as a Parliamentary Reporter.' *Dickensian*, 36 (1939/40), 211–18.

— 'An Unknown Play by Dickens?' *Dickensian*, 46 (1949/50), 94–95.

Hall, Samuel Carter. *Retrospect of a Long Life: From 1815–1883*. New York: D. Appleton and Company, 1883.

Hatton, Thomas, and Arthur H. Cleaver. *A Bibliography of the Periodical Works of Charles Dickens: Bibliographical, Analytical, and Statistical*. London: Chapman and Hall, 1933.

Hill, T. W. 'Books that Dickens Read.' *Dickensian*, 45 (1948/49), 81–90, 201–07.

— 'Dickens and His "Ugly Duckling"' [*The Village Coquettes*]. *Dickensian*, 46 (1949/50), 190–96.

— 'Notes on *Sketches by Boz*.' *Dickensian*, 46 (1949/50), 206–13; 47 (1950/51), 41–48, 102–07, 154–58, 210–18; 48 (1951/52), 32–37, 90–94.

Hooker, Kenneth W. *The Fortunes of Victor Hugo in England*. New York: Columbia University Press, 1938.

[Hotten, James Camden, and H. T. Taverner]. *Charles Dickens, The Story of His Life*. London: John Camden Hotten, [1870].

House, Madeline, and Graham Storey, eds. *The Letters of Charles Dickens*. (The Pilgrim Edition.) Vol. I (1820–1839). Oxford: Clarendon Press, 1965. Vol. II (1840–1841). Oxford: Clarendon Press, 1969.

Houtchens, Lawrence Huston, and Carolyn Washburn Houtchens, eds. *Leigh Hunt's Dramatic Criticism, 1808–1831.* New York: Columbia University Press, 1949.

Hudson, Liam. *Contrary Imaginations: A Psychological Study of the Young Student.* New York: Schocken Books, 1966.

Hugo, Victor. *The Last Days of a Condemned.* Trans. Sir P. Hesketh Fleetwood. London: Smith, Elder, 1840. Originally published as *Le Dernier Jour d'un condamné.* Paris: Gosselin, 1829.

Hunt, Leigh. *Critical Essays on the Performers of the London Theatres, Including General Observations on the Practise and Genius of the Stage.* London: John Hunt, 1807.

— *Essays.* Ed. Arthur Symons. London: Walter Scott, 1887.

'"In All the Glory of Print."' *Dickensian,* 30 (1933/34), 1–10.

Johnson, Edgar. *Charles Dickens: His Tragedy and Triumph.* 2 vols. New York: Simon and Schuster, 1952.

Kitton, Frederic G. *Charles Dickens by Pen and Pencil, Including Anecdotes and Reminiscences Collected from His Friends and Contemporaries.* London: Frank T. Sabin, 1890.

— *The Minor Writings of Charles Dickens: A Bibliography and Sketch.* London: Elliot Stock, 1900.

Langton, Robert. *The Childhood and Youth of Charles Dickens: With Retrospective Notes, and Elucidations, from His Books and Letters.* Rev., enl. ed. London: Hutchinson, 1891.

Leavis, F. R., and Q. D. Leavis. *Dickens the Novelist.* London: Chatto & Windus, 1970.

Lubbock, Percy. *The Craft of Fiction.* New York: Viking Press, 1957. Originally published London: J. Cape, 1921.

Manning, John. *Dickens on Education.* Toronto: University of Toronto Press, 1959.

Marcus, Steven. *Dickens: From Pickwick to Dombey.* New York: Basic Books, 1965.

Mathews, Mrs. Charles, ed. *The Memoirs of Charles Mathews, Comedian.* 4 vols. London: R. Bentley, 1838–39.

McMaster, R. D. 'Dickens and the Horrific.' *Dalhousie Review,* 38 (1958), 18–28.

Miller, J. Hillis. 'The Fiction of Realism: *Sketches by Boz, Oliver Twist,* and Cruikshank's Illustrations.' *Charles Dickens and George Cruikshank: Papers Read at a Clark Library Seminar on May 9, 1970.* By J. Hillis Miller and David Borowitz. Los Angeles: William Andrews Clark Memorial Library, University of California, 1971, pp. 1–69. Also in *Dickens Centennial Essays.* Ed. Ada Nisbet and Blake Nevius. Berkeley, Los Angeles, London: University of California Press, 1971, pp. 85–153.

Miller, William. 'Dickens Reads at the British Museum.' *Dickensian,* 43 (1946/47), 83–84.

— and E. H. Strange. *A Centenary Bibliography of the Pickwick Papers.*

London: Argonaut Press, 1936.

Mitford, Mary Russell. *Our Village: Sketches of Rural Character and Scenery.* 5 vols. London: Geo. B. Whittaker and Whittaker, Treacher, and Company, 1824–32.

Monod, Sylvère. *Dickens the Novelist.* Norman: University of Oklahoma Press, 1968. Originally published in French as *Dickens romancier.* Paris: Hachette, 1953.

Nicoll, Allardyce. *A History of English Drama, 1660–1900.* Vol. IV: *Early Nineteenth Century Drama, 1800–1850.* 2nd ed. Cambridge: Cambridge University Press, 1955.

Nielsen, Hilmer. 'Some Observations on *Sketches by Boz.*' *Dickensian,* 34 (1937/38), 243–45.

Poole, John. 'Early Rising: – "I'll Pack My Portmanteau."' *New Monthly Magazine,* N.S. 31 (January 1831), 25–32. Reprinted in his *Sketches and Recollections.* 2 vols. London: Henry Colburn (for Richard Bentley), 1835, I, 17–38.

— 'Preparations for Pleasure; or, A Pic-Nic.' *New Monthly Magazine,* N.S. 26 (October 1829), 372–90. Reprinted in his *Sketches and Recollections,* I, 259–314 (see above).

Rogers, Carl L. 'Toward a Theory of Creativity.' *Creativity and Its Cultivation: Addresses Presented at the Interdisciplinary Symposia on Creativity, Michigan State University, East Lansing, Michigan.* Ed. Harold H. Anderson. New York: Harper and Brothers, 1959, pp. 69–82.

Rouse, W. H. D. 'Dickens and Jorrocks.' *Times Literary Supplement,* 19 April 1934, p. 282. Replies by R. H. Case, 26 April, p. 303; Lascelles Abercrombie, 3 May, p. 322; and W. S. Mackie, 14 June 1934, p. 424.

Stedman, Jane W. 'Good Spirits: Dickens's Childhood Reading.' *Dickensian,* 61 (1965), 150–54.

Stevenson, Lionel. 'An Introduction to Young Mr. Dickens.' *Dickensian,* 29 (1932/33), 111–14.

Stone, Harry. 'Dark Corners of the Mind: Dickens' Childhood Reading.' *Horn Book Magazine,* 39 (1963), 306–21.

— 'Dickens's Reading.' Doctoral Dissertation, University of California at Los Angeles, 1955.

Stonehouse, John Harrison. *Green Leaves: New Chapters in the Life of Charles Dickens.* Rev., enl. ed. London: Piccadilly Fountain Press, 1931.

Straus, Ralph. *Charles Dickens: A Biography from New Sources.* New York: Cosmopolitan Book Corporation, 1928.

Sucksmith, Harvey P. *The Narrative Art of Charles Dickens: The Rhetoric of Sympathy and Irony in His Novels.* Oxford: Clarendon Press, 1970.

— 'The Secret of Immediacy: Dickens' Debt to the Tale of Terror in *Blackwood's.*' *Nineteenth-Century Fiction,* 26 (1971/72), 145–57.

Suzannet, Alain de. 'How Mr. Hardy of Steam Excursion Fame Made His Mark at the Great Edinburgh Dinner to Lord Grey.' *Dickensian,* 36 (1939/40), 89.

— 'Maria Beadnell's Album.' *Dickensian*, 31 (1934/35), 161–68.

Szladits, Lola L., ed. *Charles Dickens, 1812–1870: An Anthology*. New York: New York Public Library, 1970.

Tave, Stuart M. *The Amiable Humorist: A Study in the Comic Theory and Criticism of the Eighteenth and Early Nineteenth Centuries*. Chicago: University of Chicago Press, 1960.

Thomas, Gillian. 'Dickens and *The Portfolio*.' *Dickensian*, 68 (1972), 167–72.

[Thomson, Henry]. 'Le Revenant.' *Blackwood's Edinburgh Magazine*, 21 (1827), 409–16.

Tillotson, Kathleen. 'Dickens and a Story by John Poole.' *Dickensian*, 52 (1955/56), 69–70.

— 'Seymour Illustrating Dickens in 1834.' *Dickensian*, 54 (1958), 11–12.

Victoria and Albert Museum. *Charles Dickens: An Exhibition to Commemorate the Centenary of His Death, June–September 1970*. London: Her Majesty's Stationery Office, 1970.

Warren, Samuel. *Passages from the Diary of a Late Physician*. 2 vols. Edinburgh: William Blackwood and Sons, 1832; 5th ed. with additional chapters. 3 vols., 1838.

Watson, Ernest Bradlee. *Sheridan to Robertson: A Study of the Nineteenth-Century London Stage*. Cambridge: Harvard University Press, 1926.

Waugh, Arthur. *A Hundred Years of Publishing, Being the Story of Chapman & Hall, Ltd*. London: Chapman & Hall, 1930.

Wegelin, Christof. 'Dickens and Irving: The Problem of Influence.' *Modern Language Quarterly*, 7 (1946), 83–91.

[Wight, John]. *Mornings at Bow Street. A Selection of the Most Humourous and Entertaining Reports Which Have Appeared in the Morning Herald*. London: C. Baldwyn, 1824.

[—] *More Mornings at Bow Street. A New Collection of Humourous and Entertaining Reports*. London: J. Robins, 1827.

Willis, Nathaniel P. *Dashes at Life with a Free Pencil*. (The American Short Story Series. Vol. 30.) New York: Garrett Press, 1969. Originally published New York: Burgess, Stringer, & Co., 1845.

Wilson, Edmund. 'Dickens: The Two Scrooges.' *The Wound and the Bow: Seven Studies in Literature*. Boston: Houghton Mifflin, 1941, pp. 1–104.

Index

In sub-entries the following abbreviations have been used: *BL, Bell's Life in London*; CD, Charles Dickens; *EC, Evening Chronicle*; *MC, Morning Chronicle*; *MM, Monthly Magazine*; *PP, Pickwick Papers*; *S by B, Sketches by Boz*. Where a reference is to be found in both text and footnote on a page, only the page number is given; where the reference is to be found only in the footnote, the page number is followed by 'n.'

Goldsmith, Oliver 6–7, 25–26, 61, 64, 80, 91n
'Gone Astray' 11–12, 14n
Graham, Walter 31n
Grant, James 22, 24, 91n
Gray, Thomas 27
Great Expectations 74; Pip 12
'Great Winglebury Duel, The' 111, 134, 151, 154, 157; comparison with other works by CD 126–32, 143–45; dramatization of (*see also The Strange Gentleman*) 111n, 135–36; fictional techniques in 126–32, 143–45; influences on 126–27, 131–32; review of 43n; writing of 111n, 126
'Greenwich Fair' 8n, 70–71, 149, 154, 156
Grey, Charles, Earl 62n, 63
Gross, John 66n
Grubb, Gerald G. 21n
Gruneisen, Charles 91n
'Guest, The' (*The Holly-Tree Inn*) 5n
Guilford, J. P. 6n
Gulliver's Travels (Swift) 6
Gurney, Thomas 18

'Hackney Cabs, and Their Drivers' (*see also* 'The Last Cab Driver, and the First Omnibus Cad') 31n, 136–37; first reprinting of 164–66; new facts about 158–59; revisions 152, 158–64; writing of 159–60
'Hackney-Coach Stands' 67–70, 74, 149, 154, 156
Hall, Samuel Carter 1n, 16n, 21n, 24n
Hall, William (*see also* Chapman and Hall) 30, 135
Halley's Comet 105n
Hansard, T. C. 137n
Hansard's Parliamentary Debates 21
Hard Times 4
Harley, John Pritt 19, 136n
Hatton, Thomas 31n, 141n, 147n, 158, 159n
Hazlitt, William 26
Hill, T. W. 26n, 83n, 159
History of England, The (Goldsmith) 25
Hogarth, Catherine 23, 26n, 84n, 91n, 111n, 113, 115n, 121, 135, 136n, 143
Hogarth, George 23, 60, 91n, 110–12, 114–15; review of *S by B* (1st ser.) 43n, 112, 115, 135n
Holbein, Hans 7, 25
Holcroft, Thomas 143n
'Holly-Tree, The' 4–5

Holly-Tree Inn, The 5n
Hood, Thomas 26, 31
Hook, Theodore 26, 143n
Hooker, Kenneth W. 115n
Horace 7
'Horatio Sparkins' 31n, 102, 128, 131, 148, 154, 157; fictional techniques in 42, 53, 57; Horatio Sparkins 100; review of 43n
'Hospital Patient, The' 112n, 136–37, 152, 155–56, 158–60
Hotten, John Camden 91n
House, Madeline (*see also Pilgrim Letters*) 3n
'House, The' (*see also* 'A Parliamentary Sketch') 31n, 149; revisions 23–24, 90n, 133, 149
House of Correction *see* Coldbath Fields
Household Words 4n–9n, 11n
Houtchens, Lawrence Huston and Carolyn Washburn Houtchens 52n
How to Grow Rich (Reynolds) 143n
Howitt, Mary 29n
Hudson, Liam 6n
Hugo, Victor 112, 115–16, 119, 120n
Hullah, John 19, 135
Humourist's Miscellany, The 7
Humphry Clinker (Smollett) 6
Hunt, Leigh 26, 51–52, 61, 80

'I'd Rather Have a Guinea than a One-Pound Note' 9
Idler, The (Johnson) 6
Inchbald, Elizabeth 6, 8
Intelligence, modern theories of 5–6
Irving, Washington 3n, 6, 61, 80
Is She His Wife? 19
'Ivy Green, The' 26

Jack the Giant-Killer 4
Jackson, Philip W. 6n, 10n
John Jones (Buckstone) 43n
Jonathan Wild (Fielding) 6n
Johnson, Edgar 2–3, 4n, 5, 7n, 8n, 12, 18n, 19n, 21n, 56n, 60, 91n, 134n, 136n, 140
Johnson, Samuel 6, 26, 61
Jonson, Ben 67
Jorrocks' Jaunts and Jollities (Surtees) 26, 143n
Joseph Andrews (Fielding) 144

Keeley, Mrs. Robert 44n
Kitton, Frederic G. 15n, 18n, 19n, 20n, 27n, 29n, 110n
Knight, Thomas 52

Sketches of London – *continued*
humor, in 66–69, 76–79, 85, 91–92;
views of life in 65–69, 76–80, 91–92
Sketches of Young Couples 52
Sketches of Young Gentlemen 52
Smollett, Tobias 6, 10, 13, 64, 126, 131–32
Solomon Bell the Raree Showman 136
'Some Account of an Omnibus Cad'
(*see also* 'The Last Cab Driver, and the
First Omnibus Cad') 26n, 31n, 93, 95,
136n, 144n, 151, 158–59; revisions
161, 163
'Sparks, Timothy' *see* Dickens, Charles –
Writing, pseudonyms
Spectator, The (Addison and Steele) 6
Speeches of Charles Dickens, The (ed.
Fielding) 13n, 21n
'Steam Excursion, The' 31n, 126, 148, 154,
157; fictional techniques in 46–47,
49–51, 54, 58; influence of a sketch by
Poole on 47n, 170–72; Percy Noakes
100; revisions 63n
Stedman, Jane W. 15n
Steele, Richard 6, 61
Sterne, Laurence 6, 67, 69
Stevenson, Lionel 60–61
Stone, Harry 4n, 5n, 26n
Stonehouse, John Harrison 56n
Storey, Graham (*see also* Pilgrim Letters) 3n
Strange, E. H. 1n
Strange Gentleman, The (*see also* 'The Great
Winglebury Duel') 19, 111n, 135–36,
159
Straus, Ralph 27n
'Street Sketches' (*MC*; *see also* 'Sketches of
London' and titles of individual
sketches, listed 148) 23, 60, 67, 133
'Streets at Night, The' 93, 112n, 133, 151,
155–56
'Streets – Morning, The' 61–62, 70–71,
123, 133, 150, 155–56
Sucksmith, Harvey P. 119–20
'Sunday Out of Town, A' *see* 'A Dinner
at Poplar Walk'
Sunday Under Three Heads 136, 159
Surtees, Robert 26, 132, 143n
Suzannet, Alain de 27n, 63n
'Sweet Betsy Ogle' 22n
Swift, Jonathan 6
Symmons, C. 25
Szladits, Lola L. 21n

Tales of the Genii (Ridley) 6, 10, 15
Tatler, The (Addison and Steele) 6

Tave, Stuart M. 67
Taverner, H. T. 91n
Tegg, Thomas 136
Terence 7
Terrific Register, The 7
Thief, The see London Weekly Magazine
Thomas, Gillian 7n
Thomas, Owen P. 13–14
Thomson, Henry 119–20
'Thoughts about People' 80–81, 100, 149,
153, 156; revisions 76–77, 149
'Tibbs' *see* Dickens – Writing, pseudonyms
Tillotson, Kathleen 2n, 26n, 32n, 42n, 76,
82n, 87n, 90n, 91n, 95, 111n, 121n,
133–34, 141, 144n, 147n, 148n, 159n,
160, 163n, 167n, 169n, 170–71, 177
Times, The (London) 25
Tobin, Daniel 14, 16
Tom Jones (Fielding) 6, 13, 129n, 132, 144;
Partridge 10
Tragedy of Jane Shore, The (Rowe) 8
Trenck, Baron, *Life* or *Memoirs* of 6
Tristram Shandy (Sterne) 6, 88n, 89
True Sun, The 21, 25
'Tuggs's at Ramsgate, The' 31n, 111,
152, 157; comparison with other
works by CD 126–32, 142, 145;
fictional techniques in 126–32, 142,
145; influences on 126–27, 129n, 132;
writing of 111n, 126
Turnpike Gate, The (Knight) 52
Turpin, Dick 118
Tyrell, Sir John 65

Uncommercial Traveller, The 4n, 6n–9n,
13n
'Unsettled Neighbourhood, An' 9
Urquhart, John and Miss 20n
Utopia (More) 26

Vail, R. W. G. 147n
Valentine and Orson 4
'Vauxhall-Gardens by Day' 137, 153,
155–56
Vicar of Wakefield, The (Goldsmith) 6
Victoria and Albert Museum 6n
Village Coquettes, The 19, 135–36, 159
Virgil 7
'Visit to Newgate, A' 110, 134, 151, 153,
156; CD's visit to the prison 112–13;
comparison with other works by CD
119–20, 132–33, 138; fictional techniques
in 113–20, 132; influences on 112,
115–16, 119–20; praise of 111–12,

114–15; purposes for writing 112,
114–17; revisions 112, 114–16, 118n;
writing of 111n, 112–17, 133
'Vocal Dress-Maker, The' 97, 99, 101n,
102–04, 108, 112, 151; retitled 'The
Mistaken Milliner – A Tale of Ambition'
97, 151, 155, 157
'Voice of the Sluggard, The' (Watts) 5n
Voltaire, François Marie Arouet 6n
Volunteers: A Letter to Wm. Wyndham 25

Waldie's Select Circulating Library 147
Walpole, Horace 6n
Walsh, C. F. 16
Ward, Adolphus W. 129n
Warren, Samuel 120
Warren's Blacking 3, 13–14, 22n

Watts, Dr. Isaac 5n
Waugh, Arthur 141n
Weekly Dispatch, The 41, 91n
Weller, Mary 4, 5n, 6n, 8–9
Wellington House Academy 7–8, 13, 15,
17, 115
'Where We Stopped Growing' 6n, 9n,
10n
Whittington, Dick 11
Wight, John 26
Wilkinson, Mr. 43, 44n
Willis, Nathaniel Parker 112–13
Wilson, Edmund 3–4
*Wit's Miscellany, The see Bentley's
Miscellany*

Yellow Dwarf, The 4